REASON TO BELIEVE

REASON TO BELIEVE

The Controversial Life of
Rabbi Louis Jacobs

HARRY FREEDMAN

BLOOMSBURY CONTINUUM
LONDON · OXFORD · NEW YORK · NEW DELHI · SYDNEY

BLOOMSBURY CONTINUUM
Bloomsbury Publishing Plc
50 Bedford Square, London, WC1B 3DP, UK

BLOOMSBURY, BLOOMSBURY CONTINUUM and the Diana logo are
trademarks of Bloomsbury Publishing Plc

First published in Great Britain 2020

All photographs reproduced by kind permission of the Jacobs Family with the exception of the
opening of Golders Green Yeshiva (1947, photographer unknown) and New London Synagogue
(© Karen Freedman) on page 8 of the illustrations

Copyright © Harry Freedman, 2020

Published with the kind support of the Friends of Louis Jacobs www.louisjacobs.org /
www.booksof.louisjacobs.org

A catalogue record for this book is available from the British Library

Library of Congress Cataloguing-in-Publication data has been applied for

ISBN: HB: 978-1-4729-7938-4 ; eBook: 978-1-4729-7937-7;
ePDF: 978-1-4729-7936-0

2 4 6 8 10 9 7 5 3 1

Typeset by Deanta Global Publishing Services, Chennai, India
Printed and bound in Great Britain by CPI Group (UK) Ltd, Croydon CR0 4YY

To find out more about our authors and books visit www.bloomsbury.com and
sign up for our newsletters

For Bonnie and Leo: Two new stories unfolding.

Contents

List of Illustrations

Introduction

In 2005 the *Jewish Chronicle* conducted a poll of its readers to mark 350 years since Oliver Cromwell allowed the Jews to return to England. The newspaper aimed to highlight the contribution made by the Jewish community to national life, by asking its readers to decide who they thought had been the 'Greatest British Jew'.

Over the next six weeks the paper suggested candidates from the fields of science, art, entertainment, sport and philanthropy. Among the names they suggested were those of Benjamin Disraeli, Isaiah Berlin, Harold Pinter, Rosalind Franklin, Lucien Freud, Chaim Weitzmann, Simon Marks of Marks and Spencer, Montague Burton the tailor and Rabbi Dr Louis Jacobs. Readers were also invited to nominate candidates of their own choosing.

An initial field of nearly 100 names was whittled down to a shortlist of eight, from whom readers were asked to make a final choice. When Louis Jacobs won the competition, winning nearly twice as many votes as the nearest runner-up, he said with characteristic modesty that he felt 'both embarrassed and daft'.

Contributors to the *Jewish Chronicle*'s letters page were not so reticent. One naysayer described Jacobs as a 'pariah' and 'highly destructive', whose victory was 'bizarre and irrelevant'. Another correspondent thought that the poll results had made a 'mockery of Anglo-Jewish history'. These remarks were condemned in a letter the following week as illustrative of 'the festering tumour that is infecting Anglo-Jewry today'. But by far the largest number of letters simply celebrated his victory, correspondents writing of the 'tears of joy' they had shed when they'd heard the news, praising his intellect and condemning the 'obscurantists' who opposed him. Not for the first time in his career, Louis Jacobs had unwittingly divided the community.

Unlike previous occasions, the divisions did not focus on his theology or religious outlook. This time, it was personal. On one side were those who, even if they had never met him, held him in deep affection. On the other side those who, even if they had never read his works or heard him speak, were offended by opinions that others claimed, often mistakenly, that he held.

For his opponents, his victory was a reminder, if they cared, that by ostracizing him all those years ago they had alienated a large part of their community, enhanced his scholarly reputation and guaranteed his popularity. But in the main they did not care. Religious certitude brooks no compromise.

For his supporters, Louis Jacobs's victory was a vindication. For the best part of half a century he had been an outcast from the Orthodox community that had once hailed him as a genius, their brightest and most promising hope for the future. Spurned by those who could not reconcile his theology with the established creed, nor accept his refusal to compromise when it came to matters of the mind. Disparaged by former colleagues and students, who considered the conclusions he reached through intellectual prowess and depth of learning to threaten their traditions and the religious commitment of their congregations. They feared his reputation as a man of reason, a spiritual leader with his feet on the ground, a theologian who spoke the language of ordinary people, a polymath with a depth of knowledge unequalled in the British rabbinate. And perhaps most of all, since we are talking about Britain, an underdog who had been unfairly treated and who was, in words echoed by a *Jewish Chronicle* columnist, 'the best Chief Rabbi we never had'.[1]

At last, with his victory in the poll, over 40 years after the notorious 'Jacobs Affair', Louis Jacobs's congregants and supporters could claim with justification that they had been right all along, when they had said that their teacher, guide and mentor had always held a special place in the hearts of the British Jewish community. Even if, as he himself was the first to admit, only one-third of 1 per cent of the community had actually bothered to participate in the poll.[2]

For Louis Jacobs and his family, the accolade of Greatest British Jew, embarrassing and daft as it may have been, helped to ameliorate a long-standing hurt. Sadly though, it came too late to gladden the heart of their beloved Shula, his wife of 61 years, his guide and greatest ally. She had passed away just six weeks earlier. As a young bride she had been advised by one of his teachers, as if she needed any telling, that her new husband was a genius; her role, this rabbi said, was to nurture him so he could devote every waking moment to his studies. But Shula Jacobs, born Sophie Lisagorsky, had a greater insight. 'For him it was the learning, more and more. I felt it was not right and I kept pressing him to give, to teach others and not keep it all to himself.' Louis Jacobs's scholarly reputation, dozens of books, hundreds of articles and countless hours of lecturing all stem from Shula's insistence that he not keep it all to himself.[3]

Much has been written about Louis Jacobs, and much more will be. Books, articles and PhD theses analyse his thought, discuss his contribution to the various fields of Jewish scholarship in which he was active, talk about his place in the history of British Jewry – even the personal impact he made upon the lives of those he encountered. In this book I have tried to write about Louis Jacobs the man: to chronicle his life and illuminate, to the best of my ability, his personality. I was privileged to have known him for nearly the whole of my life, to regard him both as a teacher and a family friend, and to rely on his wisdom and assistance at critical moments.

Many people knew Louis Jacobs, and he was known by many names. To his family and his friends in Manchester and Gateshead he was known by his Yiddish name, Laib, or Laibel. When he settled in London he became Louis, pronounced as in French (it had always been his name, but he had rarely used it). To those who addressed him with traditional formality he was always Rabbi Jacobs, even socially; to opponents who wished to denigrate him he was merely Dr Jacobs. To most of the world, most of the time, he was Louis. I found myself referring to him by each of these titles, depending on where it was in the story. But much of the time I refer to him as Louis; it may not be the most respectful way to denote one's rabbi and teacher, but, given the aims of the book, it felt like the right thing to do.

1

An Unlikely Rabbi

Louis Jacobs was an unlikely rabbi. Rabbis, like kings and mafia bosses, tend to be the products of dynasties, their ancestry almost as important as their depth of learning. Louis Jacobs was no dynastic scion; his DNA was not that of a rabbinic elite.

That is not to say he was a stranger to religion. His parents were traditional Jews, as were most people in the North Manchester working-class Jewish community into which he was born, on 17 July 1920. With his father Harry, the young Louis would go to synagogue every week, recite *kiddush* on Friday nights and say the Grace after Meals. He attended *ḥeder*, religious school, several times a week and following his bar mitzvah he put on *tefillin* every weekday. But on Saturday afternoons, although such things are forbidden, his father would take him in the winter to watch Broughton Rangers, the local rugby team, and in the summer to see Lancashire play cricket at Old Trafford.

Many years later, when the divisive Jacobs Affair was playing out in the British press, the *Daily Express* printed a picture of his father, proudly speaking about his son. Harry Jacobs was shown sporting a large black skullcap on his head. In the cutting that Shula Jacobs placed in her scrapbook Louis has scrawled underneath: 'Not a true picture! It's a put up job.' Harry Jacobs, according to his son, would never have allowed himself to be photographed wearing a skullcap. The Jacobs family were traditional English Jews. They only wore skullcaps, or *cupels*, when praying, or sometimes when eating. They did not don them for secular activities in the middle of the week. Unless being interviewed by a journalist working for the *Daily Express*.

Louis's parents tempered their Judaism with typical English reserve. But they themselves had been brought up in a far stricter religious environment. No *shabbes* afternoon rugby or cricket for Harry Jacobs as a child – of that Louis's paternal grandfather believed he had made certain. But somehow, in their teenage years, Louis's dad and two brothers managed to slip away to the rugby most Saturday afternoons. Such desecration of the holy Sabbath would have been inconceivable in Telz, where both his paternal grandparents were born, a Lithuanian centre of Orthodoxy renowned for its yeshiva, or Talmudic college. Nor could it have been imagined even in the slightly more Westernized city of Mittau, in Latvia, the birthplace of his mother's parents.

Both sets of grandparents left their ancestral lands during the 1880s, seeking a better, safer, more prosperous future in England. They ended up in Manchester, where their children, Louis's parents, were born. Harry Jacobs and his future wife Lena Meyerstone were both educated in Manchester Jews' School. In 1910 they were married in the city's Great Synagogue. Then they waited ten years for Louis – Laib as he was known in Manchester, their only child – to arrive.

A MANCHESTER BOY

There was never any doubt that Louis would turn out to be intelligent. It was only their penurious upbringing and the social inequalities of Victorian England that had held his parents back. Even though his mother's older brothers had done well for themselves in Manchester, one establishing himself as a clothes retailer, the other as a jeweller, it was unthinkable that Lena could follow in their footsteps. As an unmoneyed woman all routes to her social advancement were closed. She concentrated instead on advancing her own self-education, and on developing her son's potential. With her prodigious memory and passion for English literature she supplemented Louis's schooling, spending hours together with him reading Arthur Mee's *Children's Encyclopaedia* and reciting the huge chunks of poetry she had memorized. Louis inherited her photographic memory and love of reading. As a young man he devoured books, spending hours in the local library reading whatever he could get his hands on, fiction as well as non-fiction. His favourites were the outstanding Edwardian authors, among them George Bernard Shaw, Hilaire Belloc and H. G. Wells. Overshadowing them all, in his mind, was G. K. Chesterton, with 'his brilliant paradoxes and defence of traditional religion, even though it was not the Jewish religion and indeed he was rumoured to be a bit anti-Semitic'.[1] With the easy simplicity of his writing conveying ideas that demanded the reader's active engagement, Chesterton was perhaps Jacobs's earliest literary role model; he would weave his epithets into his sermons and lectures whenever he could.

Louis's father's intellectual potential had also been constrained by the circumstances of his upbringing. As a child he had won a scholarship to the renowned Manchester Grammar School. But he'd been unable to take up his place, because his family needed him as a breadwinner. He worked as a machinist in raincoat factories, compensating for the lack of cerebral stimulation by attending political lectures and advocating in disputes on behalf of his work colleagues.

For a while it looked as if Louis's luck would be no better than that of his parents. Illness and poverty took a toll on his education. He was shunted from school to school, attending a total of five altogether. When his first school closed he was sent to Manchester Jews' School, where his parents had been educated. Established in 1838 to provide an education for Jewish children in the city, the school provided free clothes and meals, teaching manual trades and shorthand to its pupils alongside religious instruction.[2] But it was some distance away from where they lived, and following an attack of appendicitis at the age of eight his parents decided he was no longer strong enough to manage the walk. They enrolled him in the third of his five schools, this one nearer home.

At the age of 11 he won a place at Manchester Central High, acclaimed in the competitive Jewish community as nearly the best school in the city, second only to Manchester Grammar. But his parents couldn't afford to keep him there, so by the age of 14 he found himself at his fifth, and final school. On the whole he received an adequate, if fragmented, education, enough to equip him for a trade that might produce a modest income and help alleviate the family's impecuniousness. Had he not been fortunate enough to live in a town blessed with a remarkable Jewish teacher, such a trade was more than likely to have been his destiny.

Yonah Balkind opened his *heder*, a Hebrew school for young boys, in Manchester at the age of 19. He taught there for nearly 70 years. A phenomenally gifted teacher, who had never formally learned how to teach, Balkind's reputation is legendary amongst his former students, collectively known as 'Balkind boys'. His was not the first *heder* that the young Louis Jacobs attended; his parents had sent him to several before enrolling him at Balkind's. All would have been pretty austere places, usually just a room (the word *heder* means room) equipped with desks, some musty books, and a teacher or two reliant on a strap or ruler to keep discipline. Very few pupils found these places inspirational, but attendance a few times a week at after-school *heder* was an obligatory chore for young, nominally observant, Jewish boys in pre-war Manchester. Louis would have found one *heder* much like another. Until he walked into Balkind's. It changed his life.

Louis Jacobs described Yonah Balkind as the man he always considered to be his teacher par excellence. He made learning fun. Not simply because the *heder* doubled as a boys' club, offering billiards and table tennis alongside religious education. Rather it was Balkind's enthusiastic, practical pedagogy that captured his students' attention; play-acting biblical passages with them, holding speed-reading competitions, and most importantly sitting down with each pupil individually to ensure they had fully absorbed the day's instruction.

Learning at Balkind's was fun, and Louis was in his element. He was probably not even surprised when, immediately after his bar mitzvah, Balkind asked him if he had thought of going to Manchester Yeshiva. It was a question rarely asked of most 13-year-old, not particularly observant boys. But Balkind had long been aware that this was no ordinary 13-year-old boy.

Manchester Yeshiva was a college exclusively for young men deeply immersed in their Jewish learning. Some would go on to be rabbis, others would carry their learning with them in whichever direction life would take them. For the older students, yeshiva life was an all-consuming full-time experience, devoted almost exclusively to the study of the Talmud. But the yeshiva also ran an after-school class for younger pupils, with a curriculum that included Bible study, grammar and history. Aimed at boys unlike Louis, from strictly observant homes who would graduate to the full-time yeshiva when they left school, it was a much more immersive educational experience than he had been used to, either at school or at Balkind's. Religiously, it was far less compromising than anything he had ever known. But he loved the intensity of study, scarcely noticing that it was drawing him into a cloistered world of strict religious observance; a world that for a while would be his natural home. He always retained an affection for this strictly observant world, for the manner in which it submerged him so deeply into the depths of Jewish learning and personal piety. He never lost his lingering affection for those strictly observant communities in which he could so easily have spent his life. Had he not, as he grew older, come to consider them as medieval in their understanding and ahistorical in their outlook.

Like many young people newly exposed to intense forms of religion, Jacobs went through a phase in which he became, in his words, 'an insufferable little prig and religious fanatic'.[3] His parents were bewildered by the change in their son, by his scrupulous observance, his intolerance of anything bordering on the moderate and the demands his religious needs placed upon the household. No doubt they began to regret ever sending him to the yeshiva. But his fanaticism didn't last. Looking back, he came to believe that his lifelong intolerance of extremism was a reaction to that short, intense period.

Neither Jacobs nor his parents expected him to remain at the yeshiva beyond the age of 14, when compulsory schooling ended and young men of limited means started to earn a living. His father had negotiated an apprenticeship for him with a local printer, and had it not been for the intervention of his yeshiva teachers, that would have been his trade. Harry Jacobs did not take kindly to their suggestion that Jacobs remain in full-time education at the yeshiva; he had no intention of seeing his son become a rabbi. Nor was he particularly impressed by their assurance that the rabbinate was not the only career path open to him: Louis could, his teachers improbably suggested, become a religious journalist instead. But Jacobs senior had never forgotten how his own education had been cut short due to poverty, and he was too wise to allow the same thing to happen to his son. So, no doubt reluctantly, he agreed that Louis could become one of the 30 or so full-time students at the yeshiva. Like his biblical namesake, the young Jacobs laboured day and night for the next seven years.

MANCHESTER YESHIVA

Jacobs's teachers had always known that he was a pupil of exceptional promise. But it is one thing to excel at lessons, to be the sharpest kid in the class, impressing with one's intellect. It is quite another for students to take such an interest in their subjects that they not only seek out background material but immerse themselves in advanced, complex topics way beyond the demands of their curriculum.

So, it is likely that when the head of Manchester Yeshiva gave Louis Jacobs a book to thank him for helping to dust his library before Passover, he may have pictured the young student dipping into it from time to time. He almost certainly never imagined that Jacobs would devour Rabbi Elhanan Wasserman's somewhat specialized notes to the Talmud to such an extent that he would soon be able to master the precise, didactic methods of analysis practised in the Lithuanian yeshivas.

When not engaged in the core yeshiva activity of unsupervised Talmud study with a fellow student, Jacobs worked his way through the books in the seminary's library. He took an especial interest in collections of Responsa, often highly technical books, containing a particular sage's written answers to legal enquiries he had been sent. He was captivated by one compilation in particular, the Responsa of the sixteenth-century Egyptian legal authority Rabbi David ibn Abi Zimra, a prolific writer who composed over 2,000 replies to questioners. Jacobs, who rarely forgot anything he had read, retained a particularly strong memory of this work. Its clarity, simplicity and precision, even when treating complex theological matters, made a deep impression on him. They were the very qualities that shaped his own thinking, qualities which would define his own writing style and make his works easy to read. Forty years later, when writing his book *Theology in the Responsa*, he recognized that ibn Zimra's work, which he had found and studied on his own so long ago in the yeshiva, had been his inspiration.[4]

There were only two full-time teachers in the yeshiva. Rabbi Moshe Yitzhak Segal, the head, or *Rosh Yeshiva*, was, in the eyes of his students, a stern, forbidding figure. Jacobs developed a tremendous respect for the man's piety, though he said he never felt comfortable in his presence. For Jacobs, Segal's piety was best illustrated by his respect for his students while he prayed. Unlike many rabbis, he did not expect his congregation to wait patiently for him until he finished the private prayer that he often recited slowly and with intense concentration. It was a small thing, but for the young Louis Jacobs, who had not so long ago gone through his own intense phase of religious fanaticism, it was a lesson in how to temper piety with respect for others.

Rabbi Segal had been educated in the Novardok Yeshiva in Russia. The school subscribed to the puritan *musar* tradition in Judaism, an approach which, amongst other things, encouraged the profound internalization of ethical texts, through constant repetition and memorization, as a pathway to character improvement and religious piety. It was a severe upbringing, which, in attempting to produce upright, irreproachable, God-fearing individuals, severely suppressed spontaneity and enthusiasm. This was the environment that Segal had been taught in, and it shaped his personality and pedagogical approach. Fortunately for the students at Manchester Yeshiva, and for Louis Jacobs in particular, the only other full-time teacher at the yeshiva, Rabbi Yitzchok Dubov, a Czechoslovakian Hasid, provided a perfect counterweight to the austere Segal.

It was Rabbi Dubov, as jovial and exuberant as a Hasid should be, who injected a spirit of joy and passion into the otherwise dry atmosphere of the yeshiva. A member of the mystically inclined, life-affirming Habad sect, Dubov sparked Jacobs's lifelong fascination with Kabbalah and Hasidism, subjects on which he would write prolifically throughout his career. In later life Jacobs would keep a picture of Rabbi Dubov on his study door.

What neither Dubov nor Jacobs could know at the time, but which they would have both found ironic, is that half a century later Jacobs would become an unlikely hero to the, by now greatly enlarged, burgeoning Habad movement. His testimony on their behalf in a dramatic, widely publicized New York trial confirmed the movement's legal ownership of their previous rabbi's library, against the claims of his grandson. The account of the trial, to which we will return in due course, would have been a fitting addition to Rabbi Dubov's repertoire of Hasid tales. With his story telling, melodious voice and joyful, mystical demeanour, Rabbi Dubov commanded the respect of his students. But his easygoing manner meant that he was never held in the same sense of awe as was the strictly formal Rabbi Segal, the head of the yeshiva.

Although physically located in Manchester, the yeshiva was spiritually and emotionally rooted in the world of Eastern European Orthodoxy, a world so soon to be tragically destroyed. Louis's grandparents had been part of that world. His parents had stepped away from it, into middle-of-the-road, traditional English Judaism. Now Louis was travelling back. His teachers and fellow students at the yeshiva, and the rabbis he came across in his daily life, were dismissive of the formality of the Anglo-Jewish establishment, its 'English' rabbis (even in Scotland) with their Anglican demeanour, canonicals, dog collars and sermons delivered in a 'foreign' language (by which they meant English). It is another irony of his life that Louis Jacobs would not just end up as an 'English' rabbi but as the custodian of what he would call the 'Anglo-Jewish tradition'. Cleaving to its genteel formality throughout his career, even when the vast majority of traditional British synagogues were creeping back towards something that more closely conformed, in form if not in spirit, to the now obliterated customs of bygone Eastern European communities.

THE KOLEL IN GATESHEAD

Jacobs had no inkling in 1939 that he would one day become a custodian of the old Anglo-Jewish tradition. He would probably have laughed, had he been told. He'd been at Manchester Yeshiva for several years, and had a growing feeling that there was nothing more he could accomplish there. He was becoming increasingly interested in the methods of Talmud study practised in the Telz Yeshiva in Lithuania, the town where his paternal grandparents had come from, the methods he had read about in Rabbi Elhanan Wasserman's book. These methods, which stressed the importance of understanding the deeper meaning of texts, rather than just their superficial argumentation, demanded extreme analytical acuity – a skill he had begun to possess and wished to develop.

He was drawn to Telz, partly by his intellectual interest and the family connection, but more profoundly by a sense that there was some sort of mystical force leading him there. It first manifested when he won a book of essays published by the Telz Yeshiva, and he felt it again when Rabbi Dubov asked him to comment on an essay written by his son who was studying there. That he was being propelled towards a preordained destiny in Telz was confirmed in his mind when an emissary of its yeshiva providentially appeared in Manchester to recruit students. He met Jacobs and offered him a place as a student. His family's inability to afford the cost of sending him would be no obstacle: Louis was already so highly regarded as a student of promise that the emissary agreed to waive all fees.

Jacobs's education had already progressed so far beyond his parents' comprehension that they did not even try to stop him. He obtained a visa from the Lithuanian consulate in Manchester and began to prepare for the journey. But mystically ordained fates are peculiar things; they don't always deliver what they promise. Jacobs's destiny was not to be realized, and a good thing it was too. Britain declared war on Germany, all travel plans were thrown into confusion, and his future in Telz, where in 1941 all Jewish life was obliterated, was off the agenda. Though it wouldn't be the case for millions of others, the Second World War literally saved Louis's life.

Unable to travel to Telz yet still feeling that Manchester Yeshiva had little more to offer him, Jacobs cast around for another institution able to cater to his intellectual needs. He wrote to the rabbi of Sunderland, who was said to have known all 37 volumes of the Talmud, nearly 2 million words, by heart. Louis asked if he could become his private pupil. It was a highly speculative request, and of course Louis had no money or collateral to underwrite his application. As things turned out it was probably fortuitous that he received no reply. For it was just as Louis was feeling most downcast that he was invited to take part in a pioneering initiative, led by a man who he would always say was the most influential teacher of his life.

Eliyahu Dessler had arrived in England from Lithuania in 1928. He had taken up a rabbinic post in North London until the outbreak of the Second World War, when evacuations, military call-ups and the traumas of war dispersed the members of his community. In 1941 he received a letter from Gateshead in the North of England. It came from David Dryan, a pioneer of Orthodox education who had established a yeshiva in the town some years earlier. Reports were beginning to arrive of the Nazi persecution of European Jewry, and although for some years the scale of the slaughter would be not only unknown but beyond all imagination, Dryan realized that the days of the outstanding rabbinic colleges in Eastern Europe were almost certainly numbered. Anxious to save lives, provide a refuge for displaced scholars and ensure the continuity of Torah study, Dryan resolved to establish a centre in Gateshead where those who were too advanced for the town's yeshiva could study. He invited 20 leading rabbinic scholars to join him. When Dessler received Dryan's letter he responded with alacrity.

These days, in Strictly Orthodox communities, it is not unusual to find elite institutions where mature students engage in full-time advanced Talmudic study supported by philanthropic donations. But such establishments, known as kolels, are a relatively recent innovation; they were virtually unknown before the twentieth century. Few would have rated the chances of successfully opening a kolel in 1941, in the darkest days of the Second World War, in a remote town in the North of England with a relatively small Jewish population. But few founders of a kolel could match the commitment and enthusiasm of David Dryan, or of Rabbi Eliyahu Dessler.

Louis joined the Gateshead Kolel just a few weeks after it opened. He was the youngest of the 20 members, the only one who had not studied in a European yeshiva, and indeed the only one who came from a middle-of-the-road, Anglo-Jewish family rather than a background steeped in the minutiae of religious observance and unfathomable depths of learning. He was also probably the only one who had even heard of G. K. Chesterton, certainly the only Kolel member familiar with his works. But from its very inception Gateshead Kolel was intended to be an elite institution, catering only to the most powerful intellects in the rarefied world of Strictly Orthodox Jewish learning. Louis Jacobs – or Laib as he was still known – would never have been admitted if he had not been held in the highest regard; despite his age and upbringing he was considered to be a scholar of outstanding potential. He self-deprecatingly described himself as the 'babe of the kolel', who was treated with an 'amused tolerance', but his peers and teachers are likely to have thought otherwise.[5]

Although in its early days all members of the kolel were nominally regarded as equal, there is no doubt that the intellectual powerhouse, the man to whom all deferred, was Rabbi Dessler. Steeped in the severe *musar* tradition, with its emphasis on scrupulous ethical rigour, he is now acclaimed as one of the great thinkers of mid-twentieth-century world Jewry. To the young Jacobs he was an inspirational teacher, whose discourses reached levels of philosophical enquiry, mystical speculation and spiritual insight that would at times inspire, on other occasions subdue Jacobs throughout his career.

> Together with other youthful enthusiasts, I would uncritically swallow whole the master's very erudite and eloquent discourses, in which there was a blend of *musar*, Kabbalah and Hasidism with an added spice of caustic humour as well as an occasional reference to the theories of Freud and Einstein; the whole constituting a heady mixture that could not fail to intoxicate highly impressionable young men . . . Yet many of Dessler's ideas, especially those regarding this world as a preparation or school for life in the next, found a permanent home in our hearts and minds to influence our religious lives, tending at times to produce a mood of severe introspection, often resulting in disillusionment with the world and its glittering prizes.[6]

Although many years his senior, Dessler had a high opinion of Jacobs. Some years later, when describing the Gateshead Kolel, he wrote:

> There is one young man, a product of Manchester (he is the only native product), and it is no exaggeration for me to say that hitherto, I have never seen an *ilui* [Talmudic genius] of such depth together with the other strengths in any one . . . he is a truly great one . . . able to plumb the depths of thought.[7]

Unfortunately, other than from his own account, little is known about Louis Jacobs's time at Gateshead. Not because the kolel is reclusive; like most institutions which depend on charitable donations it is keen to publicize its accomplishments. Its website lists all the institutions worldwide where its members have gone on to teach or study. It contains a complete record of past and present members. Or at least, almost complete. Only one name is missing. The easiest way to deal with dissenting, independent thinkers is to pretend they don't exist. Louis Jacobs may have been a member of the kolel's founding cohort, and amongst its most illustrious graduates, but the time he spent there has been erased from the institution's memory, and his name from its history. One wonders what Rabbi Dessler would have thought.

Jacobs's time at Gateshead was seminal in shaping his thinking and religious outlook. Yet he was not fully of Gateshead. Younger than his fellow students and with a working-class upbringing, not born into the other-worldliness of a Strictly Orthodox lifestyle and with a wide range of literary interests outside of Talmudic studies, he was never likely to have seen his curiosity satisfied by a lifetime of arcane study in Gateshead's reclusive ivory tower, no matter how intellectually rewarding. That Jewish learning would be his life was in no doubt. But an impoverished childhood had taught him the necessity of earning a living. Before leaving for Gateshead he'd ministered on a Saturday morning to the small Shomrei Shabbos Synagogue in Manchester's Cheetham Hill. It had never earned him more than pocket money. Now he needed to find a job in which he could both earn an adequate wage and remain intellectually stimulated.

2

Becoming an English Rabbi

The obvious career path for Jacobs was to become a rabbi. He had the skills and the ability to receive ordination, or *semicha*, to be inducted into the rabbinate. All he needed was to achieve a level of fluency in the rules and regulations of the primary areas of Jewish law. It mattered little whether a candidate for ordination was any good at preaching, or whether he had the empathy necessary to carry out pastoral duties. These were things that could be picked up later – or in some cases never at all.

Jacobs returned to Manchester Yeshiva to study for his *semicha*. He received his ordination from Rabbi Segal on 23 March 1943, just a few months after returning from Gateshead. Rabbi Segal gave him a letter of recommendation, addressed To Whom It May Concern. 'Rabbi Laib Jacobs', he wrote, 'is a brilliant scholar with a singular capacity for learning and he has acquired a wide and comprehensive knowledge of Jewish Learning and Rabbinical Law and Practice . . . he is most conscientious, pious and of a kindly disposition and I have every confidence in recommending him . . .'[1]

Jacobs obtained a second *semicha* a few months later from Rabbi Rivkin, the charismatic and deeply respected head of the Manchester rabbinic court. (It is not unusual for a rabbi to be ordained more than once.) Rabbi Rivkin had studied with the acclaimed rabbinic genius Rabbi Joseph Rosen of Dvinsk, better known as the Rogatchover Rebbe, who was reputed to know the whole of rabbinic literature by heart and out of whom, the Hebrew poet H. N. Bialik had once said, two Einsteins could be carved. In old age Louis Jacobs would say that there were two great rabbinic thinkers whose works still continued to inspire him, the thirteenth-century Spanish Talmudist Menahem Meiri and Rabbi Rivkin's twentieth-century teacher, the Rogatchover Rebbe.

Throughout his education, Louis Jacobs had been fortunate in having teachers with outstanding personalities, men he looked up to both as mentors and as role models. But he decided not to follow the examples they had set him: he would not become a full-time teacher in a yeshiva or a permanent member of a kolel. He needed a different sort of role model, someone who played an active and influential role in communal life, while maintaining a reputation as a thinker and scholar. He was fortunate again. In wartime Manchester he met several men each of whom exerted a powerful influence on his life.

Perhaps the most important, in terms of his intellectual development, was Dr Alexander Altmann, the communal rabbi of Manchester. Altmann was probably the first outstanding Jewish scholar that Jacobs met who had not emerged from the inward-looking, self-contained world of Eastern European Orthodoxy. He had been educated at the Hildesheimer Seminary in Berlin, an Orthodox institution which paid regard to modern, Western scholarship, even to the extent of requiring potential students to have an advanced level of secular education before they could be admitted.

In 1953 Altmann established the Institute of Jewish Studies in Manchester. He intended it to be a research centre for Jewish religious thought, recognized by Manchester University. But as soon as the Institute's formation was announced, he found himself the subject of vitriolic attack, not dissimilar to that which would be meted out to Louis Jacobs some years later. Members of Manchester's Strictly Orthodox community saw the Institute as an initiative to reform the Jewish religion, in line with proposals Altmann had previously put forward to improve the decorum of the city's synagogue services. His opponents held a protest meeting and demanded his excommunication, setting off a long and acrimonious debate within the Manchester community and in the letters pages of the *Jewish Chronicle*. Although all this happened some years after Jacobs had left Manchester it explains why he considered Altmann a kindred spirit. He described him as a mentor and friend, who had 'electrified the intellectual members of the Manchester Jewish community with his erudition and eloquence and his courageous summons not to despair of Western culture, but to continue to assimilate it into the Jewish world view – as did the orthodox Jews in Germany, despite, or rather because of, the Nazi onslaught'.[2]

A different type of influence on Louis's development as a rabbi came from a young man just seven years older than him. When Louis received his rabbinic ordination, 29-year-old Kopul Rosen was the rabbi of Manchester's Higher Crumpsall Synagogue. He wouldn't be there long; within a year he had been invited to become communal rabbi of Glasgow and two years later Principal Rabbi of the Federation of Synagogues in London. His progress was stellar. It matched his personality.

Jacobs's plans to go to a Lithuanian yeshiva had been thwarted by the outbreak of the Second World War. Kopul Rosen, being a few years older, had not faced the same obstacle. Born in London, he travelled to the Mir Yeshiva in Lithuania, where he spent three years, returning just before the war broke out. A disciple of Rabbi Dessler, Rosen combined a charismatic and attractive personality with a sharp, open-minded intellect and a commanding talent for oratory in both English and Yiddish. For Jacobs, who had first come to know him when he had taught in the Hebrew classes of his synagogue, Kopul Rosen was a role model. Proof of what a young, contemporary minded rabbi could achieve, notwithstanding the severity of the rabbinic establishment at the time.

Kopul Rosen was the outstanding British rabbi of his generation, a man in whom the community's hopes for the future were invested. In the words of one well respected rabbi, 'he brought lustre to the rabbinate'.[3] Tragically he died young, long before he could fully realise his promise. When Louis visited him in 1962, about a fortnight before he died, they spent hours discussing the communal controversy in which Jacobs was then embroiled. Kopul Rosen was on Louis's side, though he warned him not to trust all his supporters; his was one of several voices which suggested that Jacobs was being taken advantage of by one or two people with agendas other than his own.

Jacobs came away from the meeting with Rosen overwhelmed. Not just because his mentor was dying, but because, despite knowing that his days were numbered, Kopul Rosen 'could talk brilliantly and with keen interest and sympathy about a problem which would not be resolved in his lifetime'.[4]

It is ironic that Alexander Altmann and Kopul Rosen were so prominent among the personalities who helped shape Jacobs's career. When Chief Rabbi Joseph Hertz died in 1946 a search was launched to appoint his successor. Three names were put forward. One was Dr Alexander Altmann, another was Kopul Rosen. Neither got the job. Despite his accomplishments Rosen was deemed too young. Altmann was also ruled out, the rumour being that he had been vetoed by Sir Robert Waley-Cohen, President of the United Synagogue, on the bizarre grounds that he was German.[5]

The third candidate, Rabbi Israel Brodie, was appointed. The irony is that if either of the other two had been offered the job instead of Brodie, the Chief Rabbinate would have been so different that the controversy which tore British Jewry apart and torpedoed Jacobs's career is unlikely ever to have happened.

A very different influence on the young Laib's life was exerted by an eccentric Lithuanian rabbi who arrived in Manchester shortly before the outbreak of the Second World War. Koppel Kahana, who had known Trotsky in his youth, arrived in the hope of obtaining a rabbinic position, leaving his wife and young daughter at home in Lithuania until he established himself. Tragically, in a story that is all too familiar, the war broke out before he could bring them over. They were murdered by the Nazis.

Already in his mid-forties, alone, with bad eyesight and poor English in an unfamiliar country, Kahana had no choice but to rebuild his life. He found employment in various casual roles in the Manchester community, preaching in Yiddish in the synagogues and giving a weekly Talmud class, which Laib would attend, at the home of Kopul Rosen. As these part-time appointments would never be enough to sustain him, he taught himself English and Latin, and won a place at Cambridge, where he obtained an MA in Law.

For Jacobs, Koppel Kahana brought to 'cold and dreary Manchester' the vanished Lithuanian yeshiva world he had so wanted to study in. Jacobs would talk with enthusiasm of Kahana's sharp analytical skills, his retentive memory, recalling in full passages he had studied years earlier, and his impressive ability when performing the 'pin test'. This trick, beloved of yeshiva students, involved sticking a pin into a volume of the Talmud and declaiming the passage on the page where its point emerged. The trick could, of course, only be done by someone with a photographic memory. Jacobs would explain that this was not the same as a retentive memory; Koppel Kahana had both. As indeed did Jacobs.[6]

EARNING A LIVING

Few newly ordained rabbis walk straight into a job as spiritual leader of a congregation. Jacobs was no exception. He made ends meet by teaching at synagogue Hebrew classes and at Mercaz Limmud, an educational centre that aimed to give a deeper appreciation of Judaism to young people. Many of its students were war refugees, now in Britain but preparing to build a new life for themselves in what was then British Mandate Palestine. The director of the Mercaz Limmud was a German refugee, Hans Heinemann. A brilliant scholar, he would eventually settle in Israel, where as Professor Yosef Heinemann he become the world's leading authority on Midrash, the ancient homiletical interpretation of the Bible. Laib Jacobs was privileged to meet some outstanding scholars during his formative years.

It was at Mercaz Limmud that Louis saw Sophie Lisagorsky for a second time. He had first noticed her three years earlier. He hadn't spoken to her then, and he didn't speak to her now. But once they did start talking, the conversation continued for over 60 years.

Sophie (or Shula as she was better known) had been born in London in 1922. She moved with her parents to Manchester, to be close to her sister Malka and her husband, Yank Levy. Yank, who had taken over his father's successful wine merchants, was a generous supporter of Manchester Yeshiva and its students. Louis and Sophie had first set eyes on each other, but did not speak, at a party that Yank hosted for the yeshiva students. She remembered the date: it was the Simchat Torah holiday in October 1940. Sophie was cautiously serving the food, feeling uncomfortable about venturing too far into a room full of religious young men. Louis may not even have given her more than a fleeting glance; he was a pious rabbinic student. But three years later, when they spoke for the first time, he remarked on the colour of the dress she had been wearing that evening.

At the time Shula was living on a kibbutz in Bromsgrove, Birmingham. The kibbutz was one of several set up by the religious-Zionist movement Bachad, to provide a wartime place of safety for young Kindertransport refugees, and to prepare them for life in Palestine, once they were eventually able to settle there. Shula was one of very few English residents of the kibbutz. Too young to be called up but anxious to help the war effort, the opportunity to do Land Army agricultural work in Bromsgrove's Jewish environment provided her with the best of both worlds.

Laib and Shula first spoke when Laib was invited to dinner at Yank and Malka's home. Shula was staying there while on a short break from Bromsgrove. Laib thought he had been invited so that he could take yet another look at Yank's extensive library. It didn't occur to either of them that their hosts' plan was that they should meet.

After dinner Laib went to look at the books in Yank's study. He knew he would find plenty there to occupy his attention. Somehow he got talking to Shula about the kibbutz. That was when he mentioned the dress she had been wearing three years earlier. As they spoke, she remembered a former employer of hers talking about a brilliant young man who was going to be a rabbi. And she recalled her friend Herbert Laster pointing at someone across the street, saying: 'See that fellow, he's brilliant, he's going to be a rabbi.'

Shula had been at Bromsgrove for nearly two years when she and Louis got talking at the dinner party. They went for a walk together next day. She recorded her thoughts in her diary:

> During the walk all I can say is I was absolutely enthralled being entertained by my head being filled with magical Hassidic tales and the like. I must have appeared quite ignorant in opposition to his brain, but it did not seem to worry him at all. Suddenly, here was a *yeshiva bochur*, a rabbi, and I always thought of rabbis in terms of dull, pious and old in [their] ways, [and he,] not knowing anything modern, was just the opposite. Together with a tale for every question, joked and seemed like a normal Manchester English young man. He wasn't pompous, certainly did not parade his religiousness. Talked of literature and poetry and he even liked jazz! (Well, I was not so sure about that.) He was refreshing to talk to, and yet he gave me the impression of being the spiritual type, which I admired anyway and seemed to me right away that he was Mr. Right! Lived for his learning. (Until I came along . . .)[7]

It was 26 December 1943. She was due to go back to the kibbutz on the 28th.

At 11 a.m. on 28 December, Shula was packed, with her suitcase in her hand, about to set off for the station, when the phone rang. It was Laib. 'Please do not go back to the kibbutz,' he pleaded. 'Stay in Manchester.' Someone, possibly her mother, reminded her that a young rabbinic student would never speak in vain.

Shula did not go back to the kibbutz. She and Laib were married three months later. It was 28 March 1944. Shortly before the wedding Rabbi Segal took Shula aside. He told her that she was marrying an *ilui*, a Talmudic genius. It would be her duty to take care of all his needs, so that he could devote his life to the study of Torah, without distraction or interruption. Shula had no problem with that.[8]

MARRIED LIFE

Laib was not earning nearly enough to support himself and Shula, even by their own modest standards. That was fine in the eyes of his new brother-in-law, Yank Levy, who believed that the duty of a scholar was to study. Shula's father Isser Lisagorsky must have felt the same, because, with some help from Yank, he purchased a small house for the newly-weds to live in. He presented Laib with a full set of the Vilna edition of the Talmud, all 37 volumes, in order that he could spend his days studying. Laib also picked up some casual teaching work, giving private tuition to the children of rabbinic scholars and conducting a Talmud class in Yiddish every evening at the Machzikei Hadas synagogue.

With just about enough financial security to see them through, Laib and Shula settled in to married life. The only dark cloud was their awareness that Laib's father, Harry Jacobs, did not approve. Proudly working-class, with a burning desire to see his son make something of himself in life, he thought it utterly unacceptable that Laib was living off the kindness of others instead of going to university and preparing himself for a career in the rabbinate.

It didn't take long before Harry Jacobs was vindicated. Laib's intellectual curiosity was leading him into fields away from Talmud. He sensed that the religious training he'd received, invaluable as it was in terms of developing analytical skills and detailed knowledge of Jewish law, was largely irrelevant to most British Jews. At the same time, he felt that the training undertaken by those who did minister to the British community, was sorely lacking in the very skills that he had acquired. But even as he began to dwell on these matters, formulating solutions in his mind for what he perceived as a crisis in British Jewry, working out what his own contribution should be, he became distracted by more pressing issues. Shula was soon to have a child. And her father was desperately ill. Not only was his instinct leading him towards greater communal involvement, he was about to be burdened with new financial responsibilities. One can imagine Harry Jacobs's relief when Laib told him he wanted to prepare for a career.

Louis and Shula became parents on 30 March 1945. Shula's father, who had supported them so generously, did not live to see the moment. They named the baby Isser after his grandfather – Ivor in English.

Louis Jacobs first appeared in print with a letter he wrote to the *Jewish Chronicle* in July 1944. He told his diary that his motive in writing it was 'not purely altruistic but was mainly occasioned by a desire to "get on" and to get known. Though this may seem extremely egoistic (and it probably is) yet I don't see any great harm in it.'[9]

In the event, it didn't do much to advance his name, as the newspaper, possibly short-staffed due to the war, signed him off as a Rabbi D. L. Jacob. With hindsight it is easy to see how the letter, in which he called for a synthesis between the yeshiva world and the tolerant modernity of England, foreshadowed the trajectory of his career:

In your columns you report certain reforms that the administration of Jews' College intended to take to make that institution a living force in our community. May I respectfully suggest that what our community really needs is not a new Jews' College but a modern *Yeshiva*. Every sane-minded person will readily admit the importance of many of the ideals that the College stands for. It is most important that our Ministers should possess a good secular education. It is also important that they should be capable of delivering inspiring sermons. But these things are good only when backed with sound Torah knowledge. It is here that Jews' College fails; it has succeeded in producing a new type; modelled on the parson and parish priest . . . It is not only Jews' College that is at fault. The *Yeshivas* have refused to recognise the facts [*sic*] that their exclusion of everything except Torah could not possibly succeed in the England of to-day. England is a land where, as Chesterton pointed out. 'a breach of good manners is looked upon with more abhorrence than a breach of morals'; people are less shocked at the man who doesn't believe in G-d than at the man who eats peas with his knife. The *Yeshivas* blind their eyes to this. They go on trying to instil a love of Torah and *yirat shamayim* in their pupils without giving them a practical philosophy of life . . . The time is surely ripe for a new institution, one that will combine the deep piety and love of *torah lishmah* of the Yeshiva with the polish, the modern methods and the efficiency of Jews' College.[10]

Despite calling for a new institution, Jacobs was clear-sighted enough to recognize that his best chance of getting a job was in one that already existed. When Jews' College advertised for a temporary lecturer in Bible and Talmud, at a salary of £500 per annum, he threw his hat into the ring. Inexperienced, and without a university degree, it was always unlikely that he would get the job. It hardly mattered, for by the time the rejection letter arrived he had spotted a far more likely opportunity:

REQUIRED, lecturer for Talmud and allied subjects. Rabbinical diploma, experience with adults and of Talmud Torah class work, command of English. Write immediately to Rabbi Dr. E. Munk, 680, Finchley Road, N.W.11.[11]

Rabbi Dr Eli Munk had arrived in England from Germany in 1930. Like Alexander Altmann, he'd studied and received his rabbinic ordination at Berlin's Hildesheimer Seminary. It was the Seminary's unique blend of Orthodox scholarship and Western culture which resulted in him, a German-speaking rabbi, obtaining a PhD on the religious poetry of William Wordsworth.

Munk was the rabbi of a synagogue in Golders Green with a largely German congregation. It was a predominantly middle-class, professional community adhering to the vanished traditions of Jewish Frankfurt; scrupulous in its religious observance, formal in its synagogue services, erudite and culturally literate. The only informal thing about the synagogue was that nobody called it by its official name, the Golders Green Beth Hamedrash. It was universally known as Munk's *shul*, as it is still today, more than 40 years after Rabbi Munk's death.

In his diary, Jacobs records his hesitation about accepting the post. 'At first I refused but after writing a second time to withdraw my application I again received a letter asking me to arrange a meeting and to talk over the whole matter. Shula says that this is *beshert* and he writes that it is the chance of a lifetime. I wrote to him to arrange a meeting.'[12]

Jacobs's initial hesitation was due to his lingering attachment to the belief that the best way to spend one's life is in full-time Talmudic study. His brother-in-law Yank encouraged him in this, holding forth on 'the greatness of sitting down and learning'. But with the promise of a job looming, Jacobs rapidly grasped the benefits of paid employment. 'Even if I could become really great through sitting down here in Manchester, I would still prefer to earn my own living – a small thing no doubt, but my own . . . I have visions of starting new movements, magazines, *shiurim* and so on, and I hope that something comes of this.'[13]

Jacobs joined Munk's synagogue as assistant rabbi in September 1945. It was a new world for him, in which philosophical discussions were held on Sunday afternoons in congregants' homes, while tea was taken in silver services and cakes dispensed upon fine china. It was Louis's first real taste of how a religious Jewish community could nevertheless enjoy the benefits of an English cultural life.

Louis, Shula and the baby moved into a flat in Greencroft Gardens, West Hampstead. It was a quiet, leafy road in an area that housed many German-Jewish refugees. The flat itself was a conversion in what had once been a substantial, three-storey, red-brick Victorian house. The only drawback was that they were living nearly three miles from the synagogue, necessitating a good 45 minutes' walk each way on a Shabbat morning, whatever the weather.

A few months after Jacobs joined the synagogue its rabbi and management opened a part-time yeshiva to provide advanced Talmudic tuition, in English, to pupils of school-leaving age. Jacobs was appointed to be its principal. It was not a yeshiva of the same standing as that he had attended in Manchester – few of its students were likely to graduate to the rabbinate or to full-time

Talmudic study. But it was Jacobs's first serious pedagogical role, made all the more challenging because he was teaching students only a few years younger than he.

The yeshiva's official opening took place in January 1947, five months after studies had commenced. It turned out to be the most controversial episode of the young Rabbi Jacobs's life to date. The proceedings began with Dayan Abramsky of the London Beth Din, the religious court, speaking in Yiddish to declare the yeshiva open. His choice of Yiddish was no accident; he was making a point about the school's policy of teaching exclusively in English.

Then Jacobs spoke. He told those present that he had received objections about the English-language ethos of the school. He said that, without wishing to denigrate Yiddish, he knew of no language so fluid, so correct, so full of technical terms to illustrate the finer points of an argument, as English. Torah could be taught in any language and it was untenable to use a foreign language such as Yiddish to teach English-speaking students. Furthermore, he said, 'It was quite possible, when giving instruction in higher Jewish learning; usefully to employ from many sources of English, such as Shakespeare, Shaw, or even Sherlock Holmes.'

The *Jewish Chronicle* reported that Dayan Abramsky then spoke once more, again in Yiddish. He 'commented at length and somewhat unfavourably on Rabbi Jacobs's reference to the use of quotations from Sherlock Holmes'.[14] It had been Jacobs's first run-in with a *dayan* on the London Beth Din. It would not be his last.

Jacobs introduced his students at the yeshiva to the analytical methods of Talmud study, but it is unlikely that he succeeded in engaging them as deeply as he would have wished. One of his students did enter the rabbinate, becoming the rabbi of a Manchester synagogue and eventually opening his own yeshiva in Jerusalem. Some years later he published an essay under a pen name attacking Louis Jacobs for heresy.

Shula gave birth to their second child, Naomi, in June 1947. By now Jacobs's reputation was spreading through the London community. In July 1946 he was asked to preside over the annual prize giving at Menorah Primary School, where Shula was asked to distribute the prizes. The following April he preached the sermon at the Shomrei Hadas synagogue in Hampstead, and in September of that year he delivered the traditional Sabbath of Repentance lecture in Maida Vale. Louis was a young man going places.

Like most synagogues, Munk's ran a Hebrew School for the children of its congregants. Its head teacher was Rabbi Alexander Carlebach. A favourite family story is of Ivor Jacobs lying in his pram outside Munk's synagogue. Alongside him was a pram in which lay Rabbi Carlebach's baby daughter, Tirza. The ladies of the congregation would look at the two babies cooing at each other, and foretell that one day they would wed. They were right. They did.[15]

3

A Reasonable Faith

Even before he left Manchester Louis had made up his mind to study for a university degree. He had enrolled on a correspondence course to prepare for London University's Special Entrance Exam, noting in his diary that 'everything is going fine, thank G. I find hardly any difficulty at all with the lessons and if they continue to be so easy I think I will do fine when the time comes for the exams. Nevertheless I feel just a little impatient at having to wait so long for my BA. Although on second thoughts it won't be so long, I will only be 27, please G.'[1]

Louis passed the entrance exam and enrolled on a BA course in Semitics at University College London, where he had the distinct good fortune of being the only student on the course. There was also only one tutor. Louis's degree course was intensively one-to-one, and his job at Munk's gave him enough spare time to allow him to take full advantage of the opportunity.

It came as something of a shock to Jacobs to discover that his powerful intellect, honed during years of intense Talmudic study and incisive reasoning, was not fully equipped to meet the demands of an academic curriculum. Talmud study demands in-depth analysis of arguments rooted in a single cohesive textual discipline. Semitics, Jacobs found, was far broader. It ranged across ancient and modern Hebrew literature, philosophy, grammar and history. Its study required an appreciation of context and the ability to impose conclusions deduced in one field on problems encountered in another.

Nevertheless, Jacobs came away from his final examination convinced that he had obtained a first. He had, he thought, performed well in his viva, when he was examined by three of the most erudite Jewish scholars in the country. He was therefore most put out to discover that instead of the first-class degree he expected, he had been awarded a lower second. It was a lesson in life, appended to three years of academic study.

Like many of the dominant personalities who influenced the young Jacobs, his tutor, Siegfried Stein, had been born in Germany. Religiously observant, he had been educated at the Berlin *Hochschule*, a pioneering institution in the academic study of Judaism. One of the school's principal areas of study was Biblical Criticism, a discipline that investigates the literary nature and origins of the Bible by exploring inconsistencies in the text, variant readings across different manuscripts, and the evidence of history, archaeology and language.

Stein introduced Jacobs to the critical study of the Bible, warning him that he might find some of its conclusions unsettling, but assuring him that it need not undermine his Jewish belief. He maintained that it was quite possible, as his own lifestyle demonstrated, to academically challenge the Orthodox view that the Torah had been dictated word by word to Moses in the wilderness, and yet not waver in the slightest in one's faith.

At first Jacobs happily and innocently accepted the validity of this approach to Bible study – Stein was after all an observant Jew. But as Louis pondered the problem he became increasingly convinced that it was not intellectually honest to compartmentalize scholarship and observance in this way, to act as if there were two truths, one for the academy and one for the synagogue. Nor could he accept the compromise of many Orthodox rabbis, that although one must reject the tenets of Biblical Criticism, one may study it if one is a candidate for a degree in Semitics.

Jacobs knew he was not the only person unsettled by this dilemma: some of the students at Jews' College felt the same way. He even knew of one Jews' College student who had been so disturbed by the inconsistency of this view that he rejected Orthodoxy and became a Reform rabbi. That however would not be Jacobs's response. He would take a classic Talmudic approach to the problem, seeking to reconcile the two apparently conflicting views. The solution that he gradually reached would shape the rest of his career.

Jacobs was always indebted to Stein for introducing him to academic study. But he came to realize that Stein's compartmentalization of his views was neither to avoid conflict in his own mind, nor to allow him to sit simultaneously in both the academic and the religious camps. Instead it appeared that Stein believed that holding conflicting religious and scholarly views was a legitimate philosophical position – a point of view that Jacobs was never able to accept. When the controversy over Jacobs's theological views broke out, Stein, together with eight other academics, wrote to the *Jewish Chronicle* implicitly criticizing him for not treating academia and religion as mutually incompatible. They were rebuked in turn by Rabbi Ignaz Maybaum, a leading Reform theologian, for preserving their academic views in a vacuum and making no contribution whatsoever to religious life.[2]

Louis received his degree in June 1947. Even though he had only obtained a lower second, Stein managed to obtain two teaching scholarships for him, one to the value of £55, the other for £40. He offered Louis a position as his assistant at University College, a role that he performed for a short time alongside his duties at Munk's.

Jacobs did not remain an assistant, either to Dr Stein or to Rabbi Munk, for long. At the end of 1947 he received an approach from the Manchester Central Synagogue to fill their vacant post of rabbi. The pulpit had been vacant for some years because the congregation had been unable to agree what sort of rabbi they wanted. A working-class congregation with Eastern European roots, the synagogue was split between the older members who wanted a Yiddish-speaking rabbi of the old school, and a growing contingent of younger congregants who favoured a university-educated English minister. Louis, who was only 27 years old, with a university degree, met the modernizers' criteria. But as he was also a yeshiva graduate, had been taught by traditional European rabbis and spoke reasonable Yiddish, the older members were quite comfortable with him. On top of all that, he was a child of the synagogue; he had sung in its choir as a boy.

Jacobs delivered a trial sermon at Manchester Central on 20 December 1947 and gave a lecture that afternoon. On 31 December the president of the synagogue wrote to him, saying how pleased he had been by the sermon and that he was proposing to call a general meeting of members, at which the Council would recommend that Rabbi Jacobs be invited to fill the vacant post of *Rav*, the Eastern European term for rabbi.

Jacobs was inducted into office on 18 April 1948 at a service conducted by Rabbi Alexander Altmann. The new rabbi spoke on the value of tradition. Those who believed in watering down traditional teachings to attract young people were, he said, doing a great disservice to Judaism.

MANCHESTER CENTRAL SYNAGOGUE

Manchester Central Synagogue was a congregation that tended towards the Anglo-Jewish tradition, without fully discarding its Eastern European origins. The rabbi, cantor and choir boys were all required to wear canonicals, the distinguishing feature of the Anglo-Jewish persuasion, and Jacobs preached every week in English. But twice a year, on the Sabbaths preceding Passover and Yom Kippur, he delivered a lengthy sermon in Yiddish. These were the traditional occasions when a rabbi would preach to his community; the weekly sermon being something rarely encountered in Eastern Europe. Jacobs gave these sermons in Yiddish because that was the way the older congregants remembered it. He also conducted a nightly Talmud class in Yiddish, for those whose religious learning had always been conducted in that language.

Louis had never spoken in public with such regularity. Apart from the sermons, he addressed couples getting married, delivered eulogies at funerals and in houses of mourning, exhorted bar mitzvah boys to remain true to their Judaism and spoke at communal gatherings and functions. In his autobiography he described how this 'orgy of public speaking' led him to take elocution lessons, to help him project his voice effectively.[3]

Jacobs's newly gained academic and professional status gave him the confidence to start writing seriously. He had always enjoyed writing but up to now his output had largely been letters and diary entries. Now, as a man of growing repute, he turned his attention to producing more scholarly material.

His first article, 'Laws of Marriage and Divorce in Israel', appeared in January 1949, just a few months after he had taken up his new position in Manchester. It was published in the *Jewish Review*, the journal of the Religious Zionist, Mizrachi Federation of Great Britain and Ireland, the group to which he felt most closely aligned. The article set out the legal problems that the new state of Israel would need to address if, as Jacobs hoped it would, the nation adopted Jewish law in respect of marriage and divorce. He outlined possible solutions to the classical problems: of widows who are unable to remarry because they cannot produce evidence that their husband is dead, of spouses who will not grant a divorce, and of children born from forbidden marriages. Although he drew on liberal opinions in the rabbinic Responsa to imply that solutions could be found to all these problems, he did not, at this stage in his career, come down firmly on any side. The purpose of the article was 'to show – albeit tentatively – that the difficulties are not unsurmountable'.[4]

Later in his career he was far more outspoken, arguing for legal solutions to situations that made a misery of people's lives simply because rabbinic opinion had vacillated for centuries in indecision. At this stage, at the age of 28, he was not yet ready. But even at such an early juncture in his career it was pretty clear where he was heading.

Once he began writing, new articles came thick and fast. Over the next 18 months a further seven pieces appeared. Most were for *Chayenu*, a journal published by Bachad and Torah va-Avodah, both constituents of the Mizrachi Federation; Bachad had run the kibbutz where Shula was living when she and Louis first met. The two groups worked closely together, running activities for young religious Zionists, hoping to inspire them to become pioneers in the new state of Israel.

Louis was too busy building a career in England to contemplate a move to Israel, a land where few rabbis were able to find paid employment. But he and Shula participated enthusiastically in Torah va-Avodah's social and educational activities. Apart from contributing to their journal, Jacobs was the resident lecturer at their summer schools in 1950 and 1951.

Jacobs's first article for *Chayenu* was entitled 'Judaism and Freedom'. Arguing that true freedom is to be found when one is able to exercise self-control, he invoked Buddhism, comparing it unfavourably with Judaism:

> The Buddhist urges as his solution that man should try to free himself from all his desires. Judaism has a saner solution than Nirvana. The Jewish answer is that man must learn to control himself by observing the laws of the Torah. Surely this is the meaning of the saying of the Rabbis that we should not read *Harut*, 'engraved', on the tablets of the of the law, but '*Herut*' – freedom.[5]

Most of the articles he wrote during this period were about Jewish law and its ability to respond to changing conditions. It was a theme he would return to over and again in his career. At this stage he defended Orthodoxy against 'those who state that orthodox Rabbis have not made an attempt at coming to grips with modern problems'.[6] As he became older, and more confident in his views, he would not only stress the flexibility of Jewish law, but adopt a less compromising attitude towards authorities who failed to apply this flexibility in their rulings.

In a 1951 article defending the ability of Jewish law to respond to modernity he drew both on traditional rabbinic and secular sources, throwing in ideas from, among others, Freud, P. G. Wodehouse, Rabindranath Tagore and even Rudolf Kittel –

'a contemptible toady of Hitler and the Nazis', for good measure. In his final paragraph he returned to a dispute he had previously been involved in, now reiterating his view that a proposal to reconstitute the Sanhedrin, ancient Israel's legislative body, was an example of muddled thinking.[7]

Two years earlier the Conference of Anglo-Jewish Preachers, a body that included both Orthodox and Reform ministers, had come out strongly in favour of reconstituting the Sanhedrin in the new state of Israel. Jacobs had been one of the few voices opposed, and was criticized for this opinion in the leader pages of the *Jewish Chronicle*. He had written a lengthy letter in response arguing that a reconvened Sanhedrin would not, in law, be the appropriate institution to resolve the difficult questions around marriage and divorce then facing the new state of Israel.

The fact that he felt obliged, two years later, to repeat his earlier opinion, and once again outline his case, shows how strongly he felt about the issue. A lesser man might have swallowed the *Jewish Chronicle*'s criticism and the opposition of the Conference of Anglo-Jewish Preachers, and let the matter drop. That was not Jacobs's style. Others might have formed views based on the utility of a solution, but Jacobs didn't think in that way. For him, it was all about dissecting and analysing a problem. Logic was always subordinate to humanity and compassion. But a logical solution was always preferable to one formulated because it was merely useful, or a good idea.

A LEGAL FICTION

In the weeks leading up to Passover in 1951 a remarkable correspondence between Louis and another young rabbi appeared in the letters pages of the *Jewish Chronicle*. It began when Jacobs wrote an article for the paper about the legal device which allows *chametz*, produce that is not kosher for Passover, to be sold to a non-Jew before the festival, and bought back afterwards.

In his article, Jacobs condemned those who said that the sale of *chametz* was 'fooling the Almighty', yet considered the *prozbul* – a device to circumvent the remission of debts in the sabbatical year – as evidence that Jewish law could be reformed. These people didn't realize, Jacobs said, that the *prozbul* was a legal fiction of exactly the same nature as the sale of *chametz*. He referred his readers to a book entitled *Hamoadim b'halakha*, a treatise on the laws of festivals by the renowned scholar Rabbi S. Y. Zevin.

Jacobs's assertion that the sale of *chametz* was the same type of legal fiction as the *prozbul* prompted a fierce response from Reverend Leslie Hardman, minister of Hendon United Synagogue. Hardman had been chaplain to the British Army during the war. He had witnessed the horrors of the Shoah at first hand, entering Bergen-Belsen on the day it was liberated, wholly unprepared for what he was about to encounter. He later spoke of his inability to understand how the God he worshipped could have permitted such atrocities.

Hardman wrote to the *Jewish Chronicle* in response to Jacobs's article. 'I regret to say that in stating that the *prozbul* is a legal fiction of "exactly" the same nature as the sale of *chametz* he has committed a grave error in the interpretation of *halakha* . . . The two institutions are based on entirely different notions.' He was astonished that Jacobs had described the sale of *chametz* as a legal fiction at all. Had Jacobs listened to a series of lectures given by Rabbi Koppel Kahana he would not have made such an error. Furthermore, if he had looked in the Talmud rather than in Rabbi S.Y. Zevin's book *moadim b'halakha* he would have realized that the legal-fiction theory for the sale of *chametz* was a fallacy, based on an entire misunderstanding of the text.

Jacobs wrote back the following week. Hardman, he said, 'makes the amusing, though not uncommon, mistake of assuming that the term "legal fiction" implies a dishonest or fraudulent contrivance'. Calling it a legal fiction does not imply that the sale of *chametz* is invalid. As for Hardman's criticism that Jacobs should have referred to the Talmud rather than Zevin's book; it reminded him of the gibe: '"Some people are alive; others are in the civil service" – as if Zevin's fine work is at all at variance with the Talmudic sources.' Furthermore, Jacobs had no doubt that Rabbi Koppel Kahana would agree with Zevin, and with the views that he had expressed in the article.

Reverend Hardman was having none of it. He wrote again: 'Rabbi Jacobs in his letter makes no reference at all to the matter pointed out in my first two paragraphs. Can I then take it that . . . he has withdrawn his remark "the prozbul and the sale of chametz are on 'equal terms'"?' He again challenged Jacobs's use of Zevin's book rather than quoting directly from the Talmud and insisted that the onus was on Jacobs to show what is wrong in explaining the nature of the sale of *chametz* according to the normal principles of Jewish law, rather than using a legal-fiction theory.

If Louis Jacobs replied, the *Jewish Chronicle* did not publish his letter. Instead it rounded off the correspondence with a letter from the barrister Peter Elman. He gave a lengthy explanation of the technical meaning of legal fiction before coming down firmly on Hardman's side. Avoiding both the Talmud and Zevin, he quoted from the sixteenth-century Jewish law code the *Shulhan Aruch*, before insisting that the sale of *chametz* 'certainly cannot be called a legal fiction in any sense of the word. The law of *chametz* remains as such unaffected. The mechanism of the sale is a legitimate use, not fictitious in any sense . . .'[8]

If this dispute masked any personal tension between Jacobs and Hardman, it did not last. Ten years later, when the Jacobs Affair blew up and Louis Jacobs was excluded from the United Synagogue ministry, Reverend Leslie Hardman was one of very few senior Orthodox leaders prepared to stick their necks out to support him.

A PROMISING CANDIDATE

Unafraid to speak his mind, and invariably in possession of all the sources needed to support his views, Jacobs was attracting the attention of the Jewish community's religious leadership. In 1949 he received a call from Dayan Abramsky of the London Beth Din, asking him to visit. Possibly a little apprehensive, because of Abramsky's comments two years earlier at the Yeshiva dedication, Jacobs travelled to London to meet him. Their discussion passed uneventfully, although Jacobs was not really sure why he had been invited. He found out a few weeks later, when he heard 'in a rather roundabout way' that the Chief Rabbi wanted him to succeed Dayan Swift, one of the judges on the Beth Din, who was departing for a post in South Africa. The Chief Rabbi, apparently, had him in mind both for both of Swift's jobs: his role as dayan, or judge, on the Beth Din and his position as Minister of the Brondesbury Synagogue in North West London. Jacobs now realized that his visit to Abramsky had been a closet interview for the job, so secret that even the candidate did not know he was being interviewed.

Things took an even stranger turn when Jacobs, who had neither applied for the job nor been approached officially, was invited to preach at Brondesbury Synagogue. He declined the invitation, writing that it would be unfair of him to leave his current synagogue, where he had been employed for less than two years. He found his refusal ignored, and received another letter from the assistant minister at Brondesbury, telling him he was about to be invited to interview by the Executive of the United Synagogue, the umbrella body under whose auspices the posts fell. The assistant minister suggested Jacobs telephone him, as well as Dayan Swift, the departing post holder.

As if this was not perplexing enough, he then met the Chief Rabbi, Israel Brodie. He informed Jacobs that the job he had not applied for was to be downgraded from a judge on the Beth Din to a position as the court's Registrar. Louis was left feeling distressed. 'After all I had not taken any initiative in the matter and, if the truth be told, did not want to leave the Central Synagogue.'⁹

Thirteen years later, at the height of the Jacobs Affair, Swift wrote to Abramsky recalling the incident and praising him for his foresight in 'prophesying' that Jacobs was a 'great *epikoros* [heretic]'. Of course Swift was writing many years after the event and therefore, as Elliot Cosgrove points out, his comment should be taken with a grain of salt. If Abramsky's reservations were really as strong as Swift recalled, it is surprising that the process of vetting him was allowed to drag on for as long as it did.¹⁰

Jacobs was in demand from other quarters too. He may have not wished to leave the Central Synagogue, but a short while later, when he received an approach from the Netherlands, he boarded a plane for the first time in his life and spent ten days in Amsterdam, lecturing in English and Yiddish and meeting members of the community. Ultimately though, he decided against taking the job, believing that the language barrier would be too great for him to overcome, and that in any event there were other rabbis in Amsterdam who, knowing the community better, would be better suited to the position.

Manchester Central Synagogue was a second home for Shula and Louis's older children, Ivor and Naomi. Louis may have been too busy during the Shabbat morning service to spend much time with them, but they invariably accompanied him at the end of the afternoon when he returned for the traditional final Shabbat meal. It was a memorable walk for Naomi, whose five-year-old legs were obliged to march double time when they passed the shops; 'Let's speed up here,' her father would say. 'We don't want to shame anybody.' Louis could not bear the thought of embarrassing a congregant who, coming out of a shop, where they should not have been on a Shabbat afternoon, found themselves bumping into the rabbi.

Many years later Naomi was reminded of her father's strict adherence to the principle of not shaming anyone. They were walking home from synagogue in London after a Shabbat morning service when they were caught short by a torrential downpour. As it was Shabbat they were carrying nothing; neither umbrella, nor even handkerchiefs to put over their heads. Naomi persuaded her father to take a short cut through St John's Wood High Street. He was reluctant, in case he bumped into a congregant who would be embarrassed to be caught shopping on a Saturday, but the rain was so heavy that he acquiesced. When they got home he agreed that no harm had been done. The rain was so fierce that it was impossible to see more than a few inches ahead; no one had seen them and they recognized nobody. Two days later Naomi went back to the High Street, to have her hair done. Her hairdresser told her of the consternation that had broken out the previous Saturday amongst his customers. Trapped beneath the hairdryers when they spotted the rabbi walking by, there was nowhere they could hide. When Naomi reported this back to her father, she says he was devastated.

As a communal rabbi, Jacobs could have done the job the synagogue employed him for, and left it at that. But like many Jews of his generation who had grown up in reduced circumstances, he was driven by an ambition to succeed, to throw off the constraints of his background, make the most of his potential and to acquire a name for himself. Some of his contemporaries were on the way to becoming successful businessmen or professionals; his choice had been the rabbinate, but his drive was no less for it. He became vice principal of Manchester University Jewish Society, and honorary chaplain to the local Jewish social and sports venue Waterpark Club. He chaired Manchester Mizrachi, took on a temporary role as honorary principal of the Bachad Institute for Jewish Studies, and led educational weekends and summer schools. Most significantly, he continued writing. In 1951 he joined the *Jewish Chronicle*'s team of seven anonymous writers who, in rotation, contributed weekly sermons for the paper.

In 1952 he published his first article in an academic journal. Entitled 'Evidence of Literary Device in the Babylonian Talmud', it appeared in the *Journal of Jewish Studies*. Introducing an approach now widely followed but in which he was a pioneer, Jacobs argued against the accepted view that the Talmud was an agglomeration of discussions conducted in the Babylonian academies, which later editors had linked together by adding a few comments of their own. He used the article to show that the Babylonian Talmud was deliberately edited as a literary work, given structure by its editors, who 'quite often use dramatic methods to achieve literary effect'. He compared the Talmudic discussion to the casket scene in *The Merchant of Venice*; just as in Shakespeare's play Bassanio's correct choice of casket is not introduced until the Princes of Morocco and Arragon have each made the wrong choice, so in the Talmud's discussion, the dramatic effect is heightened by keeping the ultimate refutation until the end.[11]

Jacobs found time, alongside his communal duties, extramural activities, family obligations and writing, to complete his PhD thesis. He had first registered as a doctoral student in 1947, shortly after receiving his bachelor's degree, but it took until 1950 for his chosen subject to be formally approved. He successfully defended his thesis, 'The Business Life of the Jews in Babylon from the 3rd to the 6th Century', and was awarded his PhD in June 1952.

To celebrate the award of Louis's doctorate his congregation in the Central Synagogue decided to hold a special service. They invited Dr Altmann to preach the sermon. Politely but firmly, Altmann declined. Although he was pleased to associate himself with the congregation's honouring of their rabbi, Altmann explained to Jacobs that he felt that the idea of a special service was incongruous, since the conferment of a secular degree does not call for a special celebration. He suggested a *kiddush*, a small buffet, following the Sabbath morning service, at which he would indeed speak. Jacobs, however, as the congregation's rabbi, should preach the sermon during the service.

The *kiddush*, held on 30 August 1952, turned out to be a double celebration. Just a few weeks earlier Shula had given birth to their third child, David.

In his address, Altmann predicted a marvellous future for Louis, a favourite of the Jewish community not just in Manchester but in the whole of Britain. The president of the Communal Council seconded the toast, praising Jacobs's work in the community, wide popularity and great nobility of character.

Jacobs's nobility of character was challenged a few months later. A row had broken out in Manchester over changes that Rabbi Dr Altmann had proposed to the Shabbat morning services, with a view to improving decorum. None of his changes were particularly radical, and all fell within the parameters of religious law, but that did not stop a backlash from a small section of the community who believed that this was the thin edge of a far thicker and more sinister reforming wedge. After Altmann had tried to defend his proposals through the pages of the *Jewish Chronicle*, he received a letter from the editor of the *Jewish Spectator* in New

York, asking if he would write an article for his paper detailing his proposed changes. In his reply Altmann indicated that the issue needed to be placed within a wider context, as the campaign against his proposals bore 'all the features of medieval fanaticism'. He suggested that the matter called for thorough analysis and appraisal and that he was obviously not the right person to write an article describing the full facts and implications. Instead, he proposed that Louis write the article. He told the editor that he and Louis had already discussed the matter and that Jacobs was indeed willing to write a piece.

Decorum in the synagogue was hardly at the top of Jacobs's scholarly agenda, but the criticisms directed at Altmann were not abating, and it was not in Jacobs's character to refuse. Because of constant chatter, he wrote, and due to a lack of devotion, services in many Manchester synagogues were unedifying. Few people experienced a sense of spiritual satisfaction. Altmann's suggestions, however, were not attempts to introduce Reform Judaism, as his detractors maintained. Rather he was seeking to strike a balance, retaining everything that was essential to a traditional service but eliminating practices that dragged the service out without conferring any spiritual benefit. Louis drew a parallel with recent events in the National Gallery:

> A year or two ago a process was discovered by which the paintings of the old masters in the National Gallery could be cleaned. At first there were shocked outcries of 'sacrilege'. Many of those that protested seem to have considered the very grime that had accumulated through the ages should be an essential part of the pictures. The protests went unheeded, the pictures were cleaned, the grime removed, and new beauties formerly obscured were revealed to the eye. We should keep this in mind with the approach to the renewal of Jewish life. We must never identify the dust of the ages with the living Jewish faith; but as traditional Jews, when attempting to remove the dust, we must ever be in our guard not to irreparably damage the picture of Judaism by removing the paint with our too vigorous cleansing.[12]

Although the topic had not been one that Louis would have naturally gravitated towards, and he wrote the article only to support his mentor Dr Altmann, he managed to align his argument with the journey that he was beginning to realize he had already embarked on.

> Moderation and tolerance are needed today in the religious life of Jews as never before and those who are prepared to tread the middle-path and to face the vituperations of the extremists on either side are performing a notable service to the cause of Judaism.[13]

Jacobs's choice of path was that of the middle way. Between tradition and modernity, Englishness and Jewishness, reason and belief. It was a path from which he would never deviate.

A MIDDLE WAY

Jacobs's decision to go to university, study for a PhD and immerse himself in historical–critical scholarship would not have gone down well with some of his former fellows in Gateshead. Within the Strictly Orthodox community, secular studies are a distraction from the life-affirming obligation to spend one's time studying Torah. They pose a danger in that they may weaken faith, by, for example, introducing ideas that clash with the biblical account of Creation, or that challenge the historicity of tradition. As for secular studies of sacred subjects, they are anathema not simply because they divert the student's time from Torah study. With their roots in the nineteenth-century German discipline *Wissenschaft des Judentums*, the scientific study of Judaism, they are a gateway to heretical ideas that weaken faith, poison the mind and undermine the very fabric and foundation of Judaism itself.

Jacobs had never fully accepted the Strictly Orthodox perspective on secular learning, probably not even in his teens, when he had just started at yeshiva and, with hindsight, had referred to himself as an 'insufferable little prig and religious fanatic'. His secular education, his love of literature and his natural curiosity would never have allowed him to channel his thinking along just one path, however sacred that path might be. But he was now at an intellectual crossroads. He did not want to forsake his love of Talmud, of the Lithuanian analytical methods he had yearned to learn about in his youth and studied so avidly at yeshiva. But nor could he compartmentalize his thinking. He could no more compromise his academic perspective on biblical authorship than he could forsake his sense of awe and wonder in the presence of the divine, simply because the findings of science did not always correlate with the biblical text. He was prepared neither to uncritically assign truth to tradition, just because it was tradition, nor to reject his belief in a personal God who intervened in the affairs of the world, just because his existence was not objectively verifiable.

Jacobs had begun his quest for a middle way. And increasingly he was aware that he wouldn't find it in Manchester Central Synagogue. Not because there was anything wrong with the synagogue or his congregants. But because he felt it dishonest to pursue this line of thinking in a nominally Orthodox synagogue, even if his congregants, if he put it to them, would probably agree with his way of thinking. He longed to find an environment where he could pursue his quest more freely. He briefly considered a full time role in academia. But in his early thirties, poised on the brink of a successful rabbinic career, he was no longer at a stage where he could easily slip into the ivory tower. A more realistic option was to find a synagogue where he could do his work freely 'without the burden of double-think'.[14] Unexpectedly, but right on time, the opportunity came along.

4

High Society

In August 1950 Louis was lecturing at a Torah va-Avodah summer school in the Kent port of Deal when he met the Reverend Raphael Levy. Levy was the 'minister-reader' at London's prestigious New West End Synagogue, a post he had been appointed to in 1946, at the extremely young age of 29. He and Louis had similar backgrounds: both had received a yeshiva education before taking university degrees, both had studied for a while in Gateshead, and both had an appreciation of secular Western culture. Their paths had intersected previously: Levy had ministered a congregation in Preston, from where he had travelled frequently to Manchester to complete his MA in Semitics.

Raphael Levy and Louis Jacobs became friends, and when the New West End's long-serving 'minister-preacher' retired, Levy encouraged Jacobs to apply for the job.

The New West End Synagogue in Bayswater is one of the great masterpieces of nineteenth-century synagogue architecture. Designed by George Audsley in the Neo-Moorish style and completed in 1877, the synagogue is declared by English Heritage to be:

The architectural high watermark of Anglo -Jewish architecture . . . No expense was spared when this cathedral synagogue was built and it is filled with opulence from the mosaic floor and dramatic stained glass rose window by Audsley, to the alabaster and marble walls with Hebrew texts in gilt lettering. The architect paid enormous attention to detail; no two capitals of the bimah are the same.[1]

Dramatic as the architecture was, it was not the building's aesthetic qualities that made the New West End the ideal synagogue for Jacobs. Founded by some of the most prominent figures in the Victorian Jewish community, with independent minds and resources to match, the synagogue professed a sort of High Church Anglo-Orthodoxy, fiercely wedded to its own traditions even if those traditions sat slightly on the wrong side of what others deemed acceptable in Jewish law.

The New West End fell under the umbrella of the orthodox United Synagogue, but from the outset it had made it clear that its views were its own. Its first minister had been Simeon Singer, a 'well-nigh perfect minister, loved and respected within the Community as few men have ever been'.[2] English-born, he had obtained a rabbinic diploma in Vienna from Isaac Hirsch Weiss, the great nineteenth- century scholarly historian of Judaism. He never used the title rabbi, however; during the incumbencies first of Chief Rabbi Nathan Marcus Adler and then his son and successor Hermann Adler the only person in Britain allowed to use that title was the Chief Rabbi himself. Every other minister, no matter how impeccable their credentials, was to be known simply as Reverend.

Singer's enduring legacy was his prayer book, 'The Authorised Daily Prayer Book of the United Hebrew Congregations of the British Empire', which he collated and translated into a stately Victorian English. The language of Singer's Prayer Book occupies the same status in the cultural heritage of English Jews as does the King James Bible in the Church of England. Singer's prayer book went through 27 editions and multiple revisions, until eventually the Empire became the Commonwealth. The prayer book's title changed to reflect the new reality, and the count of editions and revisions started all over again.

In 1873 Singer delivered a lecture in which he outlined three principles he considered fundamental to Judaism. One was the doctrine of *Torah min Hashamayim*. Literally meaning Torah from Heaven, Singer translated it as the 'truth of revelation'. He could not possibly have imagined that his free translation of the Hebrew phrase would align him with one of his successor 'minister-preachers' at the New West End, a man still half a century away from being born. The meaning of *Torah min Hashamayim* was the subject that, beginning just a few years after his arrival at the New West End, would dog Jacobs's life for the rest of his career. Singer's translation, indeed his whole religious outlook, was responsible for a tradition in the New West End of non-dogmatic theological enquiry; a tradition that inspired Jacobs and gave him the confidence to proceed as he developed his thinking over the coming years.

Singer's views were not outspoken for his time, although they became so in due course. His successor, however, courted controversy almost from day one. Joseph Hochman was only 24 years old when he was appointed to the pulpit of the New West End. One of his competitors for the job was the future Chief Rabbi Joseph Hertz.

Brilliant, and unafraid to speak his mind, Hochman composed a Yom Kippur sermon in 1910 in which he said that Orthodoxy had no place in religion. In those days United Synagogue ministers were obliged to send their Yom Kippur sermons to the Chief Rabbi for approval. Chief Rabbi Hermann Adler demanded that Hochman retract. Hochman duly obliged and preached a sanitized version of his original speech. But less than two months later he published the full sermon. By now the Chief Rabbi was terminally ill and unable to take any action.

When Adler died Hochman established a committee to investigate the possibility of shortening the synagogue service. He instigated a campaign for reform of the office of Chief Rabbi. This did nothing to improve his relationship with the new incumbent, Joseph Hertz, who already resented Hochman for beating him to the New West End post. They fell out again when Chief Rabbi Hertz heard that Hochman, who would ride his horse through Hyde Park on his way to weekday services, had conducted the prayers in his jodhpurs, instead of the mandatory canonicals. A few months later Hochman resigned.[3]

So the New West End to which Jacobs sent his job application was no stranger to controversy. But what appealed to him was that this was an illustrious congregation, numbering among its members some of the nation's finest, most independent minds. In this sort of company he knew, provided he got the job, that he would be free to speak his mind; to pursue the quest that was becoming so important to him, to find the elusive middle between faith and reason.

Raphael Levy encouraged Jacobs to apply for the job. The synagogue's current minister-preacher, the Reverend Ephraim Levine, was retiring after 38 years, and the congregation was seeking new blood. Levine had been a strong, dominant leader who had won the affection of the community. Described as 'the most human of Anglo-Jewish ministers', and as helping to 'preserve the delicate balance between Orthodoxy and secular British life', he was known for his eloquence and wit, outstanding talent in the pulpit, and as an after-dinner speaker. He proved a hard act for Jacobs to follow. Not least because he continued to attend the synagogue after his retirement, 'week after week, glowering, tut-tutting or gnashing his teeth (sometimes all three)' every time Louis said something from the pulpit he did not like.[4]

Jacobs was formally appointed to the New West End pulpit in October 1953. It was the culmination of a lengthy process, during which he had also been courted by the Golders Green Synagogue, just a stone's throw from Munk's, where he had served as assistant rabbi. The Golders Green congregation had, not unreasonably, assumed that Rabbi Jacobs would prefer them to the New West End. Theirs was an observant and learned congregation in the heart of London's Jewish community, an area where he was already known and had friends. In Golders Green they thought that the New West End was a little infra dig, particularly for an up-and-coming Orthodox scholar like Jacobs.

Louis received a letter from one of his friends in Golders Green alerting him to the fact that the trial sermon he had preached at the New West End had 'made a bad impression here'. He warned Jacobs that he and his family would be changed at the New West End, and not for the better. Since Jacobs had a very promising future, he should avoid the temptation to follow 'easier paths and false friends' by allowing himself to go after jobs he should avoid. 'The New West End, in my opinion, is such a job. Golders Green, on the other hand, would give you scope and opportunity'.[5]

A few days later Louis replied saying that he had discussed the matter with Shula, and after careful consideration they had decided they preferred the New West End. This, he was at pains to stress, cast no reflection of any kind upon his respect and admiration for the people at Golders Green.

Rabbi Munk expressed his distress in a letter to Jacobs. 'I am very stunned regarding your decision. Others are also flabbergasted at what could have happened to bring you to such a state of affairs.'[6]

The 'state of affairs' that Rabbi Munk regretted was the perception that members of Anglo-Jewish synagogues lacked adequate religious commitment and intensity. These congregations were considered to be unlearned, secular in outlook and insipid in their commitment to religious practice. For the most part members of these congregations, so their opponents maintained, failed to observe the rules of family purity, ate forbidden food and desecrated the Sabbath. Their children were in constant danger of marrying out of the faith. That a scholar of Jacobs's standing, who had so much to offer to Orthodoxy, could allow his learning to go to waste in such a congregation was indeed, in the eyes of his teachers and colleagues, flabbergasting.

It should be said that there were many among the 'English' Jews who were similarly disdainful of the Strictly Orthodox. They regarded them as obsessively religious, *meshuggeneh frum*, who failed to appreciate their tremendous good fortune in living in a tolerant country, where they were free to practise their faith free of persecution and contempt. Blinkered in their outlook and living in self-imposed ghettoes, they not only refused to make any meaningful contribution to wider society but also condemned those who did.

Between these two extremes however was a wider, less opinionated, middle ground, which was comfortable with the diversity of the English Jewish community. It was this middle ground that Louis and Shula instinctively tended towards; it was the environment they had both been born into. Not that the New West End would not have felt somewhat alien to them initially. Premier among the 'high church', affluent congregations of Central London, it was more 'English' than any other synagogue they had known.

The Saturday morning service was divided into two parts. Prayers began at 9.30 and paused shortly after 10, just before the reading of the Torah. At 10.15 the formal service began. The choir would sing as the dog-collared, enrobed clergy entered the synagogue. Behind them in top hats, waistcoats and striped trousers followed a slow, stately procession of wardens and synagogue dignitaries.

The service was led by the cantor and choir, the congregation joining in at key moments, though not too loudly lest they mar the choral harmony. The rabbi would preach and at 12 noon the congregation would remain in their seats, while the clergy led a further procession out of the building. They remained in the vestibule, or on the front steps, shaking hands with the congregation as they emerged. The influence of the Church of England on Anglo-Jewish congregations such as the New West End is not hard to spot.

Jacobs would not have found any one of these traditions remarkable – he would have come across each of them in the different synagogues he had visited, although perhaps not all at the same time. But the New West End's tradition of having men and women singing together in the choir, in defiance of a partially observed Talmudic stringency, would have bothered him in his youth. It didn't seem to bother him now. When asked, some years later, whether a mixed choir contradicted Jewish law, he responded in his inimical fashion by first clarifying the legal position before setting the question in its historical context: 'As for the argument that in any event a mixed choir is untraditional, this is true, but then the whole institution of a choir in the synagogue is untraditional, and was severely opposed by the more conservative rabbis when it was first introduced.'[7] He recalled a colleague who had been asked if the men and women in his mixed choir sat together. 'Sit together?' he queried. 'They don't even sing together!'

In his induction sermon on 13 February 1954, Jacobs invoked the 'great and glorious' Anglo-Jewish tradition that 'found some of its staunchest upholders among the members of this Synagogue'. This tradition, he said, was responsible for the values of the synagogue, which never faltered in 'spurning the superficial tinsel attractions of the Zeitgeist out of loyalty to the perennial ideals of our eternal faith'.[8]

As if New West End's opulent architecture, English traditions and fierce pride in its own historical importance were not enough to get used to, Louis and Shula found themselves on even more unfamiliar territory getting to know their new congregation. Louis's working-class Manchester upbringing had given him few tools to help prepare him for life in London's wealthiest, most illustrious Jewish community. Among the New West End's members were lords and ladies, baronets and dames, eminent doctors and lawyers, highly successful business people, scientists, musicians and artists. A stellar congregation that seems not to have intimidated Louis or Shula in the slightest.

They rose to the occasion. Jacobs had always been confident in his own intellectual abilities; he might not have been a top scientist, eminent doctor or successful lawyer, but he knew that intellectually he was their equal, that they would learn from him just as he would learn from them. As for the ennobled congregants, and those who considered themselves members of the English upper classes, he never had the audacity to say it, but he may well have contemplated the old Talmudic dictum: Who are the kings? The rabbis!

Among the distinguished members who warmed to Louis and Shula were Viscount and Viscountess Samuel. Herbert Samuel, who had been the first Jewish cabinet minister and the first British High Commissioner in Palestine, was a lifelong member of the New West End. He was a northerner like Louis, hailing from Liverpool, but his upbringing couldn't have been more different. His father, who had died when the young Herbert was only seven, had been a banker; he had been in partnership with his younger brother, who, as Viscount Swaythling, would also become a member of the New West End. Herbert Samuel was educated at University College School in London and Balliol College in Oxford, where, during a falling-out with his mother, he renounced all religion. Nevertheless, he and his wife Beatrice would invite the new rabbi and his wife to tea, where Beatrice at least would discuss the weekly Torah portion with Louis.

Not every distinguished member of the New West End was elderly. In 1955 Viscount Samuel found himself marking his 85th birthday at the synagogue with a boy celebrating his bar mitzvah. The boy was Daniel Barenboim. In his address to them from the pulpit Jacobs spoke about the man who was world-famous and the boy who would become so one day. Barenboim never forgot this; even after achieving global fame he would unfailingly send Jacobs a New Year's greeting card every year. Sixteen years later, when Jacobs asked if he would give a piano recital at the New London Synagogue, he accepted without hesitation.

The celebrity connections made life at the New West End interesting, but as far as Jacobs was concerned they served a higher purpose. Being surrounded by high achieving individuals gave him the impetus to develop his ideas freely, unconstrained by what he had previously described as 'the burden of double think',[9] just as he had hoped when he first applied for the pulpit.

Like any job, there were niggles. The New West End was a constituent of the United Synagogue, which employed him directly and gave him duties beyond his responsibilities to his congregation. He was formally appointed as Jewish Chaplain to St Mary's Hospital, Paddington, a duty he would have been quite prepared to undertake voluntarily, without it being part of his job description. But he resented the fact that his chaplaincy work was scrutinized by someone he had never met, in the United Synagogue head office, to whom he had to send weekly reports.

As an employee of the United Synagogue he was also for the first time under the direct authority of the Chief Rabbi. Manchester Central Synagogue had deferred to the Chief Rabbi out of respect, but were under no statutory obligation to obey him. In the United Synagogue, however, congregational ministers were effectively the Chief Rabbi's local representatives: nothing of any substance could be done without his approval. It was the Chief Rabbi who inducted Jacobs into office, and it was with the Chief Rabbi that he crossed swords when he was invited to speak at a meeting of the London Society of Jews and Christians.

As its name declares, the London Society of Jews and Christians was an inter-faith group which held regular meetings and discussions. It was the oldest such group in the country, but it was affiliated to the more recently established Council of Christians and Jews, of which the Chief Rabbi, together with several bishops, was a Joint President. When, in September 1955, Jacobs accepted an invitation to speak at the London Society, he received a short letter from Chief Rabbi Brodie pointing out that the organization was run under the auspices of the Liberal Synagogue and that neither he nor his predecessor had approved of any Orthodox rabbi associating with it. When Jacobs replied pointing out that Dr Altmann had previously spoken to the Society he received a longer letter:

> The Jewish members of the London Society of Jews and Christians are wholly or very largely Liberal Jews and it is for this reason, as well as on the grounds of its policy, that the Chief Rabbi considers it inappropriate for an orthodox Minister to address this body.

> The Chief Rabbi was not aware that Rabbi Dr. Altmann gave an address under the auspices of the London Society. If he had known of Dr. Altmann's intention to do so, he would have endeavoured to dissuade him.[10]

Frustrated but feeling he had little option, Jacobs acceded to the Chief Rabbi's request. He cancelled the engagement. He would not bow so easily to such edicts for long.

A STIMULATING CONGREGATION

In 1955 Louis Jacobs published his first book, *Jewish Prayer*. He based it on a series of sermons he had delivered at the New West End. The sermons had so impressed his friend, mentor and congregant William Frankel, who was then the general manager of the *Jewish Chronicle*, that he offered to publish the sermons as a book under the newspaper's imprint.[11] Running to just 68 pages, it was a readable yet scholarly introduction to a subject with which every practising Jew was familiar, yet whose content often appeared remote and impenetrable.

The book was an instant success both in Britain and the United States. A second edition appeared just a year later and a third in 1962. Jacobs would go on to write two further short guides in the same style, one on Yom Kippur, the other on Rosh Hashanah.

Writing always came easily to Jacobs, but the demands that his new pulpit made on his time meant that he wrote far less in his first couple of years at New West End than he might have hoped. His only serious scholarly output in 1955 was an article drawn from his PhD thesis and redrafted in Hebrew, on the economic life of ancient Babylonian Jewry. But although he was writing less, his interaction with his New West End congregation was enabling him to unwittingly lay the foundations for what would become the most important publication of his early career; a book whose impact would stay with him for the rest of his life.

Louis conducted regular classes and study sessions with his congregants at New West End, just as he had done at Munk's and at Manchester Central Synagogue. But the congregants at New West End had different interests to those at his previous synagogues, and displayed a different sort of intellectualism. Rather than delving into the depths of Talmud with his congregation, dissecting texts and commentaries to establish the principles of Jewish law and practice, Jacobs found himself being challenged on the ideas that underpinned Judaism, on the meaning of faith and the complexities of theology. It was a challenge that he relished: this was exactly what he had hoped to find when he made his decision to find a congregation where he could develop his thinking.

The interests of his congregants and his own developing maturity meant that Jacobs was growing ever more comfortable with what he had previously perceived as a conflict between traditional Judaism and the pursuit of critical–historical scholarship. His knowledge of the Talmudic sources was sufficiently extensive to help him recognize that it was possible to interpret some of the more socially problematic areas of Jewish law liberally, without stepping outside the traditional framework. The fact that liberal solutions to legal dilemmas were not being discussed within contemporary Orthodoxy did not mean that such interpretations were invalid. Earlier generations, it was clear to Jacobs from the sources, had been far less afraid of unfettered discussion.

Jacobs described his approach as a 'quest'. He discussed his ideas in study groups and lectures, aimed at young, intellectually engaged people from across London. His first series of lectures on Modern Jewish Thinkers ran for 18 months and was followed by a series entitled 'Judaism: What It Means to Me'. He drew on the services of outside speakers for many of these lectures, but always took the chair to lead a discussion on the lecture at the end. He also lectured extensively to student and adult groups outside of the synagogue, encouraging them to enquire more deeply into Judaism and developing his theme that Jewish law was sufficiently flexible to adapt to the demands of modern times.

He relaunched the synagogue magazine, calling it *Venture* and using it as a platform to generate discussion. In his editorial for the first edition he wrote, in what sounds as much like a manifesto as the credo that he declared it to be:

We are convinced there is a burning need – keenly apparent to intelligent observers of Anglo-Jewry – for what may be termed a 'middle of the road' position in our Community if Judaism is to come into its own as a vital, inspiring and ennobling faith, relevant to the spiritual needs of twentieth century Jews and Jewesses. We indignantly repudiate that the adoption of such a position is a sign of weakness, lukewarmness, ignorance or compromise. On the contrary, we affirm that it calls for both knowledge and courage – knowledge to distinguish between the eternal and the ephemeral, the essential and non-essential in Jewish life, and courage to avoid the extremes of the right and the left even though we live in a world in which extremes are popular.[12]

Jacobs may have identified a 'burning need' for a 'middle of the road' position, but the New West End congregation were not the sort of people to meekly accept such a vague proposition. In the second issue of *Venture* he acknowledged that several readers had urged him to provide a more specific, detailed account of what this middle way might be, and what its implications were for the wider community. Jacobs found himself forced him to articulate ideas that he was still developing but had consciously refrained from expressing, knowing that as soon as he did so he was likely to find himself on a path from which there may be no retreat.

Adopting a terminology that he would return to throughout his career, he asserted that it would be more correct to speak of the middle way as an attitude, a mood, rather than a detailed blueprint. On the intellectual plane, the middle way recognized that it was no longer possible to accept the old views on matters such as the age of the Earth, evolution, or the authorship of biblical books. In the synagogue, the middle-of-the-road approach combined traditionalism, in melody, language and prayer, with modernism evidenced by such things as a mixed choir, the elimination of anachronisms and the use of an organ at certain weekday services. The inflexibility of Jewish law would give way to the more dynamic methods of the great Talmudic sages. He quoted a rabbinic parable that the nineteenth-century thinker Nachman Krochmal had used when dealing with a similar issue: The Torah may be compared to two paths – one of ice, the other of fire. To tread the one is to be burnt in the fire; the other, to be frozen by the ice. What does the wise man do? He walks in the middle! Jacobs rarely quoted the contradictory view, that he who walks in the middle of the road gets run over.

Not all of Jacobs's congregants were able to adjust to the idea of a middle way. Although the New West End had always been a liberal-minded community, they knew better than to display their laxity of observance in a manner that might embarrass their rabbi. Conversely, Louis held firm to the principle of never putting anyone in a position where they might feel ashamed. One Shabbat morning, Louis and family were walking home after prayers when a green Morris Minor pulled up close to them, at a junction. The driver was a member of Jacobs's congregation. He panicked when he spotted Jacobs and in a state of confusion slammed his foot down on the accelerator. His car shot out into the main road, straight into the side of a passing vehicle. Jacobs rushed off, terribly upset that he had been the cause of the accident, leaving the rest of the family to make sure that nobody had been hurt. Jacobs and his congregant, each anxious not to embarrass the other, had achieved the opposite effect.

Louis could not have accomplished nearly as much as he did without the support of his family, particularly Shula. An English rabbi's wife in the 1950s was effectively a full-time unpaid secretary to her husband, a hostess to his visitors, a counsellor to the congregation's women, a community worker, and in Shula's case, mother to three young children. All these tasks came naturally to her. With an outgoing personality, wide range of interests, love of conversation and captivating singing voice, Shula was the perfect counterpart to the scholarly, ambitious rabbi, already confident in his abilities and his growing reputation in the community. Her upbringing in East London had been very different to that of many women in the New West End but, never one to stand on ceremony, she was as comfortable chatting at length and without inhibition to a wealthy titled lady as she was to one of her own children.

Most of the details that we know about Louis Jacobs's life during this period are due to Shula's organizational diligence. She kept diaries and wrote articles for the synagogue magazine, but little has survived from this period. What have survived are the letters, press cuttings and photos that she archived into scrapbooks and box files.

Without them we would not have known, for example, that in 1956 Jacobs received a letter from a dayan on the Irish Beth Din asking him to approach his congregant Viscount Samuel on behalf of an historian anxious for information on Sir Roger Casement, the revolutionary leader executed during Samuel's tenure as Home Secretary in 1916. Nor that in the same year Jacobs received an invitation from the Chief Rabbi of South Africa, Dr Louis Rabinowitz, to apply for the post of Rabbi of Johannesburg's Oxford Synagogue. Jacobs did not mention this in his autobiography, but Shula kept the highly persuasive letter that Rabinowitz had sent him. Among other things Rabinowitz pointed out that he would relinquish his post as South Africa's Chief Rabbi in four years' time, and he was confident that Jacobs would be a most suitable person to succeed him.

Jacobs did not pursue the opportunity. It has been suggested that he did not want to leave his parents – his mother was to die the following year. But it is just as likely that he considered the New West End a far more promising option if he was to enjoy the sort of career he hoped for, one in which he could develop his ideas and encourage the British Jewish community to develop a deeper intellectual engagement with their faith.

The New West End congregation exposed Jacobs to intellectual challenges very different from those that he had faced in Manchester. The Central Synagogue had been an observant community, familiar with the texts, prescriptions and rituals of Judaism. The questions they brought to Jacobs were those of text and practice; queries about how to understand a difficult Talmudic passage or perform certain rituals. And of course the classic question asked of rabbis in the days before pre-packed meat, as to whether or not a chicken was kosher. Few at the New West End raised such questions. Instead, their dilemmas were more likely to be about the meaning, validity or relevance of Judaism itself. He responded to some of these issues in a series of sermons themed as 'Religion and the Individual', but the sermons just led to more and bigger questions.

Much to his delight Jacobs found himself discussing, among other things, the place of religion in the modern world, how to understand biblical narratives in the light of modern scientific theory and historical investigation, and what exactly was Jewish theology.

He debated these matters with his regular study group at the synagogue, spoke about them from the pulpit and formalized them in lectures. Time and again he returned to the idea that Judaism was a reasonable faith, that reason dictates that there is a higher purpose to life. His fellow study-group members encouraged him to set out his views in a book. After he gave a further lecture on the role of reason in faith his friend Dr Ian Gordon suggested that the book he would write should be called *We Have Reason to Believe*.

HEADING FOR TROUBLE

We Have Reason to Believe was published on 2 April 1957 A second edition was published in 1962 and a third in 1965. The proximity of the last two editions, compared with the gap between the first and second, eloquently summarizes the book's early reception; most people had not even heard of it, let alone read it, until the book and its author hit the headlines in 1961.

Subtitled *Some Aspects of Jewish Theology Examined in the Light of Modern Thought*, the book is readable, concise and, as its title suggests, reasonable. It is easy to digest – the whole work is only 143 pages long, with no more than 13 pages in any of its 12 chapters. In his introduction, Jacobs tells his readers that that his purpose is to examine the challenges that modern thought poses to the three fundamental pillars of Judaism, namely belief in God, in his Torah, and in Israel's role as his people.

He warned of three pitfalls that stand ready to ensnare all who engage in Jewish apologetics: the dangers of obscurantism, religious schizophrenia and intellectual dishonesty. Obscurantism, he contended, means the rejection of 'modern thought and all its ways as of the devil'. Religious schizophrenia allows 'incompatible ideas to exist side by side in water tight compartments'. As for intellectual dishonesty, it is the postulating of 'an artificial synthesis, a queer hybrid faith which both the adherents of traditional Judaism and representative modern thinkers would repudiate'.[13]

A modern reader starting to read the book for the first time might wonder what all the fuss was about. The first few chapters contain nothing that seems even remotely controversial. He discusses Jewish conceptions of God, the various attempts to prove his existence and the traditional way in which Jews relate to him, both as a personal God who is intimately involved with the affairs of each and every one of us, and as the God of our ancestors who links us with history and generations past. The prose is eloquent, his grasp of the subject and of the writings of earlier thinkers comprehensive, his conclusions wholly acceptable to any Orthodox thinker who takes the time to contemplate the rather unfashionable subject of theology. There is not a whisper of anything contentious, no hint of dissent from traditional belief. Until one gets to chapter five.

One of the striking things about Jacobs's writing, on any topic, is its reasonableness. No matter how unconventional, innovative or contentious the point he is putting across, it always seems to follow on seamlessly and logically from what has gone before. It was a feature of his lectures and sermons too. His training in Talmudic logic, his grounding in the Lithuanian method of analysis protected him from non sequiturs and illogical connections. He was always reasonable. Even when he was accused of being wrong.

Ironically, it was Jacobs's Talmudic approach that got him into trouble. For there are certain conclusions in Orthodox theology where logic and rationalism are obliged to give way to faith. Some things, Orthodox thinkers will tell you, cannot be proved. They have to be believed. Louis Jacobs could not accept this. Granted, the existence of God cannot be proved, the Almighty stands beyond logic, one has to have faith to believe in him. But once one has made that leap of faith everything follows on rationally and reasonably from there. Even the vexed question of the authorship of the Torah. At least, that is how it appeared to Louis's mind.

Chapter five, entitled 'The Torah and Modern Criticism', begins with an analysis of what we mean by the Torah, a word that is used in three distinct but complementary senses. As the Pentateuch, or

Five Books of Moses, the word Torah includes the interpretative tradition that is considered to have been orally delivered to Moses on Mount Sinai. At other times the word Torah is used to refer to teachings from the non-Pentateuchal sections of the Bible. And Torah can also mean the totality of Jewish religious teaching. In sum, Jacobs declares, the Torah 'is 'a tree of life which, carefully tended by its devoted cultivators, nourished by its fruit, produces new spiritual fruits in each generation.'[14]

After defining Torah, Jacobs offered the first hint that he was about to adopt a controversial line. Declaring that Judaism stands or falls on the belief in revelation, he rather disingenuously stated that there is no 'official' interpretation of the manner in which God spoke to man. In support of this view he quoted the former Chief Rabbi, Joseph Hertz. Hertz had said that the exact manner of supernatural communication between God and man 'will be conceived differently by different groups of believers. Some will follow the biblical accounts of Revelation in the literal sense; others will accept interpretation of these biblical accounts by rabbis of Talmudic days, Jewish philosophers of the Middle Ages, or Jewish thinkers of modern times.'[15]

By suggesting that Jewish believers might not accept the literal, biblical account, that God spoke to Moses and Israel at Mount Sinai, Jacobs implies that Hertz had deviated from the strict understanding of that event as a matter of history. There was, until recently, complete unanimity in the belief that the whole of the Torah was given to Moses on Sinai, or at very least, at intervals during the journey through the wilderness. The Hebrew text of the Torah in our possession today is exactly that which Moses received. Despite this, Jacobs argued, there had never been a universally accepted view on the manner of revelation, nor, since at least the twelfth century, agreement that the entire Torah as we have it was revealed word for word to Moses. The whole question of how we understand revelation, he maintained, had evolved in line with the development of our critical facilities.

Therefore, and this is the crux of his argument, there is no reason to reject new critical tools and techniques as they emerge.

We should be open to the questions raised by Biblical Criticism, even though they challenge the traditional view that Moses received the entire Torah at an event in history, which took place on Mount Sinai. Not that we should necessarily accept the conclusions of Biblical Criticism. But we should strive for a synthesis between the new and old ways of understanding revelation.

Jacobs of course was not the first to argue against the historical Revelation at Sinai. Reform Judaism had rejected the Mosaic authorship of the Torah when Higher Biblical Criticism first emerged in the nineteenth century. Orthodoxy had long quarrelled with Reform over this very issue. Dr Hertz, whom Jacobs quoted as accepting that revelation was conceived in different ways by different Jewish authorities, nevertheless came out strongly, in his commentary on the Pentateuch, against Biblical Criticism. He may have agreed with Jacobs's premises; he certainly would not have agreed with his conclusions. But this was because Hertz subscribed to a view of Orthodoxy that is prepared to make a leap of faith regarding the historical nature of revelation, in contrast to Jacobs, who argued for the scientific validity of the critical method.

Jacobs knew that his position would not be accepted by Strictly Orthodox thinkers, by his old comrades in the yeshiva world. But he almost certainly thought that what he said would not be particularly contentious in the middle-of-the-road United Synagogue, with its university-educated rabbis and acculturated British congregations. His friend William Frankel disagreed. He had high hopes for Jacobs, whom he expected to be the next Chief Rabbi. He feared that immediate publication of the book would damage Jacobs's chances of being offered the post and advised him to wait until after the Chief Rabbi's retirement. Jacobs, who was probably less ambitious about being Chief Rabbi than William Frankel wanted him to be, refused to wait. His scholarly reputation and commitment to principle mattered far more to him than the trappings and politics of high office. He thought that if his views were to be deemed controversial, better to bring it out into the open now, rather than at a later stage in his career.[16]

With the exception of the *Yorkshire Post*, which recommended it, *We Have Reason to Believe* received no attention in the national or literary press. Jewish theology was not high on their list of interests. Even the Jewish press paid it scant attention. The *Jewish Chronicle*, which had published the book through its imprint Vallentine Mitchell, devoted part of a leader to it, calling it controversial and stimulating. Despite giving it less than 300 words of publicity, they hoped it would be widely read and would arouse the interest of lay and religious thinkers in the community.

The Mizrachi Journal *Jewish Review* gave the book a lukewarm reception, complaining about its excessive reasonableness, arguing that faith cannot be made to look so reasonable without depriving it of its abiding mystery. Nevertheless, like the *Jewish Chronicle*, the reviewer hoped it would be read widely: 'We need to be reminded that Judaism is as much about the mind as the belly.'[17] The Anglo-Jewish Association and the South African *Jewish Chronicle* liked it. But the most striking feature of all the reviews, even the more scholarly ones, was that nobody commented at all on Jacobs's remarks about Biblical Criticism, or suggested that the book was in any way controversial. He was already highly regarded within the London Jewish community, and it is unlikely that no United Synagogue rabbis read the book when it came out. It is far more likely that nobody at the time felt that his views were particularly unusual or unpalatable. Four years later, everything would change.

WIDENING HORIZONS

A few months after the publication of *We Have Reason to Believe*, the *Jewish Chronicle* published Jacobs's *Guide to Yom Kippur*, the sequel to his earlier book on Rosh Hashanah. He began writing scholarly articles again, diversifying his subject matter more broadly than before. During 1956 and 1957 he published articles on Freud and Judaism, piety in rabbinic literature, the Jewish view on self-sacrifice and a comparison between the economic conditions of the Jews in Babylon and Palestine during Talmudic times.

Louis's mother, Lena Jacobs, died on 28 July 1957. Louis, as the only child, now had to integrate his father's needs into his increasingly busy life. Had Harry Jacobs not been proudly independent, Louis and Shula might have felt the need to move back to Manchester. His father would not move to London.

During 1957 Jacobs began a correspondence with Professor Louis Finkelstein of the Jewish Theological Seminar and another with Rabbi Wolfe Kelman, executive vice-president of the Rabbinical Assembly. Based in New York, both organizations were keystones of Conservative Judaism, an American movement not dissimilar to Orthodoxy in terms of its synagogue services and rituals. However, unlike Orthodoxy, Conservative Judaism accepted the findings of Biblical Criticism, gave women a far greater role in synagogue life and took a less stringent approach when delivering rulings in Jewish law. Later that summer Jacobs received an invitation to attend their national biennial convention.

As far as Jacobs was concerned there was little to distinguish the approach of the American Conservative movement from his own, or indeed from that of many of the United Synagogue rabbis at the time. The late Chief Rabbi, Joseph Hertz, had received his rabbinic ordination at the Jewish Theological Seminary; indeed he was the first of its graduates, and he had spoken of his approach as one of 'Progressive Conservatism'. But although Jacobs did not consider there to be a gulf of any great significance between the Judaism of the United Synagogue and that of the Conservative movement, the Chief Rabbi did. He wrote to him on 8 August 1957:

> I am sure you cannot be aware that this body represents Conservative Judaism, and not Orthodox Judaism – its tendencies and outlook today are reformist. Several rabbis who asked me about similar invitations to attend (and lecture) to the Rabbinic Assembly which is associated with the United Synagogue of America declined the invitations on my advice. Rabbi Dr Altmann who received an invitation, similarly refused.

I hope that the report of your acceptance of the invitation was premature and that if in fact you have accepted, you will nevertheless not now be associated with this convention and thereby giving support to a movement which is endangering orthodoxy in America and elsewhere.[18]

Jacobs replied graciously, saying that he had given the Chief Rabbi's letter a very great deal of thought. He was sorry that he was unable to agree with his views on the Conservative movement.

However, I believe you know the high regard I have for you and your office and my great appreciation for the sincere guidance and friendship you have always shown me. Consequently I am noting in accord with your wishes and writing today to the Executive Director of the United Synagogue of America regretting my inability to attend the conference.[19]

Brodie had been firm with Louis, but their correspondence was respectful. He was soon to be reminded that not all sections of the community were so courteous. He'd made a speech at the ceremony to lay the foundation stone of the synagogue's new community centre, named in honour of Viscount Samuels. The *Jewish Chronicle* reported that Jacobs had said 'it was their aim to make the centre commodious enough to afford hospitality to many different points of view. They were prepared to extend hospitality to every sincere thinker after the truth, for they believed there were many interpretations of the sacred truths of the Jewish faith.'[20]

The *Jewish Chronicle* amplified Jacobs's remarks in a leader expressing disapproval of virulent denunciations of Reform and Liberal rabbis recently made at an Orthodox conference in Amsterdam. The writer believed that responsible Orthodox opinion, in Britain at least, would wish to disassociate itself from such 'manifestations of *odium theologicum*'. The attitude expressed by Rabbi Dr Louis Jacobs at the foundation stone ceremony was, the leader writer maintained, a far more worthy response.[21]

A few days later Jacobs received a letter from Rabbi J. Gould, Principal of Leeds Yeshiva, taking him to task for his 'vague statement' about offering hospitality to other points of view. It appeared, to Rabbi Gould, that the *Jewish Chronicle* assumed that Jacobs had been referring to the beliefs of 'the Reformers and Liberals':

> I, personally, cannot believe that that was your intention, but since you have caused some misunderstanding it is your bounden duty to announce in the *Jewish Chronicle* immediately (a) that your statement did not refer to the teachings of Reformers and Liberals, which are definitely heretical, (b) that you do associate with those Rabbis who attacked the Reform and Liberal anti-Torah activities and (c) to clarify what you really meant in your statements. Awaiting your kind reply in a day.[22]

The letter marks a shift in Jacobs's relationship with the world of the yeshiva, where he had once been so firmly rooted. Its unambiguous tone indicates that he had already moved beyond its orbit. Members of the Strictly Orthodox community had begun to speak of him critically when he chose to take the New West End job rather than returning to Golders Green. Nothing that he had done since had put their minds at rest. Whereas the Chief Rabbi had treated Jacobs's putative association with the American Conservative movement as an error that could be corrected, the Principal of Leeds Yeshiva already seems to have seen him as someone with whom he could not reason; all that he could do was to try to browbeat him into conforming.

Jacobs replied, briefly, saying that the matter was complicated and that he would prefer a personal discussion. Rabbi Gould would have none of it. He was not flattered to have received a letter comprising a mere two sentences. While he was willing to have a personal discussion next time he was in London, the matter brooked no delay. In no circumstances must Jacobs's statement be allowed to be interpreted as 'referring to the heretical teachings of the Liberals and Reformers'. He must set the record straight with the *Jewish Chronicle* forthwith. Needless to say, Jacobs did not.

Alongside to his communal duties Jacobs was now lecturing widely, to audiences of all ages and backgrounds. He travelled to Manchester to speak at Dr Altmann's Institute of Jewish Studies, delivered lectures to the Council of Christians and Jews, spoke as a guest preacher at other synagogues, organized courses and study groups at the New West End Centre Society and addressed University Jewish societies and the Conference of Anglo-Jewish Preachers. He composed academic articles for the *Journal of Jewish Studies*, *Judaism* and the *Journal of Semitic Studies* and continued to write regularly for the *Jewish Chronicle*. He contributed chapters on the Sources of Jewish Law and on Property to *An Introduction to Jewish Law*, a scholarly work edited by Peter Elman, who a few years earlier had brought the *Jewish Chronicle* correspondence between Louis Jacobs and Leslie Hardman to a close.

As ever, he read voraciously. His daughter Naomi, also an insatiable reader, recalls how her mother would go out leaving her and Louis each sitting in their chairs reading. Three hours later when Shula returned, she would find them in exactly the same position. Neither of them had moved.

Nineteen fifty-eight saw the bar mitzvah of Louis and Shula's eldest son, Ivor. Louis received a letter from his old *heder* teacher Jonah Balkind; in the postscript he acknowledged receipt of a thank-you letter from Ivor for a gift he had sent. 'I was pleased to receive that letter from your son, which give me the opportunity of assessing his standard in letter writing, learning (Jewish) manners, consideration and appreciation, for all of which I award him full marks.'[23]

Notwithstanding the Chief Rabbi's earlier disapproval, Jacobs remained in contact with the Conservative movement in the USA. He continued his correspondence with Wolfe Kelman. They had first met when Kelman was invited as a guest minister by the West London Synagogue, a Reform congregation not far from the New West End. Kelman was a close friend of William Frankel, editor of the *Jewish Chronicle* and a congregant at the New West End. Both men would play important roles in the crisis that was about to unfold in Jacobs's career.

All was not well in his relationship with the Chief Rabbi and the Beth Din. On 3 February 1958 he received a letter from the clerk to the rabbinic court, telling him that the Beth Din had expressed the desire to meet him 'to discuss a number of problems which have arisen'. Would it be convenient for Jacobs to attend the following Monday at 4 p.m.?

Upon receiving the letter Jacobs telephoned the Beth Din to clarify which problems had arisen. He spoke to Dayan Swift, who told him that they wanted to discuss certain opinions that Jacobs had expressed. Jacobs then wrote to Swift, saying that in his view such a discussion was not a matter for the Beth Din. Although Swift had assured him that the conversation would merely be a friendly exchange of ideas, he did not feel that such a purpose could be achieved through a process initiated by a formal letter from the Clerk of the Court and held in the official atmosphere of the Court building. Jacobs was ready to discuss his views at any time, but there was an essential difference between a discussion between colleagues and an appearance before the Beth Din. Should Dayan Swift wish to ask him to an informal discussion it would give Jacobs very great pleasure to exchange ideas.

But Dayan Swift did not wish to invite him for an informal discussion. In his reply he reiterated that his invitation to the Beth Din was in no way a summons for an 'appearance'. However they were still keen to have a chat, so perhaps Jacobs could telephone the Clerk to make an appointment, at his convenience, within the hours that the Beth Din met.

Jacobs was not satisfied:

> While I appreciate its cordial tone, the suggestions you make do not, I'm afraid, meet the serious objections I raised in my last letter to a meeting at the Beth Din. I should like to repeat my willingness to meet you and your colleagues for an informal exchange of views. If you could you suggest a place where we can

meet other than at the Beth Din itself, I should be glad to accept your invitation.

Swift replied regretting that Jacobs had not seen fit to discuss some matters with them. He had handed the correspondence between them to the Chief Rabbi.[24]

A few months later Jacobs was attending a rabbinic conference at which Swift was speaking. In the course of his speech Swift diverted from his subject, rounding on Jacobs and condemning him for teaching Kabbalah in public. Jacobs outlined the incident in a letter to Wolfe Kelman in New York. Describing Swift as a 'zealot of the first water', Jacobs reported that 'the Chief Rabbi made it quite clear in his concluding remarks that he did not side with Swift'. Kelman replied that he was 'delighted that the race is not always to the Swift'.[25]

In November 1958 Jacobs received an approach from Dr Abraham Druker, President of the College of Jewish Studies in Chicago. He had heard that Jacobs might be interested in an academic position and asked that he be in touch if that were still the case. Louis did not take the suggestion further. Other opportunities were coming into play.

5

In the Limelight

By 1958 the British Jewish press were playing their irregular game of Spot the Next Chief Rabbi. As there were still eight years before Israel Brodie, the present incumbent, was due to retire, the exercise was wholly academic. But as one of several candidates tipped by a Manchester newspaper, the gossip marked an important development in Jacobs's reputation and career.

There is no reason for believing that Jacobs was particularly interested in the job. He makes the point forcefully in his autobiography.[1] Nevertheless, popular opinion favoured him, and his fans had already come to regard him as Chief Rabbi in Waiting. When, a few years later, he was ostracized by the United Synagogue it was natural for him to be spoken of as 'the best Chief Rabbi we never had', an epithet that remained with him for the rest of his life.

Even at this early stage, Chief Rabbi Brodie and his Beth Din did not consider him suitable for the post. His relationship with them had not improved since he had turned down their summons the previous year. In early 1959 he received another stiff communication from the secretary of the Beth Din, who wrote to tell him they had received a complaint that he had attended a function at Claridge's, an upmarket but decidedly non-kosher London hotel. The Beth Din found the report hard to believe but, 'in view of the seriousness of the allegation', they requested his comments.[2]

However intellectually stimulating his job at the New West End, Jacobs couldn't help feeling constrained as an employee of the United Synagogue and by what he considered to be the high-handed attitude of the Beth Din. He had not been accused of eating at a non-kosher establishment; the complaint to the Beth Din was merely that he had been present in one. Like every other United Synagogue rabbi, Jacobs had many congregants who held functions in venues that were not kosher. It was hypocritical, he believed, for him to try to enthuse his congregation to increase their engagement with their Judaism, yet to stand aloof from their wedding and bar mitzvah parties because they did not reach the standard of observance he was trying to encourage them in. Far better, he maintained, for him to show a rabbinic face at these events than to shun the celebration. Jacobs began to wonder whether it was time to consider moving on.[3]

He remained in touch with the American Conservative movement. During the spring and early summer of 1959 he had several informal conversations with Professor Louis Finkelstein, Chancellor of the Jewish Theological Seminary. Finkelstein was keen to offer him an academic post in New York. The Jewish Theological Seminary was among the most pre-eminent colleges in world Jewry, and its faculty at the time was by any measure exceedingly distinguished. Jacobs knew that to take a position there would immeasurably advance his career. But he was conflicted.

Chief among his concerns was that to move to America would necessitate leaving his father alone in England. He hadn't pursued the opportunity in South Africa a few years earlier because he didn't want to leave his parents. Now that his mother was dead leaving his father would be even more difficult. There would also be an upheaval to his family, and, as Wolfe Kelman pointed out to him, a disparity between the salary he was likely to receive and the cost of maintaining the family's lifestyle in New York. Equally, there was the matter of his self-perception as an English rabbi of the old school. Despite his yeshiva education, after six years at the New West End, the most English of all Orthodox English congregations, Jacobs was becoming the very paradigm of an Anglo-Jewish cleric. Reserved, understated, accustomed to the genteel ways of Bayswater society, and with a very English sense of humour, how would he fare in the harsher and brasher environment of New York?

He discussed his dilemma with friends. Donald Samuel, the Viscount's nephew, who had worked with him to raise the funds for the Herbert Samuel Hall, wrote to assure him that he had a great contribution to make to the future of Judaism, but that he hoped that he would make it through Anglo-Jewry. Other voices joined in. Louis started to come under the sort of pressure that powerful wealthy people, typical of those who made up his congregation, find it so easy to exert. Eight days after Wolfe Kelman had enthusiastically written to Jacobs on 20 July discussing the practicalities of life in New York he despatched a second letter, this time to their mutual friend Gertie Frankel. Kelman expressed his disappointment that Jacobs was not coming and said that Dr Finkelstein was 'rather peeved "at being used"'.[4]

FRIENDS AND SUPPORTERS

Finkelstein hadn't 'been used', but we can understand why he might have thought so. On 22 July Jacobs had written to him asking for two more weeks in which to make up his mind about taking up his offer of a position. He was torn, indecisive. Impelling him forwards was the attraction of a new career in America, free of all the difficulties of working for the United Synagogue; holding him back were his roots and responsibilities in England, not least his ageing father.

Ultimately, it was not Jacobs's conflicts that swayed his mind. His influential friends in London, who had been putting their heads together looking for ways to keep him there, believed they had come up with a solution. Rabbi Dr Isidore Epstein, the principal of Jews' College, was soon to retire. Jacobs was without doubt, to their minds at least, the ideal candidate to succeed him. Not just that but, his influential friends believed, it was in their power to propel him into the post.

Of all his supporters, William and Gertie Frankel were the closest to Louis and the most vigorous in promoting his cause.

Popular wisdom, at the time and ever since, has maintained that Jacobs was badly advised by William, who took advantage of their friendship to sell his newspapers and advance his own agenda. If there is any truth in that, it is a simplistic one; Louis may have been among the most temperate of men, but he was always too principled and determined to act in any way other than that which he believed was right.

William Frankel had trained as a barrister and built up a substantial practice when he was asked by David Kessler, the owner of the *Jewish Chronicle*, to take over as general manager of the paper. The newspaper had become stale and dull; Kessler hoped that by in bringing someone with a background outside the newspaper industry, things might be shaken up.

Kessler was right. Frankel brought drive and ambition to the newspaper. Three years after joining he was promoted to editor with a mandate to revitalise the paper. He employed the very best reporters he could find to cover world and local news, and assembled a pool of commentators, drawn from talented young Jews beginning to make their name in the worlds of journalism, entertainment and literature. He redesigned the paper, utilized graphics and photographs more effectively and set about transforming the *Jewish Chronicle* from its staid self-declared role as the 'organ of Anglo-Jewry' into a quality, international Jewish journal of note.

He published a series of interviews with emerging Jewish writers, the 'angry young men' of the 1950s, which demonstrated not just a lack of interest in but a complete antipathy towards their Judaism and Jewishness. Frankel blamed the conservatism of the Orthodox rabbinate, which he believed had failed altogether to inspire a Jewish response to modernity. There were very few rabbis in Britain who were in tune with the changing times, who could demonstrate the relevance of traditional Judaism to a confused, post-war generation, affluent but living under the shadow of the nuclear bomb, whose lives were being transformed by technology faster than ever before. Among these rabbis, he believed, was Louis Jacobs, the minister of his synagogue, a man with whom Frankel was developing a close friendship.

Louis Jacobs was the rabbinic face that Frankel wished to display to his new generation of readers. He was uninhibited in using the paper in Jacobs's support. As the Jews' College Principal, Dr Epstein, drew close to the age of retirement, William published an editorial making it very clear what his paper was hoping for. At this early stage he didn't mention Louis by name, though it has been suggested that his use of the word 'reason' was a coded reference to Jacobs's book.[5]

> Jews' College must now consider the kind of personality whom it would wish to succeed to the principalship . . . the College needs to be strengthened in self-confidence so that it can champion the combination of traditional studies with a contemporary approach. The need is to train ministers who can reason with the laity and thereby strengthen the hold of Judaism on the uncommitted.[6]

Having control of the only significant Jewish medium was useful, but William knew that his paper's support alone would not be enough to put Jacobs into Dr Epstein's shoes. He worked behind the scenes, lobbying Sir Alan Mocatta, the college chairman, and his vice-president, Dr Solomon Gaon, the spiritual leader, or *haham*, of the Sephardi community. The college treasurer, Lawrence Jacobs, another New West End congregant, was a good friend. The only cloud on the horizon was that Jacobs's appointment would require the approval of the college President, the Chief Rabbi. On current form that did not look very likely.

Determined to keep Jacobs in London, his supporters came up with a stratagem. It would backfire badly, but of course they were not to know that yet. Rather than risk everything by putting Jacobs up for the post of Principal, the college would create a lesser position of Moral Tutor which would be offered to Jacobs. The Chief Rabbi, they were sure, would not object; he would see it as a way of relegating the troublesome Jacobs to the sidelines. Jacobs would bide his time in that post until Dr Epstein eventually retired, at which time, they believed, the Chief Rabbi would have come round to their way of thinking and would agree to Jacobs's promotion. When the plan was agreed, Jacobs wrote to Dr Finkelstein advising him that he would not be coming to New York.

Finkelstein had not been 'used'; if anybody had, it was Louis. Years later he would say that he had been misguided in going along with the plan. He would have done far better, he wrote, to have stayed at the New West End until Dr Epstein retired. If the Chief Rabbi had blocked his appointment at that stage, he would at least still have had the New West End pulpit, a position he now had to give up to take the post of Moral Tutor:

> It was simply not true, as my opponents later hinted, that I was only bent on using the principalship of Jews' College as a stepping stone to the Chief Rabbinate, a position which would become vacant on Rabbi Brodie's retirement. I may have been calculating, but if to that extent and with the aim of eventually securing the office of Chief Rabbi, I would have been far better advised to remain at the New West End, then the premier synagogue in the United Synagogue movement.[7]

Those who knew Jacobs best insist that he never had an ambition to be Chief Rabbi. He would have taken the job if they'd appointed him, but it would have been through duty, not desire. He would have greatly preferred to be principal of Jews' College, where he could have trained a new generation of rabbis, than to represent the community on the national stage, and deal with the day-to-day headaches that accompany political leadership.

A MORAL TUTOR

Jacobs was appointed to a specially created post of Moral Tutor. His appointment was so curiously contrived that at first it was not at all clear, either to him or the college, what his exact role would be. In the letter offering him the position, the college secretary wrote: 'it is not possible at this stage to give you details of the duties which will be required of you at the College, as these have to be worked out more fully, but it is intended that in addition to acting as Tutor to the students you would be expected, amongst other things, to give lectures on Pastoral Theology to the students.' The details of his salary would also need to be discussed with him 'when the future is known a little more fully'. The letter suggested that since it would take him time to disengage himself from his New West End duties, the role would be part -time initially.[8]

To an outside observer, renouncing his pulpit at London's premier congregation in order to take up a part-time staff role at Jews' College could not have appeared a wise career move. He wasn't certain himself, and he took the job in a 'divided state of mind'.[9] But Jacobs's friends and colleagues reacted warmly to the news. Even Dr Finkelstein, peeved as he may have been, was gracious in his congratulations. Jacobs's long-term correspondent Jakob Petuchowski, who had been his contemporary at University College, expressed his relief. Now living and teaching at Hebrew Union College in Chicago, Petuchowski wrote to say he had been worrying about Anglo-Jewry's future. But now, with Jacobs training the next generation of rabbis at Jews' College, he was reassured that all was not lost.[10]

Louis's reply to Petuchowski shows the extent to which the United Synagogue's treatment of its rabbis influenced his decision to leave the New West End and obliquely set in train the events of the next few years:

> For some time now I have felt a growing sense of frustration at the way in which a Minister's time, over here, is fritted away on trivialities leaving him no time for anything like serious scholarly work. Two offers were made to me . . . It was no easy thing to decide which to accept but I have finally decided to go to Jews' College and so continue to work in the community in which I was born.[11]

The honorary officers at the New West End, who were aware of the political artifice behind Jacobs's appointment, took the news resolutely. They noted his new position with regret but congratulated

Jews' College on their 'acquisition'. Their true feelings might be gauged from their reluctance to negotiate Jacobs's departure; seven weeks after his appointment was announced Jacobs was still chasing them to find out the date on which they would formally release him.

Jews' College was an Orthodox establishment that did its best to remain open to modern scholarship without straying beyond the boundaries of Orthodoxy. Amongst the Strictly Orthodox the college was regarded as such a bastion of heresy that Rabbi Dessler, Jacobs's former teacher in Gateshead, could declare without any sense of irony that no God-fearing young man would contemplate attending it. Yet its condemnation by the Strictly Orthodox did not imply that the college agreed with the views that Jacobs had set out in *We Have Reason to Believe*. It had world-renowned scholars on its faculty but all, without exception, either prioritized religious belief over academic scholarship, or regarded the two areas of discourse as mutually incompatible: one could no more apply reason to faith, or faith to reason, than hear the colour red or taste a part of speech.

This meant that Jacobs was obliged to walk a fine line. He passionately wanted the job of College Principal, believing that the college shared his view that the development of Judaism could best be investigated through the tools of modern scholarship. He wanted to encourage the students to appreciate that a non-fundamentalist approach was perfectly respectable, both Jewishly and academically; that 'knowledge of Judaism as a developing religion was perfectly compatible with piety and observance'.[12]

Whether he could succeed in this mission, even were he to have been appointed Principal, is not at all certain. One former student recalled him as evangelical in his approach:

His weakness was that he had a bee in his bonnet about Pentateuchal criticism and took every opportunity of arguing that one could be Orthodox and still accept the documentary hypothesis about the origins of the Torah. Like all those who newly convert to an idea, he became a missionary for it . . .

I objected to his views at that time, adopted them later, and finally concluded that speculative historical and literary theories should not be used to challenge traditional beliefs, nor can such beliefs be employed to confute scientific ideas. They simply operate on different planes.[13]

His evangelism did not bother everyone. Some of his students saw him as a breath of fresh air in the college:

In the middle of 1959 there was great excitement and interest when Rabbi Jacobs was appointed as 'Moral Tutor and Lecturer in Pastoral Theology.' There had never been any such subject in the curriculum of Jews' College, which invited lively discussion. His charismatic personality and dynamic nature permeated the classrooms, the corridors and the canteen whenever present. He was eager to build a positive and close relationship with the other lecturers and students based on trust and honesty. He was young and energetic with a great deal of enthusiasm, openness and interaction with students; eager to understand, help and clarify their problems and conflicts.[14]

Many years later he told his daughter Naomi that he had gone to Jews' College with hopes and wishes to build it into an outstanding institution that would attract the very best students for the Anglo-Jewish ministry. His priority that all British rabbis should have a good all-round education is evident from the curriculum notes he compiled for his course on ministerial training. Alongside the self-evident requirement that trainee rabbis be fluent in Hebrew Language, Biblical Literature, Rabbinic Texts and Jewish History, he included a separate category headed General Culture. This included English Classics, History, Philosophy, Psychology, World Literature, Art, Music and Architecture. Jacobs's paradigm of the ideal English Minister was a man schooled in the totality of European civilization: both the Jewish world and the wider world beyond. The gaps in this curriculum which stand out today from a Jewish perspective, even if they did not in 1959, include Israel, non-European cultures and an understanding of the other great world religions.

Louis Jacobs, the English Minister, set an example that he hoped others would follow, engaging with his students and taking an interest in them. For it was the personal element, he believed, just as much as any religious or academic scholarship, that would lead to a rabbinate moulded into the shape that he was hoping to cast.

> He was considerate, kind and tolerant and had no problem with any challenge that we might throw at him . . . Louis would have made a wonderful Chief Rabbi, or Principal of Jews' College, but the decisions about his future became wrapped up in communal politics, as much as if not more than in theological trysts . . . Louis and his wife Shulamit were the most charming of individuals and, unlike most of the College teachers, they actually invited the students to their home. I was truly saddened when he resigned at the end of my first year.[15]

Louis took up his position at Jews' College in January 1960 while continuing, for longer than he had first expected, to serve as Minister to the New West End. He did not preach his final sermon there until 11 June.

As the New West End embarked on a search for his successor, Jacobs suggested that they consider approaching Wolfe Kelman in New York. The impetus for the idea came from Gertie Frankel, who had been corresponding with Kelman while Jacobs was mulling over whether to accept the offer to take up a post at the Jewish Theological Seminary. She seems not to have known that Jacobs was considering a move to New York, because she wrote to Kelman on 17 July telling him in strictest confidence that the New West End post was about to become vacant and asking if he might be interested 'if it can be wangled this end'. Kelman of course knew that Jacobs was corresponding with Dr Finkelstein about a position, so he may have wondered why Gertie was writing to him in such a cloak-and-dagger manner, particularly since she adjured him not to breathe a word to 'Finky'.

Oddly, Gertie's letter to Kelman included handwritten footnotes from both William Frankel and Louis Jacobs. William wrote that he thought that it would be a tough fight to try to get the synagogue to offer the post to Kelman, a leading Conservative rabbi who had recently spent a sabbatical at the Reform synagogue in London's Upper Berkeley Street. The appointment could not be made without the Chief Rabbi's approval, and it was almost certain that Brodie would not countenance a rabbi of such a pedigree. Jacobs however was optimistic, believing that Brodie could be persuaded by some of the movers and shakers in the community.[16]

Jacobs's faith that Brodie might be persuaded touches on one of the most intractable questions in what was to follow. Much has been written about Brodie's personality, his leadership skills, his attitude to the views put forward by Louis Jacobs and about whether he was his own man, or whether he was pushed and pulled by others. He was appointed as Chief Rabbi, according to Chaim Bermant, because he was 'British born and bred . . . a Balliol, Oxford man, who spoke the King's English with a beautifully chiselled diction . . . an amiable man with a pleasant, easy-going, English temperament, who could be expected to approach the problems of his office in a sensible English way . . .'[17] Even though he turned out to be relatively weak, giving way at key moments to Jacobs's critics within the Strictly Orthodox community, Brodie had a mind of his own. He was anxious to ensure that others knew it.

> That I did have misgivings in respect of the appointment of Dr. Jacobs at Jews' College is shown by my decision not to allow him to lecture on Bible studies – the subject on which Dr. Jacobs was going astray. I wished to be helpful, and as I said in an interview in July 1962, '. . . I consented to his appointment as Tutor though I knew that some of his views were not completely acceptable, but bearing in mind his background and early training, I felt that an act of faith on my part would be justified, and with the passage of time and with further study of Jewish sources and continuing research, he would modify his views.'[18]

JEWISH VALUES

Had they managed to pull it off, Kelman's appointment would have been a coup for those, including Jacobs and the Frankels, who wished to see a greater rapprochement between the American Conservative movement and the United Synagogue in England. In the event the matter was not put to the test. Kelman, although declaring he was flattered, declined. He told Jacobs that he did not relish the thought of placing himself in a subordinate position to the Chief Rabbi, and informed Gertie that his wife did not wish to be the role model for ritual observance among the congregation's women.

Jacobs was now more deeply mired in communal politics than ever before. Yet he had never seen himself as a political operator; it wasn't in his nature to manipulate or campaign. He believed passionately in harmonizing traditional Judaism and modern scholarship, to show that one could be a faithful, fully observant, non-fundamentalist Jew. But education, not politics, was the tool he chose to accomplish this, through lectures, sermons and publications. And so it was that, while still ministering to the congregation and running study groups at the New West End, teaching at Jews' College, writing regular articles and reviews for the *Jewish Chronicle* and lecturing at synagogues and universities across the country, he somehow found time to sit down and write four books.

Three of the books reflect much-neglected aspects of Jacobs's scholarship. The controversies over his theology of revelation have, in public perception, dwarfed the equally important work that he did on ancient texts, mysticism and Hasidism. Blessed with a retentive memory that allowed him to recall almost anything he read, no matter how obscure, Jacobs's command of ancient and medieval Jewish literature was encyclopedic. It allowed him both to bring long-forgotten texts to light, and to construct cogent counter-arguments against what he saw as the fossilization of Jewish law, basing his reasoning on sources beyond the reach of many of his disputants.

The first of the books to be published, in 1960, was his translation of and commentary on the sixteenth-century kabbalistic tract *Palm Tree of Deborah*. Written in Hebrew by Moses Cordovero, a kabbalist in the Galilean town of Safed, it ranks as one of the primary texts of Jewish mystical literature. Jacobs's translation, introduction and analysis was his first major contribution to the scholarship of Jewish mysticism, a field he would return to repeatedly during his career.

Two of the books he worked on at this time, neither of which would be published for several years, dealt with eighteenth-century thinkers from the Lubavitch, or Habad, branch of Hasidism. One was a translation and commentary on the kabbalistic *Tract on Ecstasy* by Dov Ber, the second dynastic leader of the Habad movement. The other book, *Seeker of Unity*, was a monograph on the Habad theologian Aaron Horowitz of Starosselje, whose life and works may have remained virtually unknown had Jacobs not taken an interest in him.

Much as these books appealed to his scholarly interest, none reflected Jacobs's distinctive religious philosophy as closely as the fourth book he wrote during this period, *Jewish Values*. Less controversial than *We Have Reason to Believe*, *Jewish Values*, published in 1960, ranks in chronology if not in stature as the second of Jacobs's major works.

In writing *We Have Reason to Believe* he had tried to close the gap between traditional theology and modern thought. In *Jewish Values* he did the same in respect of beliefs. Judaism, he maintained, was not medieval; it had always responded to new knowledge and ideas, and would continue to do so. Yet Judaism in modernity had fallen behind in its responses. The modern believer, who is challenged by new knowledge that is not addressed in the traditional interpretations, 'will tend to read his Bible with critical aids, his Talmud with the works of historical investigators to assist him, his Kabbalah with the recognition of its Gnostic and Neo-Platonic elements . . .'[19] Covering subjects ranging from Fear of Heaven and Love of God to Humility and Peace, he showed how each topic had developed in Judaism over the centuries, before proposing its relevance to Jewish life today. It was a technique that he would draw on time and again in his later works.

Jewish Values appeared to mixed reviews. The *Jewish Chronicle* made use of it to explain the paper's perspective during the trial of the captured Nazi Adolf Eichmann. Noting that voices had been raised urging the state of Israel to show him mercy, the paper published a short extract from *Jewish Values* in which Jacobs, having first demonstrated that compassion is a distinguishing feature of Judaism, outlined its limits: 'The first is in regard to Justice . . . In the name of compassion itself, the judge must decide in accordance with Justice alone, for were the Law to fail, the unjust would find no hindrance to their evil schemes . . . The second limit to compassion is to those who lack compassion themselves . . . the hatred of evil is a good.'[20]

The Jewish Observer and Middle East Review was not so impressed. The reviewer expressed his somewhat facetious disappointment in the book's emphasis on theological values rather than the pressing ethical issues of the day, notably the morality of nuclear war. The book, he said, was somewhat unrealistic.

Jewish Values was published shortly after Jacobs took up his position at Jews' College. But it was *We Have Reason to Believe*, three years after its rather quiet and unobtrusive publication, that was now receiving attention, by no means all favourable. He received a stern letter from Rabbi Emanuel Rackman, a prominent American scholar. Rackman took him to task for proposing Higher Criticism, the academic analysis of the composition and authorship of biblical passages, as a means of resolving difficulties in the Pentateuchal text.

I do not believe it is more intellectually dishonest to accept the divine character of the Pentateuch despite several of its inexplicable portions than it is to accept the reality of God's goodness despite his toleration of evil . . . Your way out of the dilemma however jeopardizes the entire structure of Judaism and I do not believe you need it.[21]

It was this perception, that *We Have Reason to Believe* undermined the 'entire structure' of Judaism, the fundamental belief that God had given Moses the Torah at Mount Sinai, which caused the greatest stir. Particularly at Jews' College, where he had now been for over a year. Things were not working out as he had hoped. Largely because Chief Rabbi Brodie had only just begun to pay attention to his book, and, even now, only because others were encouraging him to do so.

6

Jews' College

Jacobs had taken the position of Moral Tutor in the expectation that Dr Epstein would soon retire as Principal, whereupon he would be appointed as his successor. But Dr Epstein showed no sign of retiring. Ostensibly he was remaining in post until a suitable successor was found. But it was common knowledge that Jacobs was waiting in the wings and it was becoming common knowledge that the Chief Rabbi was uncertain about appointing him. Even though on a personal level it appeared their relationship was amicable enough, Jacobs felt that Brodie resented, was possibly even jealous of, his presence in the college. The Jewish press were continuing to tip Jacobs as Brodie's successor, which, given their history, may well have added to the Chief Rabbi's displeasure.

The college had other problems too. In May 1960 its Council was told that during the previous year only one person had applied to train for the ministry. When told, they weren't too worried: the college had received a sufficient number of applications in previous years; there was no evidence of a downward trend. By July however their equanimity had turned to concern. Dr Epstein warned that it was a delusion to imagine that the situation could be remedied by reforming the College's outlook. He declared that the ideal aim was to make use of the best and most constructive findings of modern scientific research and study without being bludgeoned into accepting the 'often conflicting theories of the critical schools, which, in the last analysis, were found to be based on subjective

judgments, false premisses, and unproved suppositions'.[1] Epstein
was referring to the theories of Higher Biblical Criticism, to which
Emmanuel Rackman had also alluded in his letter to Jacobs. By
refuting the traditional belief in the divine revelation at Sinai,
Higher Criticism was irreconcilably in conflict with traditional
Orthodox belief.

The *Jewish Chronicle*, which as we have seen was outspoken in
its support for Rabbi Jacobs as the college's next Principal, seems
to have taken Dr Epstein's words as a dig at Jacobs. In his editorial,
William Frankel criticized Epstein's 'dogmatic scorn' for critical
theories. The college, it declared, requires a theological position.
'To attempt to equate the search for religious truth with heresy is
ultimately to make Orthodoxy synonymous with obscurantism.'
This broadside at the college was too much even for Jacobs's friends
in the rabbinate. The following week the paper published letters
from Rabbis Alexander Carlebach, whom Jacobs had worked
alongside at Munk's synagogue, and Kopul Rosen, criticizing the
editorial's tone and its implied rejection of Orthodoxy.

Whether the *Jewish Chronicle* was right to take Dr Epstein's
words as a criticism of Jacobs is open to question. As Rabbi
Dr Jeffrey Cohen, then a student at the college, recalls, Dr Epstein
had entrusted Jacobs with the sensitive subject of teaching Textual
Criticism. The students, believing that it was Dr Epstein who had
drawn Rabbi Brodie's attention to the views Jacobs set out in *We
Have Reason to Believe*, wondered 'whether his intention was to give
him as much rope as he needed!'[2]

In fact, it was not Dr Epstein who had first drawn the Chief
Rabbi's attention to *We Have Reason to Believe*. Dayan Isidore
Grunfeld of the London Beth Din had suggested to Chief Rabbi
Brodie that it would be inappropriate for the future Principal
of Jews' College to profess the views that Jacobs had outlined in
his book. Despite having a rabbinic qualification, the scholarly
Dr Grunfeld had worked as a lawyer in Germany. He moved to
Palestine in 1933 but was unable to find satisfactory work. In 1934
he and his wife Judith arrived in London, where he eventually was
given a part-time position as minister of Finsbury Park Synagogue.

Devout and strongly principled, he was uncomfortable with the lenient Orthodoxy of the United Synagogue; he had even once refused to preach at the New West End because of its mixed-gender choir. The then Chief Rabbi, Dr Hertz, considering him an ideal counterweight to the liberal-minded lay leadership of the United Synagogue, recruited him onto the Beth Din.[3]

Grunfeld obtained a copy of *We Have Reason to Believe*, marked up in red all the passages he regarded as heretical, and gave it to Brodie. But unlike Brodie, Grunfeld took time to engage with Jacobs, inviting him to his home, attempting to persuade him to retract his views. Where Brodie appeared paralysed in dealing with Jacobs, Grunfeld recognized the importance, if it could be done, of bringing Jacobs onside. If Louis would only amend his views, it would allow him, in Orthodox eyes, to assume the leadership role in British Jewry that his scholarship and intellectual ability qualified him for.[4]

Dr Epstein had still not announced his retirement and Jacobs continued to work part-time at the college. He wrote articles for the *Jewish Chronicle* and contributed regularly to their Sermon of the Week column. He lectured at community organizations and preached at synagogues across London, including a period as acting rabbi at the Western Synagogue. But this rather disjointed life was not satisfying. When Dr Epstein announced in September 1960 that he would retire the following year, Jacobs believed there may be light at the end of the tunnel.

The tunnel however would prove to be longer and far darker than it first appeared.

OBSTRUCTION

The faculty at Jews' College were wary of Rabbi Jacobs. Two of the other long-standing lecturers were known to harbour ambitions to succeed Dr Epstein when he retired, while the Principal himself, who would have preferred to remain in post for as long as he lived, was manifestly cold towards Jacobs. Although the College Council seem not to have taken much notice of the faculty's opinion, some wrote expressing their joint opposition to Jacobs's prospective appointment.[5]

Despite the personal rapport that Louis developed with the students, several of them were not easily won over to his point of view.

> I well recall the lively debates that we had with Louis on that subject. I think we acted as if it was our sacred mission to defend the Orthodox position, which, I have to say, was a trifle disingenuous considering that we had spent the past three undergraduate years studying Bible and employing therewith the tools of higher and lower textual criticism! Perhaps we justified our position on the grounds that we had been simply studying and regurgitating the scholarly view, without emotionally engaging with it, whereas, for Louis, it was an article of faith.[6]

Jacobs was a patient man, but by December 1960 even he was becoming impatient. Three months had now passed since Dr Epstein had announced his impending retirement. Jacobs's influential supporters continued to express confidence that he would succeed Dr Epstein, but Chief Rabbi Brodie, in whose hands the appointment rested, showed not the slightest interest in offering him the job. Indeed, Brodie was sounding out scholars in Israel and the USA to see if they would be interested in the post. In October 1960 a mutual contact was asked to approach Efraim Urbach, Professor of Talmud at the Hebrew University in Jerusalem. A month later a similar approach was made to the rabbinic scholar Mordechai Margoliot, who was then at the Jewish Theological Seminary in New York. Meanwhile the chairman of the college, Alan Mocatta, was trying his hardest both to put pressure on Rabbi Brodie and to restrain Jacobs's growing impatience.[7]

In December 1960 Mocatta met the Chief Rabbi, together with Ewen Montagu, President of the United Synagogue. After the meeting Mocatta wrote to Jacobs telling him that Brodie had agreed to grant him an interview, and that the Chief Rabbi had spoken kindly and appreciatively of him. 'Much', he declared, 'must inevitably turn on your discussions with the Chief Rabbi.'[8]

Jacobs's meeting with the Chief Rabbi proved inconclusive. Rumours began to circulate that Dr Brodie was considering an interregnum prior to the appointment of a new Principal. During this time he would act as the head of the college, just as the previous Chief Rabbi had done during the Second World War. In April the *Jewish Chronicle* published an article in its Personal Opinion column warning against such an arrangement. It would, claimed the columnist, be bad for the college, the Chief Rabbi and the whole community. The following week it repeated the call in an editorial, cautioning against any delay in making an appointment. An interregnum might have been acceptable in 'more spacious' times, but given its inability to recruit students 'the critical needs of the College do not permit of delay and, since the search for a successor was announced many months ago, it should, by now, be reasonably clear who is available.'[9]

The *Jewish Chronicle* thundered impotently. On 15 May the College Council agreed that Chief Rabbi Brodie be appointed Acting Principal until a permanent successor was found. Alan Mocatta noted that no candidates to date had applied for the vacant post. The *Jewish Chronicle* proclaimed that the news of the interregnum would be received by the community 'with dismay'. It pointed out that Dr Brodie had previously said that the duties of the Principal were so great that the burden could not be carried by one man.

> Yet, in the next breath, he asserted his own ability to direct the College for an indefinite period in a few hours of each week . . . He has reported unsuccessful inquiries in Israel and the United States, which is hardly surprising and somewhat disingenuous. Our community, which maintains the College, may well regard it as strange if Dr Brodie does not now look nearer home.[10]

Dr Brodie did not look nearer home. In October he asked an intermediary in the USA to approach Rabbi Dr Norman Lamm, to see if he was interested in the position. Dr Lamm declined.

DISTRACTION

The politics of Jews' College were frustrating but they did not stop Jacobs from getting on with the things that mattered to him. In addition to his guest preaching and lecturing, he was writing profusely. The trial in Jerusalem of Adolf Eichmann dominated the news, and although nobody doubted the importance of the trial, from a rabbinic perspective Jacobs could see significant ethical and halachic issues that needed to be aired. Among the sermons, articles and book reviews he wrote for the *Jewish Chronicle* was a piece in which he asked whether proceeding against the Nazi was a morally justifiable act of vengeance, and if convicted, whether Eichmann should be executed. He argued that the true purpose of the trial was 'to remind the world that men can sink below the level of beasts' and to find the 'most effective way of reminding humanity that it must strive constantly to be truly human'. Quoting Deuteronomy, 'And those that remain shall hear, and fear, and shall henceforth commit no more any such evil,' he concluded that rather than the death penalty, the best outcome would be for Eichmann to be condemned and left to endure his miserable existence. Shunned by God and man; in Isaiah's words, 'an abhorring unto all flesh'.[11]

In July Louis took up an invitation from B'nai B'rith of America to lecture at their Institutes of Judaism across the country. It was his first overseas speaking tour. Travelling without Shula he lectured from Washington to Texas, where he was declared an honorary citizen; a distinction conferred upon him by the Governor because he had lectured at two Institutes in the State. He spent several days at the B'nai B'rith Institute at Wildacres in North Carolina. On his return Shula quizzed him for the details:

> Can you imagine . . . the ranch at Wildacres. Located picturesquely in the pinnacle of a mountain in the Blue Ridge of Western Carolina . . . the most beautiful scenery in the Eastern United States. In the curriculum golf, swimming and hiking go with learning . . . The lectures were on God, Torah and Israel. All afternoons were free, culture being put aside for enjoyment and parties . . .[12]

Jacobs's American trip was even featured in *Newsweek*, but not for reasons he might have anticipated. The country was in a nervous state over aircraft terrorism; there had been a spate of successful and attempted hijackings; only recently a Pan Am flight from Houston to Mexico had been abducted to Cuba. A few hours after the hijack Louis, short, dark-skinned and with a jet-black beard, was in the waiting room at Houston airport when several passengers decided that his appearance was of concern. They alerted a policeman who declared that Louis's appearance was a textbook profile of a terror suspect. Despite Jacobs protesting his innocence in his best British accent, the officer arrested him. It wasn't until an airport official confirmed that he was in fact a distinguished British theologian that the police acknowledged their error. Jacobs later commented that wearing a beard was a distinctly un-American activity.[13]

While waiting to find out whether he would be appointed Principal of Jews' College, Jacobs published two new books. The previous year he had received a strange letter from Achille Onge of Worcester, Massachusetts, a man of whom he had never previously heard. Onge's hobby was producing miniature books. He was hoping to publish one describing all the Jewish holidays. The rabbi he had engaged for the task had let him down and he had been given Jacobs's details by Dr Solomon Pfeffer of the Jewish Theological Seminary in New York. Onge wondered whether Jacobs would be prepared to step in. The book would measure two inches by three inches, the description of each festival would occupy 300–500 words, and a limited edition of 2,000 copies would be printed. Onge could not offer Jacobs payment for the work but would be willing to present him with 50 copies.

Many people would have declined the offer, particularly as at the time Jacobs was writing his next major book, *Studies in Talmudic Logic and Methodology*. But he agreed. It was, after all, a project of Jewish education.

Published in September 1961, *Studies in Talmudic Logic and Methodology* was Jacobs's first book-length academic publication. In a theme that he would return to in later scholarly works, he analysed the structure and logic of the Talmudic text, arguing that the work is a literary creation in which earlier material was skilfully reshaped by later editors. Like his 1952 article 'Evidence of Literary Device in the Babylonian Talmud', the book advanced an approach to Talmudic criticism that would become a staple of academic scholarship in the following decades.

The *Jewish Chronicle* used the publication of *Studies in Talmudic Logic and Methodology* to shine a spotlight on Jacobs and the continuing problems of academic leadership at Jews' College. In a feature on him under the banner *Silhouette*, the paper compared Jacobs's synthesis of yeshiva learning and modern critical scholarship to unnamed 'famous Jewish scholars in other lands'. The article warned that he had received offers of employment from seminaries and pulpits overseas but had, to date, turned them down because he considered it his duty to remain in Britain. But he now stood at a turning point in his career. Anglo-Jewry, it cautioned, would need to show the wisdom to make use of his rare qualities, if it did not wish to regret the loss of yet another of its spiritual leaders.[14]

REACTION

As 1961 drew to an end Jacobs's frustration became palpable. He'd had several meetings with Alan Mocatta, now Sir Alan as a result of his appointment in October as a High Court Judge. Mocatta advised patience, but from Jacobs's perspective the cards seemed to be stacked against him. Dr Epstein had retired, Dr Brodie was Acting Principal, and the mild-mannered, scholarly Rabbi Dr Zimmels had been appointed Director of Studies. It was known that Zimmels hoped to be appointed Principal, but despite his scholarly credentials and lengthy service at the college his age counted against him, as did the fact that he was not home-grown.

Another meeting was arranged with the Chief Rabbi, at which he again refused to sanction Jacobs's appointment. Louis felt that all was now lost, that he had spent two years of his life fruitlessly pursuing his dream of imbuing a new spirit of enquiry into candidates for the British rabbinate. He went home to write Sir Alan his letter of resignation.

Dated 14 November 1961, the letter expressed his deepest feelings of regret in tendering his resignation from the staff of Jews' College:

You will recall that two and a half years ago I was invited by you and your colleagues to come to the College as Tutor. You pointed out at the time that it was the intention of the Hon. Officers that I should be appointed Principal after the retirement of Dr Epstein, though there could be no definite promise on their part since the appointment depended, under the Constitution on the Chief Rabbi's approval. Since Dr Epstein's retirement last July, the Chief Rabbi has been asked to give his approval for the appointment, but has failed to do so on various grounds, the one recurring most often being that views I have expressed in writing render me unsuitable for the position. These views are contained in my books *We Have Reason to Believe* and *Jewish Values*. I remain firmly convinced that the approach to traditional Judaism I have sketched in these books is one that must commend itself to all who are aware of modern thought and scholarship. I have tried to show that intense loyalty to Jewish tradition and observance need not be synonymous with reaction and fundamentalism. Furthermore, I will claim that no reputable scholar in the world has an approach that is basically different from mine.

What I had hoped to do at Jews' College was to help train men able to hold their own in the field of objective scholarship and, at the same time, imbued with the spirit of *yirat shamayim*; who would realize, in some measure, at least, the implications of the verse: For this is your wisdom and your understanding in the sight of the peoples. In this task intelligent Jews everywhere are engaged. It will be sad if Anglo-Jewry with its traditional breath of wisdom were not to participate in such a presentation of Judaism.[15]

I want to express my thanks to you and your colleagues for your confidence in me.[16]

Sir Alan Mocatta tried to persuade Louis to reconsider. He asked him to wait until the College Council had discussed the matter. Chief Rabbi Brodie wrote to Sir Alan asking him not to tell the Council that Jacobs had resigned and suggesting that the whole matter be put on hold until April, when he would have returned from a trip to Australia. Sir Alan declined the suggestion, writing to the Chief Rabbi that he 'could not justify withholding such an important matter from the Council for such a long time'.[17]

Louis did not retract his resignation but he did agree to wait until the Council meeting before making his decision public.

The Council met on 18 December. Sir Alan, producing Jacobs's letter, proposed 'that this meeting of the Council of College respectfully requests the Chief Rabbi to give his consent to Rabbi Dr Louis Jacobs being appointed Principal of the College as from October 1, 1962, with Dr Zimmels as Director of Studies.' The Chief Rabbi immediately intervened, asking that the matter not be discussed that evening.

> I have many reasons for making this request but I will only say this. As I look around the table I know that opinion will be divided, and that it will be most unfortunate for the college if this particular motion is discussed and decided upon. It has been put on the agenda against my wishes and since in a few days' time, I shall be away from the country for a while, I consider that it would not be right to have this matter considered at present.

Sir Alan pointed out that Jacobs had already tendered his resignation and that he would be lost to the college if they were not prepared to appoint him as Principal. The Chief Rabbi then insisted that he would not consent to the appointment of Dr Jacobs. When pressed, he suggested that the matter not be discussed until his return in April from his forthcoming trip. Pointing out that by April Jacobs may well have secured another post elsewhere, Sir Alan insisted that he was not prepared to accept a situation that would lead to the loss of Jacobs not only to the college but also to the country. 'Here we have an outstandingly successful minister, a man who appeals to young people, a man who himself leads a pious life, and whose object it is to teach others to do so, a man born and bred in this country. He would be admirable in the post of Principal.' Should Jacobs not be appointed, Sir Alan warned, he would resign as Chairman of the College Council at the next Annual General Meeting. Jacobs's former congregant at the New West End, Lawrence Jacobs, also announced his intention to resign.[18]

The evening ended with the Council resolving to send a delegation to Jacobs asking him to reconsider. It was a fruitless mission, as Jacobs made clear in a statement to the *Jewish Chronicle*:

> I have been asked to withhold my resignation until the return of the chief rabbi from Australia in April. The Chief Rabbi has been aware of my intention to resign on this issue for some weeks. But ever since I came to the college, two and a half years ago, he has had the opportunity of considering whether or not I would be a suitable Principal.
>
> During the last few months particularly, the Chief Rabbi has had many and lengthy discussions with me and others on the subject. The facts of the matter are therefore all within his knowledge. The only answers the Chief Rabbi has given to requests that my appointment should be made have been that he would 'consider the matter' or that he hoped I would change my views. Latterly, and at last Monday's meeting, he said that he would consider the matter again in three months' time. This has introduced nothing new and still gives no indication when or indeed whether finality can be achieved. Nor does it commit the Chief Rabbi to anything that cannot be other than a delaying tactic which will lead to further delays.
>
> The appointment of a Principal to such an institution as Jews' College cannot be made in this undignified fashion. Moreover, self-respect and my regard for the College prevent me from accepting an offer if it could only be made after elaborate

deliberations as to my alleged suitability. I was therefore unable to withdraw my resignation.[19]

Over the course of the next few days further announcements of impending resignation from the Council took place. They included the other Joint Treasurer, Felix Levy, and Louis's good friend and colleague Reverend Dr Isaac Levy, Honorary Secretary of the College and Minister of the Hampstead Synagogue. The only Honorary Officer not to resign was Dr Solomon Gaon, whose position on the Executive was by virtue of his status as *haham*.

The following week the *Jewish Chronicle* published a selection of letters it had received in support of Jacobs. In a footnote it added that it had received none in support of the Chief Rabbi. The Mizrachi journal, *Jewish Review*, challenged the veracity of that statement, pointing out that the holiday period would have made it difficult for letters supporting the Chief Rabbi (but not, it seems, those opposing him) to arrive prior to publication. The strictly orthodox Agudas Israel Organisation opined that the footnote could not testify more clearly to the spiritual poverty of the Anglo-Jewish community.[20]

Jacobs's postbox overflowed with letters of solidarity, some expressing outrage, others their sadness and disappointment with the manner in which he had been treated. Jacobs was not short of support, or affection. Yet the matter was not yet concluded. Jacobs was adamant that he would not withdraw his resignation, but the Chief Rabbi had indicated he was still to make up his mind. Indeed, although he was now in Australia he instructed his office to announce that he was prepared to defer any decision for yet another year, adding even more fuel to Jacobs's charge of procrastination. In the meantime, in a state of some limbo, Jacobs continued to work out his notice at the college. He remained on the staff until the end of the academic year in 1962.[21]

7

Friends in Need

Arguably, the blame for Jacobs's situation lay in the subterfuge behind his appointment as Moral Tutor. His supporters had hoped they could ease him past the Chief Rabbi into the Principalship by first establishing him as a fixture in the college. They had assumed that by the time Dr Epstein retired the Chief Rabbi would have adjusted to Jacobs's views – a not unreasonable assumption given that Dr Brodie had raised no objection when Jacobs's initial appointment was first mooted. They believed that Jacobs was not so outspoken within the intellectual context of the time, as evidenced by the fact that he had gained the support of several other Orthodox rabbis. However, they had not reckoned with the Chief Rabbi's tendency to defer to louder voices on the right. Nor with his lengthy prevarication over Jacobs's views in *We Have Reason to Believe*, expressing an opinion neither for nor against them, until the crisis was already upon him.

The affair hit the national press. The London *Evening Standard* knew where to apportion blame for the 'rumpus': it was in no doubt that the Chief Rabbi had been under pressure from more Orthodox Jews who considered Louis too Liberal. The *Daily Express* declared that it had brought into the open a long-standing rivalry between 'liberal and orthodox elements'. The *Manchester Evening News* took a local perspective, pointing out that the crisis made things awkward for the Inter-University Jewish Federation, at whose national convention in the city

Jacobs was due to speak. The *Daily Telegraph* devoted the most space to the crisis, quoting from Jacobs's letter of resignation. *The Times* caused some offence by quoting a 'leading member' of the Jewish community who claimed that the rift was due to a number of Jewish scholars recently arrived 'from abroad' whose outlook was very different to that of tolerant Anglo-Jewry. In his autobiography Louis expressed regret at the tone of the insinuation, declaring that had he been consulted he would not have been party to it.[1]

But it was the *Jewish Chronicle*, of course, under William Frankel's editorship, which declaimed most expansively:

> Jews' College was founded to further traditional Judaism. It is also an institution of higher learning affiliated to London University. There is something incongruous in a situation that permits the appointment of the head of such an institution to be subject to an ecclesiastical veto. It is, moreover, absurd that while laymen alone appoint the Chief Rabbi, they should not be able to appoint a Principal of Jews' College. In this case, the Honorary Officers unanimously recommended Dr. Jacobs as Principal, not *in spite of*, but *because of*, his views, for they believe that only an approach such as his can make traditional Judaism intellectually acceptable and provide the College with the leadership it sorely needs . . .
>
> It is no secret that in this, as on other issues, the Chief Rabbi allows himself to be guided by the extremists of the right. Our right-wing, like all other sections of the community, is entitled to its own views. But their opinions are neither in theory nor practice acceptable to the majority of thinking Jews. They are, moreover, opinions at variance with the benevolent Anglo-Jewish traditions of tolerance and reasonableness. From a *kulturkampf* against Reform, our extremists have passed to heresy-hunting within Orthodoxy, hence the opposition to Dr. Jacobs's appointment.[2]

Among the many letters of support that Jacobs received was one from Ewen Montagu. Montagu, who had just announced his forthcoming resignation as President of the United Synagogue over an internal management dispute, apologized to Jacobs for letting him down. Henceforth he could only back Jacobs personally, not in an official capacity.[3] However he had not yet left office, and now, as he prepared to go on the attack, he was still President of the United Synagogue.

Ewan Montagu's ire was ignited by the London Beth Din. In an intervention into the Jews' College dispute, which many interpreted as a calculated attempt to tie the Chief Rabbi's hands, they had published a statement saying that some of Jacobs's views were 'in conflict with authentic Jewish belief and render him unacceptable'. Ewen Montagu was furious that they had involved themselves in a matter beyond their jurisdiction. When he criticized them at a United Synagogue Council meeting they issued a further statement accusing him of a 'disrespectful and captious attitude to the rabbinate and the members of the Beth Din, which is calculated to undermine the foundations and authority of the Court of the Chief Rabbi'.[4]

Montagu, a former naval intelligence officer whose real claim to fame was the brilliant deception he foisted on the German Army in the Second World War (as recounted in the film *The Man Who Never Was*),[5] riposted scornfully:

> The Chief Rabbi is the religious authority of the Orthodox community. In that enormous responsibility he has the benefit of being able to ask for, and to consider, the advice of his Beth Din before *he* makes *his* decision.

> The slightest degree of loyalty to their Chief Rabbi – even the slightest decent feeling – would have told the *Dayanim*, his advisers, that they of all people could not possibly publish their views on the point, especially when he has asked for time in which to make up his mind.

'Pressure!' It will need all the courage of a great man for the Chief Rabbi now to give his decision if, on reflection, it conflicts with that of the Dayanim. We all respect the Chief Rabbi and have a deep affection for him because of his wisdom, sincerity, self-sacrifice, and devotion; we also trust that he may have our admiration for his courage and strength in his own views, the expression of which forms the appalling burden of his high office, now made so much heavier for him.[6]

A pivotal letter of support came from Ellis Franklin, a former congregant at the New West End. A nephew of Viscount Samuel and father of the brilliant biophysicist Rosalind Franklin, whose all-important role in the discovery of the structure of DNA was not fully acknowledged until after her untimely death, the merchant banker Ellis Franklin would prove influential in the next stage of Louis's career.

Looking to the future, Franklin told Jacobs that he was letting fresh air into the community, that his tenure at the New West End had marked the start of a new era. He urged him not to leave the country; the community was looking to him for leadership.

FURORE

Although he was obliged to teach at Jews' College for the remainder of the academic year, Jacobs was adamant in his own mind that he would no more retract his resignation than he would repudiate the theology he had set out in *We Have Reason to Believe*. Many of the key protagonists in the affair did not believe he would be so principled. Should Dr Brodie, on his return, consent to Jacobs's appointment as Principal of the College, they were confident that he could be prevailed upon to reconsider.

The affair showed little sign of abating while Dr Brodie was out of the country. Week after week the *Jewish Chronicle* carried readers' letters commenting on the situation. Most, but by no means all, were supportive of Rabbi Jacobs or critical of the Chief Rabbi. The paper published a letter written to the Chief Rabbi and signed by 38 prominent academics pointing out that Jacobs 'probably more than any other teacher in the Anglo-Jewish community' possessed the intellectual skills and sincerity to engage with students seeking answers to their theological questions, to reassure them in their Jewish identity and prevent the 'continual draining of the lifeblood of the community'. They believed that the 'needs of the community . . . manifestly point to his selection as the Principal of Jews' College'.[7]

The *Jewish Review*, perceiving a lack of balance, took exception to the *Chronicle*'s coverage of the issue; in an article headed 'Fair Play' they noted that cuts had been made to some letters supporting the Chief Rabbi. Among these was a submission, highly critical of Jacobs, from Immanuel Jakobovits which the *Jewish Review* now published in full. In the portion of the letter that the *Jewish Chronicle* had excised, Dr Jakobovits had written that Jacobs's letter of resignation had been 'bombastic, betraying a lack of humility ill-befitting a rabbinical leader'.[8]

Professor Cyril Domb levied a similar accusation in an article for the *Jewish Review* in which he accused Jacobs of misappropriating the word 'scientific' by confusing immutable scientific facts, like the melting temperature of copper, with theories like Higher Biblical Criticism that by their very nature 'are temporary frameworks which will be verified or refuted as new facts emerge'.[9]

Louis and Shula had much to feel hurt about at this time, but few things hurt them as much as the *Jewish Review*'s coverage of the affair. Referring to itself as the National Organ of Religious Jewry, the *Jewish Review* was the house journal of the Mizrachi movement, the religious Zionist faction in the British Jewish community with which Louis and Shula most identified, the group to which they had been devoted in their younger years and where they believed their closest friends still were. The Bromsgrove kibbutz where Shula had lived was under Mizrachi auspices, Louis had chaired Manchester Mizrachi and been honorary principal of Mizrachi's Bachad Institute for Jewish Studies. Even before he joined Munk's, Louis had looked upon Mizrachi as the antidote to the cloistered outlook of the yeshiva world, with which he was growing disenchanted.

This movement [the Mizrachi] and its sister movements, particularly the Bachad, is doing wonderful work among the youth of today. Indeed they are really the only movement to do anything at all for *Yiddishkeit*. Yet they are either completely ignored by our great *rabbonim* or in many cases vigorously attacked, though mostly behind their backs.[10]

The *Jewish Review* was one of the journals in which Jacobs had published his earliest scholarly articles. Yet now, not only had they published Professor Domb's article and the full text of Rabbi Jakobovits's letter, they had opined, in an editorial headed 'Sour Grapes':

> It is a fact that there are scholars of eminence who consider that Jacobs's published works fail to display qualities of outstanding scholarship and leadership.[11]

Louis's daughter Naomi recalls how disappointed he was when he realized that Mizrachi had turned against him. 'With the wind they changed. They wouldn't say a word for him, not a word.'

Chief Rabbi Brodie returned to England at the end of April. On 7 May he addressed the Annual General Meeting of Jews' College. He made it clear that he would not consent to Jacobs's appointment as Principal of the College, and regretfully accepted his resignation.

William Frankel's *Jewish Chronicle* declared that the Chief Rabbi's speech 'marked a climacteric for Anglo-Jewry':

> The truth is that Dr Jacobs's explicit rejection of the fundamentalist thesis of verbal revelation has provoked the hostility of a small group of right-wing extremists who have succeeded in exerting a dominating influence over the Chief Rabbi in recent years . . . One would have thought that an English-born rabbi with the qualities of scholarship and leadership possessed by Rabbi Jacobs would have been nurtured and encouraged by the Orthodox community, but the reverse has so far been the case . . . It has decided that Dr Jacobs cannot become Principal so long as Dr Brodie remains Chief Rabbi. The constitution of the College gives the Chief Rabbi a veto

from which there is no appeal, irrespective of the feeling among the community at large. But Dr Brodie's tenure of office is likely to extend for only three years more, and the election of his successor, not being subject to a rabbinical veto, could reflect more closely the type of Orthodoxy which this community wants to have for itself and its children.[12]

The furore rumbled on for months, in the press and in communal gatherings. At a fractious meeting at Jews' College, the Joint Treasurer, Felix Levy, delivered a strongly worded statement setting out the reasons why he and the other honorary officers, Sir Alan Mocatta, Lawrence Jacobs and the Reverend Isaac Levy were resigning. He declared that even before Jacobs had started teaching at the college, 'a campaign of denigration began. It has continued and grown and has now achieved its object, that of smashing the academic career and destroying the livelihood of an honourable man'. A few minutes later the Chief Rabbi intervened, saying he must 'protest most vehemently'. Turning to the *Jewish Chronicle* reporter he declared that he did not want 'any of this' published.

The Chief Rabbi would have done better to have said nothing. Scornfully, the *Jewish Chronicle* not only printed much of Mr Levy's speech, they reproduced the Chief Rabbi's intervention verbatim.[13]

Jacobs had kept a low profile since his resignation letter in November the previous year, neither wishing nor believing it prudent to make a public statement. But as argument raged around him and his term of employment at Jews' College drew to a close, he began to feel that his discreet silence might be misinterpreted. He realized that it might be interpreted as an admission that he was in the wrong. With the encouragement of his friends and supporters he decided to address a public meeting.

The meeting took place on 4 June at the New West End Synagogue's Herbert Samuel Hall. The room was packed, the doors to the hall were closed 20 minutes before the meeting even began. Despite a seating capacity of 500, over a thousand people managed to get in, standing in the aisles and crushed against the walls. Many more were turned away. Jacobs's theme was the title of his book *We Have Reason to Believe*. He spoke for an hour and a half, without notes, arguing that Judaism had always accommodated diverse views.

> We have always had room in Judaism for the Rashis of France, who were content with the Revelation as a command of God, and for the giants of Spain, who, although firm and steadfast in their Jewish faith, tried to find reasons for it . . . Judaism is rich enough and complex enough to contain within it many views . . . My thesis is that many of the greatest Jews throughout the ages believed that reason should be our guide and should even be applied to Revelation itself, even though there were, and are, others who argued differently and believed that it would be wrong to do so . . . Up till now the Jewish people found room within it for both points of view, and I would claim it to be a serious departure from the grand and tolerant tradition in Jewish thinking when the protagonists of one point of view are hunted by the others as heretics when, in fact all of them are seekers after the truth . . .

> It is, of course, true that the Talmud contains a statement that a person who does not believe that every letter in the Bible was given by God to Moses is a heretic who forfeits his share of the world to come. It is also true that Maimonides repeated that statement . . .

> But people who argue that way forget that in the times of Maimonides everybody believed it and that the aim of the statement was to stress the Divine purpose of the Bible. I do not believe that every single letter was dictated by the Almighty. But that does not affect the Divine purpose of the Bible nor its spiritual value. The question is not what Maimonides said 800 years ago, but what he would have said had he lived today. I have no doubt that if he were alive today he would have grappled with the perplexing questions of our time with the same courage and intellectual integrity with which he faced the problems of his own age.

Jacobs concluded his speech to prolonged applause. Ellis Franklin, who presided over the meeting, said that the speech would remain a landmark in the life of all who had listened to it. 'Dr Jacobs stuck to his faith and he lost his job.'[14]

Out of a job, Jacobs found that most of his time was taken up in scholarly correspondence both with leading Jewish thinkers around the world and, more parochial but no less challenging, with supporters and detractors in the Jewish community at large. The *Jewish Chronicle* also kept him busy, with book reviews, articles and sermons. But enjoyable as it was, the life of a gentleman scholar could never be enough, either for his bank balance or his ambition. Getting a new job was a priority. He was forty years old with a wife and three children to support, and his overriding concern was how to provide for his family. He was insistent that he did not wish to leave the country. Family reasons made it impractical, and by now he had invested too much emotion in the ideal of the Anglo-Jewish rabbinate to simply walk away. While waiting for the Chief Rabbi to announce his decision, Jacobs had turned down the offer of a call to become Chief Rabbi of the United Hebrew Congregation of Johannesburg. He remained adamant that he would not take the job once Rabbi Brodie's decision was made known.

His friends and supporters, anxious to keep him in the country, were of course relieved. But they knew that in the absence of a worthwhile position in England, Jacobs would not be able to resist overseas offers for ever. He had remained in touch with Wolfe Kelman in New York, and it was not beyond the bounds of possibility that he would be offered a post at the Jewish Theological Seminary. Interest had also come from Canada and Australia.

Ellis Franklin and William Frankel canvassed Jacobs's most prominent supporters. They proposed creating an independent scholarly position for Jacobs in London, supported by an adequate salary, enabling him to lecture and write. A longer-term strategy to bring about more enduring reforms within the Orthodox community would, they hoped, be devised in due course.

On 20 September the *Jewish Chronicle* announced the formation of the Society for the Study of Jewish Theology. Louis would be its

Director. Its Sponsoring Committee was composed of prominent academics, communal figures and members of the New West End Synagogue. Jacobs's predecessor at the New West End, Rev. Ephraim Levine, was a member, as were all the former honorary officers of Jews' College and Sir Alan Mocatta, the former President of the United Synagogue. Only one woman was on the Committee, Ethel Wix, the Joint Treasurer. The first woman to be appointed general commissioner of income tax, and one of the first women partners in a firm of solicitors, Ethel Wix quietly pioneered the entry of women into the patriarchy of 1960s Anglo-Jewry.

THE SOCIETY FOR THE STUDY OF JEWISH THEOLOGY

The Sponsoring Committee declared that the aim of the Institution was to encourage the study, based on sound scholarship, of the teachings of traditional Judaism. A first meeting was held at the Kensington Town Hall, on 24 September 1962, when 700 people turned up to hear Jacobs lecture on 'The God of Abraham, Isaac and Jacob'. Ellis Franklin presided, as he had done at the earlier meeting in June.

Jacobs introduced his lecture by discussing the word 'theology'. Ellis Franklin had noted in his introduction that the Society's title had been scoffed at, and Jacobs indicated he had some sympathy with such a view, since historically Jews had rarely engaged in systematic theological investigation. But it would be a mistake to conclude from this that Judaism has no theology, or that Jews have no interest in religious questions.

> There is a keen interest today in religious thought . . . people want to know what it is that we, as Jews, are expected to believe. People are no longer satisfied with what is vaguely called 'a Jewish way of life' . . . You need to think through your faith if it is to be meaningful to you. You need to face up to the challenges which are presented to your faith by the world in which you live, unless you are prepared to opt out of the 20th century . . . If we are not prepared to opt out of the 20th century . . . then we cannot fail

to recognise that there are problems . . . Above all, a good deal of serious thinking is needed. It is this matter of serious thinking about Judaism to which our Society wishes to call attention . . . We hope to form a panel of speakers . . . We hope to be able to publish their researches . . . And we hope that, as a result of our efforts, many thinking Jews and Jewesses in the community will be stimulated to apply themselves, to apply their minds, to very great problems we have to face in order for Judaism to come into its own as a faith that recognises and faces courageously the challenges of our age.

Turning to the theme of his lecture, Jacobs explained that he had chosen the title 'God of Abraham, Isaac and Jacob' because each symbolizes a different approach. His thesis, he explained, was that there is room in Judaism for different tendencies, that there are in fact three separate paths, each symbolized by one of the Patriarchs. Abraham represents the person who has no tradition, who works everything out for himself. Isaac is the person who receives the tradition from his parents. And Jacob is the one who experiences faith at its most vivid, who has to struggle with his faith, to wrestle with himself. But it is Jacob who sees the ladder reaching to heaven. Drawing on the phrase that came to define his approach, Jacobs declared that they were embarked on a quest – for the meaning of Judaism in their lives. 'We are traditionally minded Jews. We love the Jewish tradition. We believe, none the less, that there are new problems that have to be solved in the light of Jewish teaching and Jewish tradition. We welcome new ideas. We welcome new thinking. We only wish to God that there would be more people in our community who engage in this kind of thinking.'[15]

As Director of the Society it fell to Jacobs to create a programme of activities to actualize his ambitious vision. He was at some advantage, due to the financial backing of his supporters and his own high intellectual profile. The financial support ensured that in addition to his own stipend he was able to run a professional office and promote his activities widely. It even offered him a little time in which to write.

He began work on the book that would become his next major publication, an analysis of Maimonides' *Thirteen Principles of Faith*. Entitled *The Principles of the Jewish Faith*, the book was planned by him as a detailed investigation of each of Maimonides' 13 fundamentals. The book's originality, as he put it in his preface to the second edition, was that it constituted the first attempt to consider not only what Maimonides intended when he formulated the *Principles* in the twelfth century, but also how much of what he said then was still relevant for the Jewish faith in the modern world.

Jacobs's growing reputation as a religious thinker with something new and challenging to say inspired others of a similar calibre to associate with him and take part in the Society's activities. Painful as it had been, the support and publicity he received during his Jews' College embroilment did wonders for his profile, catapulting him into the fashionable circles of the intelligentsia. This was early 1960s London, society was changing in many ways, and Louis Jacobs, a young rabbi with an original brain, a way with words and media exposure, was up there among the exotic new thinkers ushering in an optimistic new future.

Jacobs summed up his vision, and his aims for the new Society, in a pamphlet entitled *Creative Judaism*:

> In the Jewish religious world today there are two basic attitudes. One is represented by those who believe that Jewish observance depends on a fundamental interpretation of the Bible and the other by those who, unable to accept fundamentalism, argue that Jewish observance can no longer claim allegiance with the force of a Divine command. Both these attitudes are guilty of the fallacy of judging religious institutions merely by their origin. We, together with other observant Jews all over the world, believe that a completely free and objective approach to the origins of the Bible and the other classical sources of Judaism does not deprive Jewish observance of the Divine power, since it matters more not what an institution once was, but what it has become.[16]

The Society's most frequent activities were Jacobs's lectures, delivered mainly in synagogue halls in London. His topics were diverse. In an eight-week period in the autumn of 1963 he spoke on Existentialism, Linguistic Analysis, Comparative Religion and Freud, while running weekly classes on the Mishnah and a four-lecture series on Judaism and Modern Thought.

He brought in outside speakers to deliver keynote lectures. Among them were the distinguished scholar Reverend James Parkes, who specialized in Jewish–Christian relations, Professor Raphael Loewe, doyen of medieval Jewish studies, the grammarian and archaeologist Professor Jacob Weingreen, the orientalist Professor Bernard Lewis and the Reform theologian Rabbi Ignaz Maybaum.

Jacobs's regular speakers, all United Synagogue ministers sympathetic to his point of view, included Reverend Dr Isaac Levy of Hampstead, Dalston Synagogue's Rabbi Isaac Newman, Reverend Leslie Hardman from Hendon, Rabbi Dr S. Lehrman of the New Synagogue in Stamford Hill, Reverend Dr Chaim Pearl, who had succeeded Jacobs at the New West End, and St John's Wood's Rabbi Dr Solomon Goldman. Their themes ranged from series on Judaism in World Civilizations and The Synagogue as a Communal Institution to individual lectures about theology, modernity and prayer.

Rabbi Lehrman, minister of the New Synagogue on Stamford Hill, had prefaced his remarks at one of his lectures, saying that his presence did not mean that he completely endorsed Jacobs's views but was speaking 'primarily as a manifestation of my rooted dislike of any attempt made at what has been called "ecclesiastical heresy hunting"'. This did not stop one of the wardens of his synagogue from publicly criticizing him, saying that it was regrettable that of all the ministers in the district, 'ours should have decided to speak to the Society'. These comments in turn drew a sharp rebuke from Reverend Hardman, who saw it as another proof of the 'master and servant' relationship between laity and clergy. There were few ministers capable of giving such high-quality lectures. For Dr Lehrman to be pilloried in such a way was, he said, shameful and completely unwarranted.[17]

Altogether the Society ran one or two events each week during the academic terms and published an erudite quarterly bulletin comprising learned articles and transcripts of the major lectures. Although few, if any, of the Society's activities added to the controversy around Jacobs's beliefs on Revelation, as expected it found itself the target of hostility. When he first heard of the Society's formation Louis's friend Reverend Kenneth Cosgrove, minister of Glasgow's Garnethill Synagogue, expressed his fears in a letter to William Frankel. He told him that the Chief Rabbi, the Beth Din and 'the Jewish Review boys'

> want to discredit Louis as an orthodox rabbi and it just suits them to have him outside . . . I emphasised to Louis that that he must have a *shool* [synagogue] . . . As long as Louis does not have a pulpit the dogs have barked with success and the unjust status quo they want and wish to preserve remains. *Shool* not school will frustrate them. School without *shool* will give the jackals a feeling of victory.[18]

A few months after the Society's launch, Dr Chaim Pearl was due to deliver a lecture for the Society at Edgware Synagogue, where Dayan Swift regularly worshipped. Swift, who had been instrumental in the Beth Din's intervention in the Jews' College dispute, told the Synagogue's honorary officers that if the meeting went ahead, he would in future worship elsewhere. The honorary officers promptly banned Rabbi Pearl's lecture. On hearing that his lecture had been cancelled Dr Pearl expressed outrage: 'I was bowled over by this piece of news. If there is any feeling on the part of the Establishment that ministers should not lecture to the Society it is a lot of nonsense. I lecture to all sorts of people . . . I won't be told by anyone where or to whom I may lecture.'[19]

Jacobs's frustration was palpable. At a lecture to mark the first anniversary of the Society he complained that the Society had been misrepresented, treated intolerantly and characterized as following in the footsteps of antisemitic nineteenth-century German Bible critics. He complained of the either/or attitude which had been most forcefully expressed by Samson Raphael Hirsch over a hundred years earlier: either one believed that every word of the Bible was God-given, or one should give up Judaism altogether. 'Has Anglo-Jewry become so pragmatic', he asked, 'as to not see the value of investigation of its faith?'[20]

Turning to the theme of his lecture, to which he had given the title 'The Sanction of the *Mitzwoth*', Jacobs took issue with each of the major Jewish religious trends of the time. He argued that it was not just rigid Orthodoxy that was misguided. Classical Reform had reduced Judaism to a series of moral propositions, impoverishing and emaciating Judaism. The Historical School only saw the practice of Judaism as means of ensuring the survival of the religion, while Reconstructionism justified it in terms of human and sociological values.[21] What Judaism needed, he argued, was a fifth approach which recognized that God had revealed himself not only to the prophets, but also to the people of Israel through history, and that the real sanction behind the commandments was their importance in Jewish life throughout the ages and in their spiritual influence bringing people closer to God.

Jacobs's first public humiliation occurred one Shabbat morning in January. He was in Manchester, to give a public lecture on a Saturday evening. Although he would have liked to attend Shabbat services in his old community at the Central Synagogue, the current rabbi, a former pupil of his, had written a pamphlet attacking him. Feeling it would be embarrassing for them both if he turned up at the Central, he went instead to the Holy Law Synagogue, where the rabbi was an old friend. The rabbi welcomed him. But the honorary officers of the synagogue refused to call him to the reading of the Torah, despite this being an honour customarily bestowed upon a visiting rabbi. It was the first time he had been snubbed in this way. It would not be the last.

Whatever disappointment Jacobs may have felt was to some extent ameliorated by the attendance at his lecture that evening. Over 500 people braved 'fog, ice and snow on one of the worst winter nights for many years' to hear him speak.[22] He spoke on Judaism in the twentieth century, but the topic was not as many in his audience had imagined it would be. His good friend Sidney Hamburger wrote to him after the talk urging him to tone down the theological content and concentrate more on the sociological problems of Judaism and its relationship to economic difficulties. He told him that laymen were unable to absorb the full implication of his theses; what they really wanted was answers and a guide.[23]

Given the depth of feeling in the Jewish community over the Jews' College fiasco, it is understandable that Jacobs encountered hostility from some in the Strictly Orthodox camp. But he also found himself garlanded. He and Shula were Guests of Honour at a B'nai B'rith dinner in Leeds, and again at the Annual Banquet and Ball at the Hammersmith and West Kensington Synagogue. In Glasgow they flocked to hear his lecture. Tickets for the 500-seat venue were fully booked two weeks before he arrived.

In his mind Jacobs had put controversy behind him. Although he was not currently minister of a synagogue, he was teaching and writing, and it suited him for the present. Others, misunderstanding this, hoped that he might be a white knight, their champion in whatever battle they might be fighting against the religious authorities. In an address he gave at Manchester Reform Congregation he sidestepped questions encouraging him to condemn Orthodoxy. When he made a visit to Garnethill Synagogue in Glasgow, where the minister, Dr Kenneth Cosgrove, was a close friend and staunch ally, Jacobs found himself caught up in a dispute the congregation was having with the London Beth Din over the authorization of marriages.

Some members of the community, believing that onerous restrictions were being placed on one couple whose Jewish status was uncertain, were arguing that the synagogue should no longer place itself under the Chief Rabbi's jurisdiction. They had hoped Jacobs might declare common cause, supporting them in their campaign. But Jacobs would not be drawn; he kept as far away from the politics of the community as he could, restricting his lecture to the meaning of Jewish tradition and its openness to new ideas. If he was controversial at all it was in his closing remark, when he said that while the Anglo-Jewish community should not loosen its allegiance to the real, authentic religion of Jewish tradition, it should loosen the facile allegiance to authority for the sake of authority.[24]

Jacobs's commentary on the kabbalistic *Tract on Ecstasy*, which he had begun writing when he joined Jews' College, was finally published in late 1963. He received appreciative letters from scholars around the globe, including Gershom Scholem, Mordechai Kaplan and Alexander Altmann. A few weeks earlier he had been awarded the prestigious Abramowitz-Zeitlin prize in Israel, for his book *We Have Reason to Believe*. The prize had been established to reward the writers of literary works who clarified the Jewish faith for people 'brought up on the knees of science'. In his letter to Jacobs, Dr Altmann expressed his delight at the award 'for more than one reason'.

FÊTED OVERSEAS

The following year Louis returned to the USA, once again at the invitation of B'nai B'rith, to be their Guest Scholar for 1963. It was a longer trip than his previous visit, and Louis's profile was now much higher. Shula went with him, leaving the three children, now aged 18, 15 and 10, at home with her mother, who lived with them. Over the course of five weeks Shula and Louis travelled across 22 states, taking 37 flights, with Jacobs lecturing daily, sometimes twice, in nearly every major city. Shula was so overwhelmed by the hospitality they received, the reception given to Louis, the vibrancy of American Jewish life and the size of both the buildings and the food portions that nearly 30 years later she was still able to write two lengthy and enthusiastic accounts of the trip, detailing nearly every place they stopped, the friends they made and even the names of the restaurants they ate in.[25]

Jacobs had prepared a lengthy list of lecture topics, ranging from 'Modern Challenges to Faith' and 'Does God Answer Prayer?' to 'How the Talmud Came into Being'. As always, he spoke without notes, Shula explaining to her readers that he did not want to be pinned down to one fixed lecture and could not bear to voice the same thing over and again.

One of the lectures he delivered was in Waco, Texas to a group of Christian preachers, some of whom had travelled 500 miles to hear him. His theme was 'Preaching Texts for Christian Congregations from Rabbinic Sources'. The local synagogue who hosted him had billed him, in a somewhat exaggerated manner, as 'Formerly Professor at Jews College and Professor in Semitics at University College London, now Candidate for Chief Rabbi of the British Empire'.

It was a whirlwind trip and the press reports and letters of thanks that Louis and Shula received were rapturous. The letters they wrote home were enthusiastic, Louis telling his children how fabulous New Orleans was and how exciting it had been to have gone to the Old French Quarter to hear the jazz. He wrote about their visit to the Mayor's office in New Orleans, where he was made an Honorary Citizen and was given a key to the City. Just once Shula admitted in a letter to the children that they were feeling homesick. The kids, on the other hand, didn't seem to mind their parents' absence at all. Years later their daughter Naomi recalled:

Our parents' American tour in 1963 was great for us! Ivor was eighteen and had been driving for just a year, and so with our parents in America, Ivor got to drive 'full-time' for 6 weeks. And we went to a lot of places. We even collected our parents from Heathrow, on their return home. We were really able to do as we pleased but, as our mum said, she trusted us and we were really good kids. Our [maternal] grandmother lived with us so she cooked for us etc. and she loved it when we brought friends over. *Pesach* was just the 4 of us for both seders, and yes we were brought up very well and knew exactly how to conduct the Seder. And to get everything ready for Pesach.

Dad wrote us great letters from this American trip and I quote from one of them:

'Dear Ivor, Naomi and David,

Here we are staying at this absolutely fabulous hotel in Beverly Hills. Everything is in the height of luxury including a white telephone next to the toilet. You can imagine how mum squeaked with delight . . . Last night we went to a party at a "fabulous" house – five bathrooms and a basketball court in the garden. At midnight they began to cook cheese blintzes which they served at one o'clock. They eat the blintzes with jam. Horrible . . . The services in the Synagogue are too funny for words. On Friday night after I had spoken and the Rabbi had spoken the President went into the pulpit and began to tell jokes. . . . The latest joke here is that a Jewish man named Mr Lang had a neon sign. He was an old man so they it called it "Old Lang's sign"!

Ta ta for now, All our love,

Daddy'[26]

The tour ended with a lecture to the faculty and students at the Jewish Theological Seminary, where Jacobs had previously been offered, and rejected, a position. He spoke for nearly two hours to a distinguished audience before completing the trip with, as Shula wrote in a postcard home, 'an enormous press conference . . . Everyone has heard of Dad, I didn't know he was so famous! Two writers have been accompanying us to get material from Dad on books they are writing. I don't know what it will be like just to live in Oakwood Court after all this VIP treatment and luxury hotels.'[27]

Shula needn't have worried about returning to an eventless life. The glow of their American trip had barely faded when his career took a new, unexpected, and for a short while, decidedly unwelcome turn.

8

A Bigger Affair

Towards the end of 1963, Revd Dr Chaim Pearl, Jacobs's successor at the New West End, announced that he was resigning as the synagogue's minister. He later explained that he had felt constrained in his role, unable to do anything he wanted, that he was 'less than an office boy' in some of his ministerial duties. He announced his intention of taking up a position in America, where he would earn less but at least feel that he was minister in his own synagogue.[1]

Jacobs's powerful friends at the New West End were of one mind. The prominent industrialist Emmanuel Kaye wrote to the honorary officers expressing the hope that Jacobs would be invited to return. The honorary officers agreed entirely with his sentiments but explained that there was a process to be followed for appointing a new minister. It might take a little time, but they were sure that every effort would be expended to facilitate Jacobs's return to the synagogue.

The United Synagogue advertised the vacancy on 13 December 1963 at an annual salary of between £1,600 and £2,000. Applicants were to be under the age of 45, unless already employed by the United Synagogue, and to hold, or be able to obtain, the Chief Rabbi's certificate authorizing them to serve as a United Synagogue minister. Rabbi Jacobs qualified on all counts; the Chief Rabbi's 'certificate', a confirmation that the applicant was a fit and proper person to hold the post, had been granted to him when he first entered the New West End pulpit in 1957.

On 31 December he wrote to his old friend Jakob Petuchowski, telling him that the vacancy had just opened up and that the members were keen to have him back, 'naturally on my terms, which include, of course, as much independence as possible'.

> If this comes off it would be in the nature of a revolt from within and, as you can imagine, the 'opposition' are rallying their forces in order to block the appointment. But I understand that the synagogue will brook no nonsense.[2]

Jacobs's cautious optimism was misplaced. Although the Synagogue's Board of Management voted unanimously to offer him the position, the recommendation had to be approved by the United Synagogue's Ministerial Appointments Committee. Jacobs had not formally applied for the post and so it was not until the Appointments Committee had reviewed all the other applications that the New West End delegates were able to announce that the only candidate they were interested in was Louis Jacobs. The secretary of the United Synagogue declared that Jacobs had not applied for a new Chief Rabbi's certificate and therefore could not be considered. When the New West End members argued that his previous certificate was still in force, the secretary referred the matter to the Chief Rabbi for clarification.

Had the United Synagogue secretary not intervened in this way, Louis's appointment might well have gone through on the nod. That was certainly the hope of the New West End honorary officers, who assumed that as long as the Chief Rabbi was not put on the spot he would turn a blind eye to Jacobs's appointment. Nobody wanted to exacerbate the tensions in the community. The New West End had always been an idiosyncratic community, and from Dr Brodie's point of view there were good reasons for allowing Jacobs to effectively be put out to pasture there. It would keep him out of the Chief Rabbi's hair and enable him to promote his views directly to his own loyalists rather than travelling round the country as the troublesome Director of the Society for the Study of Jewish Theology. Having Jacobs safely embedded in his own community, where he could lecture at will, would also put an end to the ongoing row over who had the right to speak in synagogue halls. The dispute, which many regarded as yet another symptom of the divided nature of Anglo-Jewry, had been growing steadily more fractious since Dayan Swift's opposition the previous year to Dr Pearl's prospective lecture in Edgware on behalf of the Society.

But the secretary to the United Synagogue, Alfred Silverman, put paid to such hopes. Jacobs believed that he intervened because he was a stickler for the strictest application of the organization's by-laws. The *Jewish Chronicle* took a less charitable view. In a savage article headed 'Man in the News' they described him as a man who understood rules better than their consequences. 'He might not commit himself on whether the Torah was given on Mount Sinai but he treats the constitution of the United Synagogue as if it were. To that extent, certainly, he is a fundamentalist. His own beliefs, whatever they may be, do not enter into it. Whoever commands the United Synagogue commands the service of Mr. Silverman.'[3]

The day after the Appointment Committee meeting, Silverman wrote to the Chief Rabbi asking whether Jacobs's certificate was still valid, and if not, whether a new certificate would be granted in respect of the New West End vacancy. The Chief Rabbi replied a week later:

> In reply to your letter of the 17th January, I have to inform you that my Certificate is not in being for Dr. L. Jacobs in respect of the New West End Synagogue. It is with the deepest possible regret that I am compelled, owing to the views which Dr. Jacobs has expressed publicly both by written and spoken word, to answer your second question by stating that my Certificate will not be forthcoming for him for the above vacancy.[4]

On 17 February the New West End Council sent a letter of protest to the new President of the United Synagogue, Sir Isaac Wolfson. The letter informed him that the Council were unanimous in their resolve to appoint Jacobs as their minister. They were anxious to maintain and enhance the Chief Rabbi's authority but refused to accept the justice or accuracy of the Chief Rabbi's imputation that Jacobs was anything other than a pious and devout traditional Jew who had served his congregation in the past with distinction and inspired the religious spirit of its members. They hoped that reason and moderation would prevail, but if not, they would not be deterred from 'taking whatever steps may be necessary' to appoint the minister of their choice.[5]

Wolfson, a tough, no-nonsense, Glaswegian philanthropist who had gone from market trader to owning one of the country's largest retail empires, was not a man who looked for compromise. Whatever he thought of the personalities involved, and there is apocryphal evidence that he sympathized with Jacobs, the Chief Rabbi was *his* Chief Rabbi, and he would fight his corner with the same gusto as had made him one of the wealthiest men in Britain. He challenged the New West End Council's analysis of the United Synagogue by-laws, declaring that the threat in their letter 'while serious from the point of view of the challenge to authority that it constitutes, is quite ineffectual'. He demanded that they give tangible signs of their anxiety to enhance the Chief Rabbi's authority by proceeding 'in the normal way' to appoint a minister.[6]

The following week the honorary officers of the New West End Synagogue convened an Extraordinary General Meeting. Of the 260 people present, only five dissented from the resolution giving unqualified support to the board of management in their efforts to secure Jacobs's appointment. Oscar Davis, who presided over the meeting, expressed his appreciation to the *Jewish Chronicle*, which had remained uncharacteristically silent for several weeks while a resolution to the dispute was sought. They had only broken the story the day before the meeting, and even then, only in a short, albeit front-page article. A week later they published the story in full, including copies in full of the correspondence between the synagogue officers and Sir Isaac Wolfson.

The national press now covered the story too. The major broadsheets gave it a few lines. Both the *Guardian* and *Telegraph*, quoting verbatim from the same source, declared: 'it is understood that questions of theological orthodoxy are involved'. The *Evening*

Standard, in an explanation that probably troubled Jacobs more than it did the United Synagogue, declared that he was a theologian who had written and preached against the 'fundamentalist doctrines of the Orthodox Jewish hierarchy'. The *Sunday Times*, seeing a parallel with the 'Honest to God' controversy which had riven the Church of England the previous year, splashed it across the front page. They published photos of as many prominent New West End members as they could fit into five columns, even if they'd had nothing to do with the dispute. Headshots of Lord Swaythling, Lord Marks, Ewen Montagu and Barnet Janner MP all appeared alongside those of Chief Rabbi Brodie and Sir Isaac Wolfson. The only photo missing was that of Louis Jacobs. The paper published Alfred Silverman's hapless attempt to redress the balance. The Chief Rabbi, he said, 'had done everything to help Dr Jacobs'.[7]

Silverman's defence of the Chief Rabbi was challenged at a United Synagogue Council meeting later that month. 'Is it true', asked H. A. (Toddy) Simons, a life-member of the Council, 'that a month ago Rabbi Dr. Louis Jacobs was refused permission on the instructions of the Very Reverend the Chief Rabbi from officiating at a funeral of one of the members of the New West End synagogue although the deceased's family had asked Dr. Jacobs to officiate? If this is true how is this consistent with a statement in the non-Jewish press that the Chief Rabbi has done everything possible to help Dr. Jacobs?'[8]

Silverman's remarks were similarly challenged in a correspondence between United Synagogue President Isaac Wolfson and his son Leonard. Leonard Wolfson, who was a warden at the prestigious Central Synagogue, wrote to his father on 10 March registering a formal complaint 'concerning the remarks of Mr Alfred Silverman, the Secretary of the United Synagogue. Permanent officials are not supposed to be policy makers nor to give statements to the press.' When Isaac Wolfson mollified his son with an assurance that it would not happen again, Leonard requested that Silverman be persuaded 'to apologise to the congregation of the New West End for his ill-advised comments'. He hoped that Sir Isaac would find it possible to instruct Mr Silverman to make the necessary apology, as he would not like to embarrass his father 'in any way at a Council Meeting'.⁹

Sir Isaac however did not instruct Silverman to apologize. Instead he told the United Synagogue Council that he'd had specific instructions, both from the Chief Rabbi and himself, to respond to press enquiries. 'My confidence in his ability to distinguish between the occasion on which to speak and on which not to speak is quite unshaken.'¹⁰

A few weeks later Jacobs received a letter from Dr Edward Neufeld, a rabbinic colleague in the USA. Enclosed was a cutting from the *New York Times* reporting the story. Dr Neufeld, who when they had last met had strongly suggested that Jacobs stay to fight his corner, now asked him to disregard that advice. He urged him to move to the United States, fearing that otherwise he would have a nervous breakdown. Jacobs did not reply immediately. He didn't feel that he was on the point of a nervous breakdown and he was waiting to see how events would unfold.

Jacobs had deliberately refrained from making any public statements while waiting for a resolution of his appointment. Once the press got hold of the story, he broke his silence in the *Jewish Chronicle*. When the paper asked him why Dr Brodie opposed his appointment he somewhat disingenuously replied: 'I wish I knew.' He explained that although his views would not be shared in Strictly Orthodox communities, he did believe that they were fully compatible with the religious outlook of the United Synagogue. It was a restatement of his contention that the United Synagogue had never repudiated its openness to non-fundamentalist ideas, expressed by the former Chief Rabbi Dr Hertz as 'Progressive Conservatism, i.e. religious advance without the loss of traditional Jewish values and without estrangement from the collective consciousness of the House of Israel – the Anglo-Jewish position in theology'.¹¹ Like, Dr Hertz, he said he saw the United Synagogue as an umbrella; offering shelter to different points of view but working together to strengthen traditional Judaism.

In its editorial, the *Jewish Chronicle* expanded on his comments, claiming that Jacobs's views were no different in essence from those voiced by the Chief Rabbi himself 'in a recent television interview', that they were identical to opinions expressed in the New West End pulpit 70 years earlier, and were still shared by influential United Synagogue ministers at the present time.[12]

Two days after the synagogue meeting Jacobs received a call from the Reverend Ephraim Levine, his long-serving predecessor at the New West End. Levine told him he had been in discussion with the Chief Rabbi and had managed to broker a solution. All that was needed was for Louis to sign the letter that he had prepared for him. Opening with the statement 'I am writing this letter entirely at my own volition,' the document was a declaration that Louis had been mistaken in his views and now recanted them. Louis gave it one glance and refused to sign.[13]

Feelings were running high, but both sides kept talking. The synagogue agreed to wait a few weeks. Sir Isaac and the Chief Rabbi were both due to be in Israel over Passover and they would discuss the matter together. The Pendennis column in the *Observer* duly declared that Sir Isaac was travelling to Israel to persuade the Chief Rabbi to change his mind; an assertion which drew an angry denial from Wolfson.[14]

On 13 April the New West End Synagogue Council reconvened. The United Synagogue's position had not changed, and the New West End had already warned that they would take whatever steps they considered necessary to appoint the minister of their choice. They resolved to appoint Rabbi Jacobs to the post, with immediate effect, and invited him to speak from the pulpit the following Saturday. The following day Jacobs replied to Rabbi Dr Neufeld, telling him that he was very close to agreeing with him that a move to the USA would be the best solution, but that 'practically the whole congregation at the New West End are fully determined to have me as their Minister even if it means fighting the Chief Rabbi and the United Synagogue Constitution. In fact, only last night the Board of Management of the Synagogue, with the full support of the whole congregation, invited me to serve as Minister to the Congregation, and I begin my duties this coming Sabbath.'[15]

In fact, Jacobs had delivered an address in the synagogue the previous week, two days before the Board of Management meeting. As the synagogue had no permanent Minister he had addressed a boy celebrating his bar mitzvah. The honorary officers of the United Synagogue instructed Alfred Silverman to write to their opposite numbers at the New West End warning them that they were in flagrant breach of the United Synagogue Constitution. Should this persist, the honorary officers 'will have no choice but to bring the matter before a Special Meeting of the Council of the United Synagogue for action under clause 51A of the scheme scheduled to the United Synagogue Act of Parliament'.[16]

Many United Synagogue ministers were unhappy. Louis's friend Dr Isaac Levy of the Hampstead Synagogue sent him a draft of a letter he had composed with two colleagues, Dr Solomon Goldman of St John's Wood and Rev. Isaac Livingstone, the retired minister of the Golders Green community. The letter, addressed to the Chief Rabbi, was to be circulated to all United Synagogue rabbis and ministers for signature before being sent on. The letter declared their deep anxiety about the danger to the unity of the United Synagogue should Jacobs not be appointed. They argued that consenting to his appointment would be less harmful than refusing to accept it, and that the controversy would only die down were he to be confirmed in the post.

Isaac Levy preached a sermon in support of Jacobs in his synagogue. He described his treatment as 'an injustice being perpetrated in the name of religion'. A smokescreen had been 'thrown around the case in order that those who wished to see him punished may prevent the community from ascertaining the whole truth'.[17]

CRISIS IN THE COMMUNITY

The last two years had been difficult, for Louis, the Chief Rabbi and everyone involved. The communal mood was fractious, feelings were running high and there was little middle ground. It was almost impossible to be a member of the Anglo-Jewish community without gravitating towards one side or the other. Yet all this was a pale foreshadowing of what was about to come.

On the Friday after the New West End's decision the *Jewish Chronicle* headlined with the words: 'Dr Jacobs Returns to New West End: US "unconstitutional"'. The paper published the full text of the Board of Management's resolution, declaring that the United Synagogue's refusal to approve Jacobs's appointment was 'morally unjustifiable' and contrary to the organization's 'constitution, by-laws and traditions'.[18]

The *Sunday Times* jumped on the story, literally. As Louis, accompanied by his sons Ivor and David, walked through Holland Park to preach his first sermon after his controversial appointment, a photographer leapt out of the bushes. Their picture appeared at the top of the front page, headlined 'The Rabbi Marches Into Battle'. The paper reported that Louis entered the synagogue to a hero's welcome, handshakes and smiles. But it cautioned that all might not turn out well. It warned that there was much speculation in the community as to how long it would be before the United Synagogue, and its president, Sir Isaac Wolfson, deposed the congregation's Board of Management and uprooted Rabbi Jacobs from the pulpit.[19]

The answer was, not long at all. By the middle of the following week the national press had heard that the United Synagogue Council was to meet that Thursday, with a view to removing the New West End's Board and installing its own interim team of managers.

A RED HERRING

Jacobs did not believe in the literal truth of every Bible story; it was the idea behind the story that mattered, not the narrative. He illustrated this to a questioner who asked which species of fish had swallowed Jonah. 'The fish that swallowed Jonah,' Jacobs replied, 'was a red herring.' He may have thought of this conversation on the day a parcel arrived at the family flat at Oakwood Court.

Over the past few weeks Louis and Shula had been receiving late-night threatening phone calls from cranks and extremists, hoping to intimidate them. So when they picked up the parcel to find wires hanging out of it, they immediately called the police. Two squad cars arrived. As instructed, the Jacobs family lay on the floor, trying as best they could to poke their heads round the door to see what was going on, while one of the policemen, in an inspection that would scare the wits out of any bomb squad officer today, gently used his penknife to cut open the parcel.

Exposing more wires, the policeman continued cutting until he reached something wrapped in layers of paper. Gingerly he extracted it until suddenly he yelled an expletive and jumped back.

Holding his nose, he picked up and displayed a rotting, stinking herring. There was no note, no clue as to who had sent it, or whether it was connected to the threatening phone calls. The police made a few notes and left.

It was a testing time for the Jacobs family. David, the youngest, was affected most badly, with his parents not really knowing what to do. Looking back, Ivor Jacobs says: 'They were naive parents, taking advice from well-meaning congregants, who had no idea of the life of a poor family, especially a Rabbi's.'

Naomi believes that the affair impacted Shula profoundly. 'Till the end she was dad's biggest fan and she definitely saw the role of Rabbi's wife as a full time job. She always totally encouraged and supported his every step.'

While I think my parents were very upset I do not think I was emotionally affected because I looked at it as a great story to tell my friends! In retrospect I would imagine part of their distress would have been what the police must have thought of Jewish people playing such a disgusting trick. We received anonymous abusive calls. One time a ranting woman told me what a terrible man my dad was. I was so proud of my dad and knew the best thing was to put the phone down. However David, who I don't think was even ten yet, answered one of these abusive calls and was very distressed. From then on David was asked not to answer the phone . . .

I remember very well the headline in the papers 'Rabbi Marches into Battle' with Ivor and David by each side. When I got to school on the Monday morning I was immediately called to the Headmaster's study . . . The Headmaster wanted me to convey to my father that when he saw the picture in the paper he right away saw that David was wearing a Holland Park School blazer. And he was very pleased we attended his school. . . . So I was really happy.[20]

At the time Ivor was national chairman of the Jewish Youth Study Groups. When Chief Rabbi Brodie visited the movement's summer school, at the height of the Jacobs Affair, it fell to Ivor to make the welcome speech. Deciding that he did not want to discuss events in the news, he instead reminded Brodie of the speech that he had delivered at his bar mitzvah, when he had addressed him for 45 minutes from a lofty pulpit, requiring the 13-year old Ivor to peer upwards at him, cricking his neck. After the speech Brodie assured Ivor that he would not remember anything he had told him; now six years later Ivor took pleasure in proving him wrong, repeating back everything he had said.

But Ivor's reluctance to draw attention to the row between his father and the Chief Rabbi at the summer school belied the long-term impact the affair had upon him:

My overwhelming feeling was support for my dad, so it did become difficult for the family when we saw friends later gradually retreat into their comfortable worlds . . . I think it true to say that all the family felt a duty to do what we could to protect my dad so he could 'get on'? with his work and writing.[21]

The threats and hoaxes were distressing, but support came in equal measure. When the New West End first announced that they would be appointing him, Louis's postbag overflowed. Old friends, congregants, even people he had never met and had never heard of, wrote to tell him how delighted, overjoyed and thrilled they were to hear of his appointment to the synagogue. They wished him every success in his new ministry; they were certain he would thrive and flourish. It would only be a matter of a few days before many of them wrote again, this time expressing their commiserations.

The United Synagogue Council met, in a stormy three-hour meeting, on 23 April. It was a Thursday evening, meaning that the weekly *Jewish Chronicle* had no time to include a report in its issue the next day. The daily press were able to move faster. 'Rebel Jews Sacked' proclaimed the *Daily Mail* on Friday 24th, announcing that the United Synagogue had removed the entire New West End board of management from office. The *Daily Telegraph* reported that a new four-man team had been installed by the United Synagogue in their place. Sir Bernard Waley-Cohen, a former Lord Mayor of London, told the paper that the motion had only been passed by a small majority, and that he was very unhappy about the way in which the matter had been handled. Edmund de Rothschild expressed similar sentiments to the *Daily Express*.

The next day Jacobs issued a statement to the press:

The Chief Rabbi has refused to allow me to serve as minister to the New West End Synagogue because I accept the finding of modern biblical scholarship. The United Synagogue Council by upholding the Chief Rabbi's decision and deposing the board of management loyal to my attitude, has committed the United Synagogue, for the first time in its history, to an official religious position of fundamentalism, which denies the right of freedom of inquiry into the sources of Judaism and Jewish thought. As a rabbi in Israel, responsible by Jewish tradition to God alone and to no other rabbi, I shall, of course, continue to expound my views, confident that very many thinking Jews in this country and outside it have too much love and respect for Judaism to wish to see it tied to such a theory.[22]

Louis's father wrote to him, saying that he was pleased to hear that he had so many prominent people backing him up, and that it wouldn't be long before he and Shula were settled down again happily with their friends. He mentioned that he had been sitting in Goldstone Park with some of his own friends when two men from the *Daily Express* had approached him asking for an interview. He enclosed a copy of the article with his letter.

Shula, who kept copies of everything, pasted the page from the *Daily Express* into her scrapbook. Most of it was taken up with a photo of Harry Jacobs sitting on his bed, studiously examining a book. On his head was a black yarmulke. At the bottom of the page Louis had scrawled 'Not a True Picture! *Zaid* never wore a *cuple*. It's a put up job.'

The *Express* remarked on the pride with which Harry Jacobs spoke of his son. 'Of course he is Orthodox. He just believes in progressive thinking. He decided he wanted to become a rabbi. I slaved for years at £2-5s. at the tailoring bench to keep him at school. Now, because he has expressed these views he has been kicked out. He has written telling me not to worry. But what can a father do?'[23]

It was left to the *Jewish Chronicle* to spin the matter to its own satisfaction in its edition the following week.

Last week's special meeting, summoned at two days' notice, with the press excluded, debate stifled, and a secret ballot denied, was conducted with all the thoughtlessness and harshness of panic. The issue was one on which the future of the United Synagogue might depend. It would have been reasonable to assume that every *modus vivendi* would have been explored and every compromise examined. But the motion to refer the whole matter back, which might have given the opportunity for further and better thoughts, supported by such figures as Mr. Edmund de Rothschild, Sir Bernard Waley-Cohen and the Hon. Ewen Montagu, was defeated. It was a triumph for the machine over reason.[24]

Whether that was a fair analysis hardly mattered. One could equally argue that it was a victory for the new, self-made generation of Anglo-Jewish leaders over the old-moneyed, Jewish aristocracy headquartered at the New West End. Ever since the large waves of Jewish immigration in the late nineteenth century, the wealthy, interconnected families, the Cousinhood as Chaim Bermant had styled them, had been the de facto leaders of British Jewry. The immigrant families from Eastern Europe had known their place; they had not disturbed the status quo. But new waves of immigration in the 1930s and 1940s tipped the balance. Their children of the refugees were not prepared to live in an Anglo-Jewish community that mirrored the rapidly outdating social divisions of English society. Class distinctions were levelling out, both in wider society and among Britain's Jews. The schism between Jacobs and the United Synagogue may never have happened had it not been for the disparity in social background of the lay leadership involved.

By the time the *Jewish Chronicle* editorial appeared, things had already moved on. A group of Louis's most ardent supporters from the New West End, motivated more, it has to be said, by their sense of the injustice done to Louis than by any great theological commitment, had gathered several times at Blooms Restaurant in Whitechapel. They had reached a decision.

THE SPLIT

On Tuesday 27 April, reports appeared in the national press that the 'rebels' planned to set up a rival synagogue. Louis's postbag swelled again. Among the many personal letters of support that he and Shula received was one from Muriel Franklin. Her husband Ellis, who had supported Louis so determinedly during and after the earlier Jews' College crisis, had passed away a few weeks earlier. 'You have had so much to stand up to', she wrote, 'but I know you won't lose heart now. You have very real friends who care in a personal as well as a general sense and I think you know I am one of those, as my dear Ellis would have been.'

From New York, Rabbi Seymour Segal told Jacobs that he and his colleagues at the Jewish Theological Seminary would be grateful of the opportunity to assist in any way. Michael Hunter and Dr Jonathan Frankel, of the Inter-University Jewish Federation, sent him a copy of a petition being prepared, protesting against the treatment meted out to him. Reverend William Simpson, General Secretary of the Council of Christians and Jews, expressed his distress. Chelsea Synagogue, the Hillel Foundation and the Younger United Synagogue Association all expressed their support. David Franklin wrote to tell him that funds had been raised to support him and that he need not feel that financial embarrassment was to be added to his other worries.

On 28 April, the day that Harry Jacobs's interview appeared in the *Daily Express*, Isaac Kaska, the secretary of the New West End, wrote to all the members informing them that, since the synagogue was now under emergency management, the scheduled annual elections of honorary officers and board of management would not take place. There would however be a meeting the following Sunday to elect the synagogue's representatives to various communal bodies.

Only eight synagogue members turned up to vote in the election. The remaining 350 or so were on their way to a meeting called by Oscar Davis, the senior of the deposed honorary officers, who had invited the community to hear a report on the situation and consider further action.

The meeting, held on 3 May at the Rembrandt Hotel in Kensington, was asked to pass a resolution to form a new congregation. It would be called the New London Synagogue. The congregation would follow the traditions of the New West End under the spiritual guidance of Rabbi Dr Louis Jacobs. In proposing the resolution, Bernard Spears, another of the deposed honorary officers, suggested that, at the same time as establishing the new congregation, they should all remain members of the New West End Synagogue, in order to fight within the United Synagogue to restore it to its traditional position of tolerance.

Jacobs stood up to speak, to resounding applause. He said how moved he had been by the support that had been shown to him; few men had ever enjoyed such friendship. He stressed that the Orthodox nature of the new synagogue should be emphasized from the start. In typical fashion he defined his terms, pointing out that the word Orthodox means different things to different groups. What mattered in this case was the meaning of the term Orthodox in the context of Anglo-Jewry.

> If Orthodoxy means a fundamentalist attitude which is inhospitable to all modern thought and scholarly inquiry, then we are not Orthodox and are proud not to be called Orthodox: but if the term is equated with what the preamble to the by-laws of the United Synagogue describes as Progressive Conservatism and which implies respect and loyalty to tradition, we are as Orthodox as the next man.[25]

The resolution was overwhelmingly passed, with only 11 dissenting voices. Even the dissenters did not oppose the principle of establishing a new congregation, they merely believed that further efforts towards reconciliation should be made before embarking on what might turn out to be an irrevocable split. As a result, Jacobs met with Sir Isaac Wolfson a few days later. Although they both believed it would be futile, the two men drafted a letter to the Chief Rabbi, begging him to have second thoughts. It had no effect.

On 5 May the Chief Rabbi addressed a meeting of United Synagogue ministers. He complained of the denigration of authentic Judaism and religious authority in the Jewish press, which had contributed in no small measure to the current situation. He said that he had supported Jacobs during his earlier ministry at the New West End as an 'act of faith', despite having to speak to him on several occasions about his views. He deeply regretted that his hopes for Jacobs had not been realized. He referred to the lecture, 'The Sanction for the Mitzwoth', which Jacobs had delivered the previous year. In Rabbi Brodie's view it demonstrated just how far Jacobs had travelled from the accepted norms of Judaism. Furthermore, it now appeared that Jacobs had been 'used as a central figure by a few resolute individuals who have openly declared their intention of trying to bring about a new orientation in our community'. Although he had received significant messages of support, he nevertheless sympathized with those who had asked him to reverse his decision, for the sake of the community. But a new congregation outside of his authority had been established and he had been obliged to make a decision with 'a heavy heart but in all conscience . . . We pray that time and circumstances will bring healing and understanding, discipline and unity to our beloved community.'[26]

BREAKAWAY

In its 8 May edition, the *Jewish Chronicle* carried a full report of the previous Sunday's meeting at the Rembrandt Hotel. At the foot of the page an advertisement appeared announcing that the 'New London Synagogue, an independent Orthodox congregation under the spiritual leadership of Rabbi Dr. Louis Jacobs' was now holding Sabbath services. Louis's supporters had wasted no time.

The first services of the new congregation were to be held in a hall attached to the Spanish and Portuguese Synagogue in Maida Vale. The advertisement invited 'all members of the community' to apply for membership. The address to which membership applications were to be sent was that of Muriel Franklin. New London Synagogue had hit the ground running. It did not slow down for several years.

The split in the community was unprecedented. Never before in Anglo-Jewry had nearly all the members of a synagogue resigned to set up a new congregation. Never before in England had a rabbi aroused such strong passions, among both his supporters and detractors. Eight weeks after the New London Synagogue was established, Louis wrote to his friend Jakob Petuchowski, telling him that the spirit of his congregants was as enthusiastic as ever; the loyalty of his people really amazing. After something of a sticky start, things had moved remarkably quickly during those eight weeks.[27]

9

New London Synagogue

By one of those fortuitous coincidences the Torah reading for the new congregation's first service contained the memorable phrase 'proclaim freedom'. Jacobs took it as the theme for his sermon, extolling his congregants' decision to 'speak their minds' rather than 'mind their speech'.

The philanthropist Ralph Yablon arranged the loan of a Torah scroll for the service. Just a few weeks earlier Yablon had paid the ransom and brought to London over 1,500 Torah scrolls that had been seized by the impecunious Czech government. In an ironic twist, the rebel congregation, shunned and in search of a new home, heard the weekly portion of the Torah portion read from a scroll that itself had just been liberated.

Two hundred and fifty people were present in the Montefiore Hall for the first service of the New London Synagogue. Most of them arrived unaware that the service had nearly not taken place at all. The lay leaders of the Spanish and Portuguese congregation had willingly offered the fledgling synagogue a home, but in the absence of the *haham*, the spiritual leader of the community, his deputy was reluctant to confirm the arrangement. Although the Spanish and Portuguese community was not under the authority of the Chief Rabbi, the *haham*'s deputy did not want to be seen taking sides. Nor did Jacobs wish to cause him embarrassment.

As it turned out the venue was not ideal. The service was assaulted by a neighbour playing his record player as loudly as possible; in Jacobs's words the neighbour believed it was a '*mitzvah* to interrupt the devotions of the heretics, even if it meant profaning the Sabbath'.

The national press, who had been covering the story for weeks, turned up in force. The photographers, who had been firmly told that they could not enter to take pictures, poked their cameras through the windows instead. Photos of the service appeared in the following day's *Observer* and *Sunday Telegraph*. Oscar Davis wrote letters of complaint to their editors. On seeing the photos, a churlish correspondent wrote to the *Jewish Chronicle*'s editor, attacking Jacobs for being seen 'dressed in his ministerial canonicals disgorging his religious principles on Shabbat'.[1]

After the service the leaders of the new congregation agreed that the Montefiore Hall presented too many difficulties. They announced that in future the congregation would meet in the annex of the Prince of Wales Hotel in Kensington. The *Jewish Chronicle* helpfully told its readers that the entrance was opposite 25 De Vere Gardens.[2]

It took time to sink in, but finally Louis had achieved a degree of security and freedom. He was now an independent rabbi of an unaffiliated congregation, no longer answerable to any higher authority on earth. Gradually he found the time to return to his academic interests. With so much else happening during the past few years he had not been able to write as prolifically as before, but he did have a new book, *Principles of the Jewish Faith*, that he had written when Director of the Society for the Study of Jewish Theology. It came out on 5 June, just five weeks after the establishment of the New London Synagogue. In a letter to his occasional correspondent, the pioneering Indian scholar of Islam Asaf A. Fyzee, Jacobs confessed that the book was 'rather an ambitious work, possibly over-ambitious'.[3]

A week before the book came out Jacobs received a letter from Dr Altmann at Brandeis University. He told Jacobs that the New West End affair had been much discussed in the USA and that he had often been asked to comment on it. The fact that the New London Synagogue considered itself Orthodox, conforming to the spirit of 'progressive conservatism' exemplified in the United Synagogue Bye-Laws,[4] would allay fears of a tie-up with the American Conservative movement. It should lead, he was sure, to a modus vivendi with the Chief Rabbinate in the future. The same week Jacobs had heard from Professor Raphael Loewe, who was teaching at Brown University. Loewe enclosed a copy of a letter he had received from the future Chief Rabbi, Immanuel Jakobovits. Jakobovits told Loewe that he had consulted with 'others concerned in this matter' and that they would use every influence in their power on their friends in London to bring about an amicable solution, provided that a public statement were made 'renouncing any intention to establish a Conservative movement in England and any designs on the Chief Rabbinate and its authority'. The possibility that Jacobs might establish a branch of the Conservative movement in England was a real and present fear in the minds of the Orthodox rabbinate.[5]

The most influential personality whom Rabbi Jakobovits had consulted was Rabbi Joseph B. Soloveitchik, the unofficial leader of North American centrist Orthodoxy. Unbeknown to Chief Rabbi Brodie, the London Beth Din had approached Jakobovits, asking if he could obtain a statement from Soloveitchik supporting Brodie's position. Jakobovits wrote to Brodie on 16 April, indicating that Soloveitchik would support him, but would prefer an official body to issue the supporting statement. He told Brodie that Soloveitchik had not been impressed by Jacobs.

> Incidentally, Rabbi Soloveitchik – having now read some of Jacobs's utterances – was quite struck by the mediocrity of his scholarship and surprised that a man of such modest scholastic stature should now present any serious challenge.[6]

Brodie replied to Jakobovits on 30 April. He said that although up to now he had held back from seeking support in 'an issue which is domestic, the publicity which has been given to the whole matter . . . does make it necessary for spiritual leaders of the stature of Rabbi Soloveitchik to make a statement.' He said that he would rather have a statement from Rabbi Soloveitchik and other individuals than a pronouncement from official Orthodox bodies, and that he had that day written to Soloveitchik in such a vein.[7]

A week later Jakobovits wrote to Brodie confirming that Rabbi Soloveitchik was now willing to make a statement, and that he believed he could persuade Professor Saul Liebermann, one of the most distinguished scholars of the Conservative movement's Jewish Theological Seminary, to join him. He also suggested that Rabbi Soloveitchik be invited to visit England, together with Chief Rabbi Unterman of Israel. Unrealistically optimistic about mainstream Anglo-Jewry's regard for rabbinic learning, he wrote:

> By concerting the visits of the two chief Orthodox spokesman in the world, the rebellion might be crushed by sheer weight of intellect and mass-solidarity. Such a unique demonstration of superior scholarship and universally recognised authority could well provide embattled Orthodoxy in England with the requisite *hizzuk* [strength] to ensure its triumph and consolidation.[8]

A month later Jacobs received a second letter from Raphael Loewe. He too had been to see Rabbi Soloveitchik. Loewe told Jacobs that Soloveitchik had:

> Torpedoed a letter, the draft of which he showed me, which the Orthodox Rabbinical Assembly intend to send to Brodie. By withholding his signature he makes it impossible for the letter to be sent. He has also refrained, he tells me, so far from replying to a letter that he has received from Brodie, with similar motives . . . He also deplored the level upon which the argument has come to be conducted, and did not exonerate you here – he indicated that there had been too many, and too facile statements to the press and, so to speak, manifestoes although he indicated his appreciation that the personal treatment that you have received was all too prone to goad you somewhat . . . Soloveitchik's advice was to pipe down – no more statements or encouragement of

publicity, and in particular that the *Jewish Chronicle* should take you out of its headlines. He wants to help . . .[9]

Loewe added that Soloveitchik had also undertaken to convey a message to Chief Rabbi Brodie asking him to grant New London Synagogue a marriage licence. This was a thorny issue that the New London Synagogue had recognized from the very outset it would need to confront. British civic law recognizes the validity of marriages performed in those synagogues which the Board of Deputies certifies as 'professing the Jewish religion'. The Board of Deputies in turn relies upon the Office of the Chief Rabbi to confirm whether the congregation does indeed profess the Jewish religion.[10]

The New London feared, correctly as it turned out, that Chief Rabbi Brodie would demand that they place themselves under his authority in return for his confirming the validity of their religious commitment. After all that had happened this was not something they were prepared to do.

Despite his helpful intentions, Rabbi Soloveitchik's intervention did not persuade the Chief Rabbi to issue his certification. For two years, the Board of Deputies mediated between the New London and the Chief Rabbi to try to resolve the dispute. During this time the New London was obliged to request that a civil registrar attend each wedding ceremony they performed. They did not obtain a certificate until after Dr Brodie's retirement, when Dr Immanuel Jakobovits succeeded him as Chief Rabbi.

In his letter to Jacobs, Raphael Loewe enclosed the draft of a statement he had prepared which he thought Louis might be willing to make 'as an olive branch' to Dr Brodie. It was a lengthy document which defended Jacobs's position on modern scholarship, committed him to not publicizing his views on biblical authorship from the pulpit, but reserved the right for him to speak his mind as necessary and to feel free to discuss controversial theological issues with congregants who were troubled by them. It committed Jacobs to publishing a further book 'emphasising the comparative insignificance of the question of biblical scholarship as compared with the transcendent message of the Bible for the Jew and its consequent place within Judaism.'[11]

Jacobs's reply was appreciative of Professor Loewe's efforts, but unequivocal in his decision:

> Frankly, my considered opinion (and I have discussed this with William Frankel, who agrees with me) is that there is not the remotest possibility of Brodie agreeing to any sort of rapprochement. More than one person, close to him, has used the word 'obsession' with reference to his attitude. Every one of us has leaned over backwards to enable him to save face even after he had made the most elementary blunders. Isaac Wolfson has pleaded with him on many occasions, all to no avail. I found your report on what Soloveitchik said interesting, but Brody has told a number of his Ministers that he has had a letter from Soloveitchik supporting his stance.[12]

Rabbi Soloveitchik did not issue a public statement. It would have made little difference if he had. Despite his standing within the rabbinic community, most British Jews knew very little about him. And at the end of the day this was not a matter that would be resolved either in the court of public opinion, or by rabbinic edict. Positions were entrenched on either side. They would continue to harden.

Vera Sharpe, a long-standing member of the New West End, wrote to Chief Rabbi Brodie. She told him that the earlier attempt by Ephraim Levine to get Jacobs to sign a letter renouncing his views could not have been carried out by a 'worse emissary'. Nevertheless, she knew that Jacobs was still anxious to lead the New West End and suggested that Rabbi Brodie might send her a list of what he needed in order that Jacobs might return to the pulpit. She suggested that these would include Jacobs's acceptance of the Chief Rabbi's authority and his undertaking to preach 'entirely according to the traditions of the United Synagogue'. She was sure that Jacobs would assent to both conditions. She sent a copy of her letter to Louis, to make sure. Nothing came of her initiative.[13]

Arguments over the New West End affair, Jacobs's theology, the actions of the Chief Rabbi, the United Synagogue and the Beth Din reverberated in the Jewish media for months. Even in the middle of July, nearly three months after the New West End controversy came to a head, the *Jewish Chronicle* was still reporting on a community riven by rancour and bitterness. But for Jacobs and his family, life was returning to some sort of normality. He was no longer on the front pages of the national press, the threatening phone calls had subsided and nobody had seen fit to send him another rancid herring. The New London Synagogue was meeting regularly in its temporary home in Kensington. Jacobs was firmly established as an independent rabbi who could plough his own furrow.

All that was lacking was a permanent home for the congregation. There was no doubt that they would find somewhere; it was only a question of identifying suitable premises. Few imagined it would be controversial. But it was.

A NEW BUILDING

'This day will be a landmark' declared Bernard Spears at a meeting of New London Synagogue members, on 28 June. Spears, a warden of the synagogue, was reacting to the meeting's unanimous approval of a resolution to purchase the building in Abbey Road recently vacated by the United Synagogue's St John's Wood Congregation.

Constructed in 1876, built in the Byzantine style and fronted by a colonnade of arches, the building, although not quite as striking as the New West End, was a classic of Victorian architecture. A contemporary journal, *The Builder*, enthused over every detail of its construction:

> The heating and ventilation have been carefully considered. Pure air is admitted into the building in the vertical direction, either at a cold or warm temperature, and the impure or vitiated air is carried off by means of ventilating ducts which have been provided over and under the galleries and in the main ceiling, an

upward current being induced by means of Bunsen's gas-burners
. . . The builders are Messrs Kirk & Randall, Woolwich and Mr
H. H. Collins FRIBA is the architect.[14]

The United Synagogue, for whom the building had been
constructed, were not at all keen to see the building sold to the
New London. They had agreed a sale of the building, together with
approved plans to build 31 flats on the site, to E. Alec Colman,
a Jewish property developer. Colman was reluctant to demolish
a house of worship and so was delighted to receive an approach
from the New London for the building.

The sale by the United Synagogue to Colman had been
agreed two years earlier, long before the New London was even
conceived. There could have been no inkling in anyone's mind as
to the eventual outcome. But this did not stop protests from irate
members of the United Synagogue Council, who were particularly
piqued to discover that Mr Colman had sold the building to the
New London for only £175,000, exactly the same price as he
had bought it. This, in the eyes of the United Synagogue's critics,
was clear evidence of collusion. Ewen Montagu scoffed at this,
declaring that he hoped it would not go on record 'that the United
Synagogue was willing to sell a property and did not mind if people
started a betting shop, a casino or anything else on the site except
an Orthodox synagogue'.[15]

One protester took matters more firmly into his own hands.
The synagogue building was only a few hundred yards from the
official residence of the Chief Rabbi; it had been the regular
place of worship for both Dr Brodie and his predecessor,
Dr Hertz. The Chief Rabbi's seat, enclosed in carved panels, was
in a prominent position facing the congregation, at the front of
the synagogue.

One night, after the St John's Wood congregation had vacated the
premises, a pious and committed, if somewhat excitable member of
the departing congregation broke into the building with an axe. He
chopped up the Chief Rabbi's episcopal seat. It would have been
sacrilege, in his eyes, for the boards and cushions which had once

graced the *tuches* of the Chief Rabbi to perform the same function for Louis Jacobs.

INSPIRATION

The axe-wielding supporter of the Chief Rabbi was not the only one to break into the building. Victor Stone, a solicitor and one of Jacobs's staunchest allies, had acted for the New London's acquisition of the building. Arriving in Abbey Road on completion of the purchase he discovered that he had been given a set of keys that did not fit. Undaunted, he scrambled up the fire escape, removed a piece of the leaded light with a penknife and climbed in. Unbolting the doors from the inside, he admitted a small squad of ladies, formerly congregants at the New West End, now founder members of the New London. Well-to-do gentlewomen whose own homes were invariably cleaned by daily helps, they had turned up with an unfamiliar burden of mops and buckets, defiantly scouring the premises as a tribute to the justice of their cause.

But mopping the floor turned out not to be enough. The Chief Rabbi's vandalized seat was the least of the building's defects. It quickly became obvious that extensive work needed to be done, both to the building's structure and internally. The previous owners had removed the fixtures and fittings, including all the stained-glass windows. Fortunately, Louis Mintz, one of Jacobs's closest supporters, had managed to buy the pews back from the United Synagogue, and reinstalled them in the New London. It proved to be a controversial donation; Mintz was a warden of Marble Arch Synagogue at the time, a flagship constituent of the United Synagogue.

At a meeting of the United Synagogue Council, the body's treasurer publicly berated Mintz for disloyalty and a lack of integrity. Mintz responded by accusing the treasurer of making unfounded statements without checking the facts; he had bought the seats in good faith after a previous sale to Wembley Liberal Synagogue had fallen through. Ninety-one members of Marble Arch then wrote to their board of management demanding an extraordinary general meeting, to pass a vote of no confidence in Mr Mintz and require his resignation. The Marble Arch board met, and unanimously passed a vote of confidence in him.[16]

The Inter-University Student Federation, of which Jacobs was an Honorary Life Vice-President, heralded the opening of the synagogue with an editorial in their magazine *Babel*. They declared that the Dark Ages of Judaism were passing, as evidenced by the reaction of Jewish students to the 'injustice' done to Rabbi Jacobs.

> There is little doubt that the Chief Rabbi is sincere in his persecution of Our Rabbi (as most of us have come to think of him) but there can be even less doubt that many who support the Chief Rabbi do so more from a fear of upsetting the status-quo than from any deep religious conviction . . . History will thank Dr Jacobs, not for saying anything greatly original but for allowing himself to be martyred for saying what many have worried about for years.[17]

The first services at the New London's Abbey Road home were held on 29 August, just a week before the New Year Holidays. The synagogue engaged George Rothschild, who had been at the Bayswater synagogue, to lead the prayers. Initially engaged just for the High Holiday, he stayed, with just one short break, for over 35 years, building a lifelong friendship with Louis. A choir was formed under the direction of Martin Lawrence, composed of men and women just as it had been at the New West End.

The synagogue was packed to overflowing for the New Year services. George Rothschild describes the atmosphere as contagious. Jacobs saw it as a heaven-sent opportunity for him to set out his aims and ambitions for his new congregation – one he made full use of. Taking as his theme the New London's self-proclaimed status as an independent, Orthodox congregation, he addressed each of these three terms in turn:

> There can only be one theme for this morning's sermon as we face the future with a prayer for God's guidance in the year ahead and

His blessing upon our efforts. What do we stand for? What kind of congregation do we desire to create? . . . Let us discuss first the term 'Orthodox', because it is the one which has given rise to most misgivings. It was said of the Holy Roman Empire that it was neither holy, nor Roman, nor an empire. There is no doubt that we are sturdily independent. That we are a congregation is self-evident. But are we justified in calling ourselves Orthodox?

First, it is essential for us to bear in mind that the term 'Orthodox' . . . was originally used as a term of reproach by the early Reform Jews, who characterized by it the upholders of the older tradition as hidebound in their thinking and practice . . . Within the context of Anglo-Jewry we are fully entitled to describe ourselves as Orthodox, without making a fetish of the term. We believe in the three tremendous ideas upon which traditional Judaism is based: God, Torah and Israel. We are fully observant in our congregational life and in their personal lives our members are as observant as the members of other Anglo-Jewish congregations which claim to be Orthodox . . . Where we differ from some congregations is in our refusal to equate Orthodoxy with the refusal to think and inquire . . .

We are Independent . . . We have decided to take our destiny into our own hands, to work it out for ourselves . . . I am glad, though unworthy, to have a congregation composed of independent thinkers and men of action. Controversy will not be entirely avoided in this pulpit, particularly controversy of the healthy and stimulating kind . . . True religion is a vital force and its power over human lives is such that after having been brought under its influence they can never be the same . . .

We are a Congregation. A distinction is frequently drawn between a crowd and a congregation. A crowd is formed of people with no common aim who just happen to be present together at a certain place and time. . . . A congregation, on the other hand, is composed of individuals who pool their varied experiences for the enrichment of one another and for the furtherance of ideas and ideals they hold in common . . . We are in truth a congregation. We have struggled together, we have come to respect one another as fighters in a common cause, we have encouraged one another in difficult times and we intend to work together in the hard but exciting times ahead. . . . We have an excellent opportunity of building not alone a synagogue but a *kehillah*, a congregation devoted to the Jewish ideal in all its ramifications and to its realisation in our corporate life. Many are the tasks ahead and great the opportunities. May we rise to them as we have risen to the initial challenge.[18]

Jacobs's congregation, inspired by their rabbi, energized by their courageous breakaway and amazed at their good fortune in acquiring ideal premises, were more than ready to rise to the challenge he set them. They would not just become a replica of the new West End, albeit independent of the Chief Rabbinate. Like Louis, they would seek to integrate modern thought with the ancient ways. New London was about to emerge, not just as a synagogue for open-minded, Orthodox worship, but as a vibrant intellectual and cultural centre; a quintessential 1960s venue, projecting radical London through a Jewish lens.

QUEST

Jacobs believed firmly that Judaism was a quest, 'a great venture into the Unknown', that the 'quest for Torah is itself part of Torah'.[19] He was determined that the New London would epitomize this quest; whatever other cultural activities the synagogue members organized, as far as their rabbi was concerned, informed, open-minded study of Jewish texts, thought and tradition was paramount.

In January 1965 the synagogue advertised a series of Shabbat morning sermons that Jacobs would deliver over the coming months. This was unusual. Most rabbis used their pulpits to encourage their congregants ethically or religiously, linking their topic to the weekly Torah reading, a major public event or a celebration within the community. Few thought more than a week ahead; they often had little idea each time they concluded a sermon, what they might speak about the following week. But Jacobs had different ideas; his sermons were educational, designed to demonstrate how the practice of traditional Judaism walked hand in hand with a contemporary outlook and modern scholarship.

The theme that Jacobs chose for his series of sermons was 'The New Picture of the Bible'. Over successive weeks, starting on 23 January, he discussed 'Isaiah's Vision', 'An Ancient Code of Laws', 'The Story of Creation', 'The Lord is my Shepherd' and 'The Second Isaiah'. Although this was not the first time he had delivered a series of themed sermons, the timing of this one was partly conceived as a distraction from a renewed bout of controversy over the previous weeks.

It came in the wake of an address Jacobs had given to the luncheon club of the Anglo-Jewish Association, an esteemed body whose members included many leaders of the British community. In his speech, Jacobs had controversially called upon those who refused to take sides in theological debate to stop sitting on the fence. While other sections of the British public encouraged the spirit of quest, it was being frowned upon in the Jewish community, where irrationalism prevailed. He called on the community to choose between Jewish irrationalism and Jewish suicide.[20]

When the Chief Rabbi read a report of Jacobs's address in the *Jewish Chronicle* he wrote to express his dismay to the president of the Anglo-Jewish Association, the Member of Parliament, Maurice Edelman. He called upon the AJA to disassociate itself from the speech, which 'has saddened and angered many members of the community judging by the telephone calls of protest which have reached my office'.[21]

The following week Mr Edelman issued a statement to the *Jewish Chronicle*, insisting that the AJA bore no responsibility for the views of its speakers, that its luncheon club was not a suitable platform for partisan controversy and that Jacobs's address 'in no sense reflects a collective view of the AJA'. The *Jewish Chronicle*, in an editorial printed far more prominently in the paper than

Edelman's statement, called it 'a pusillanimous surrender to establishment pressure'. Noting that the luncheon club had often hosted controversial speakers, the paper hoped that henceforth the AJA would be more courageous in upholding its proud traditions.[22]

Although Louis was never shy of stirring up intellectual controversy, insisting on defending rather than withdrawing from a position he sincerely held, he tried to keep away from political strife. When the family of one of his recently deceased congregants wanted him to conduct a tombstone dedication ceremony at a United Synagogue cemetery, he was refused permission to officiate by the Burial Society. The family wrote to the Chief Rabbi asking for him to intervene, but were told by his secretary that he was not prepared to give permission for Jacobs to conduct the ceremony. The tombstone was consecrated with no minister present, the family conducting the proceedings themselves.

It would have been natural, given the distress caused to the family, for Jacobs to try to make political capital. Instead he said not a word; even the *Jewish Chronicle* took three months to hear about it. When they did, they discovered that it was not the first time that Jacobs had been barred from conducting a funeral. A similar incident had occurred a few months previously. On that occasion Toddy Simons had written directly to Sir Isaac Wolfson declaring: 'It seems obnoxious, and even tantamount to slander, to even suggest that a former Rabbi of the United Synagogue, a great scholar accepted by the Chief Rabbi as a teacher at Jews' College, is now unsuitable to even bury a former congregant'.[23]

By now Chief Rabbi Brodie was only a few months away from retirement. Jacobs of course was no longer being touted as a possible successor, but events over the past year had so traumatised the Jewish community that it was nigh impossible for those who had been tasked with making a suitable appointment to put the 'Jacobs Affair' out of their minds.[24] Among the many criteria they sought was a man with the temperament and ability to heal the split in the community, ideally to bring Jacobs and the New London back into the United Synagogue's fold. The trouble was that now he had tasted independence Jacobs was more than content to tread his own path. He had a community where he had the freedom to teach without being ideologically constrained, where he could engage without too much distraction in his own studies, write his books and articles and pursue his quest for Torah without being answerable to an umbrella synagogue body or a Chief Rabbi.

Nor did the members of the New London show any desire to be reabsorbed. Their ambition was to rekindle the light of Judaism that they had felt was in danger of being extinguished in British Jewry. Their goal was a thought-provoking religion for every day of their lives, and they would achieve this, not just through religious education and services, but also through cultural, literary, musical and philanthropic activities.[25]

Shortly after the synagogue's foundation, Louis invited two congregants, the composer Joseph Horovitz and his wife Anna, to discuss the idea of including music in the cultural life of the community. Although there is a prohibition on playing music in Orthodox synagogues, because of the ceremonial role it had once played in the long-destroyed Jerusalem Temple, Louis ruled that, provided the ark and Torah scrolls were screened off, the hall could be used to play 'Jewish' music, loosely defined as works by Jewish composers or with some sort of Jewish association.

The first concert was held in the afternoon of Sunday, 21 March, with Joseph Horovitz conducting his chamber orchestra Philomusica of London. They performed works by Handel and Haydn, a composition by Joseph Horovitz and Max Bruch's *Kol Nidrei*. A second concert was held a fortnight later, the same orchestra performing works by Bach, Marcello, Barber and Oedoen Partos. Louis introduced both concerts quoting Psalm 150: 'Praise Him with blasts of the horn; praise Him with harp and lyre. Praise Him with timbrel and dance; praise Him with lute and pipe.'

Somewhat predictably, Chief Rabbi Brodie condemned the events. He was on the point of retirement and the concerts had taken place in a synagogue not under his aegis, but he felt so wounded by events of the past couple of years that he could not help but make his feelings known. Arguing against the view that music was a good ancillary to religion he declared that playing secular music in a synagogue was repugnant to the Jewish idea of holiness.

Jacobs did not respond, but Toddy Simons, a life member of the United Synagogue Council and a stalwart member of New London, wrote a scathing letter to the *Jewish Chronicle*. He listed occasions going back as far as 1837, when secular music had been played in English synagogues under the Chief Rabbinate's supervision. This led to a lively correspondence as to the religious nature of these occasions and the actual position in Jewish law.

The final word came from Rabbi Alexander Carlebach in Belfast, who had worked alongside Jacobs at Munk's synagogue and whose younger daughter Tirza would, some years later, marry Louis and Shula's eldest son Ivor. Writing in the *Belfast Jewish Record* he quoted rabbinic sources showing that concerts in a synagogue do not contravene religious law and ended by saying: 'by extending the use of the synagogue to such functions as concerts, lectures, symposia and the like, one extends the realm of the sacred to the wider fields of human sensibility and experience from which religion in the narrow sense of the word can but profit.'[26]

Over the next 19 years the New London hosted 13 concerts. Among the artists who gave their time were Daniel Barenboim, whose bar mitzvah ceremony Jacobs had conducted at the New West End in 1955, the Amadeus Quartet, and Yehudi Menuhin, who, with his sister Hephzibah, gave a piano and violin recital. Recalling the concerts, Anna Horovitz wrote: 'To hear works such as Bloch's *Nigun* and Ben-Haim's Sonata in the setting of the Synagogue was the real purpose of our concerts, to hear such artists playing them made this a unique event'.[27]

On a lighter occasion the popular entertainers Donald Swann and Michael Flanders joined forces with Joseph Horovitz in 1970 to put on a family concert at which the children's choir of the synagogue performed. Among the pieces at the children's concert was *The Tale of Bontzye Shveig*. Based on a story by the Yiddish author I. L. Peretz, the music was composed by Donald Swann (who was not Jewish) and the libretto written by Leslie Paul, author of the Paul Report into the Church of England and a founder of the children's educational movement Woodcraft Folk.

Children's education took place in Hebrew classes on Sunday mornings, just as it had done at the New West End. Jacobs showed little detailed interest in the classes' activities, addressing the assembly at the beginning of the morning four or five times a year and attending Purim and Chanukah celebrations. He was not aloof, he always had an easy rapport with children. But as Leslie Wagner, a former headmaster of the classes, explains: 'Louis's philosophy was that Judaism was a grown-up religion that could only properly be understood by adults and that most *hederim* put children off Judaism so that they did not take it seriously later in life.' And of course Jacobs himself had had a very different *heder* experience. At only two hours a week, New London Synagogue Hebrew classes could never expect to inspire or engage children in the way that Jacobs had been inspired at Balkind's *heder*.[28]

London's housing crisis became a national talking point when the activities of the slum landlord Peter Rachman were exposed in the press and the BBC aired *Cathy Come Home*, a hard-hitting play about homelessness. Members of the New London, led by the antique dealer Philip Blairman, decided that this was too big a social issue for the synagogue to ignore, and as a prosperous London congregation it behoved them to play a part in solving the city's accommodation problem. In 1967 they established a housing trust, purchased two houses in Stoke Newington for £10,500, converted them into flats and let them out at affordable rents.

The Trust rapidly outgrew the level of the resource that the synagogue could provide. When, in 2018, it celebrated its 50th anniversary it owned 8,000 properties, valued at over one billion pounds, all rented out as social housing. Apart from a mention on the Trust's website, the only remaining connection with the synagogue is in the organization's name; its founders had the foresight to name it the Newlon Housing Trust. Philip Blairman's name no longer appears in its publicity.

The New London was just as ambitious about literature as it was about music. In September 1965 the first edition of the synagogue's new publication, *Quest*, appeared. Making sure that nobody could confuse it with a run-of-the-mill synagogue newsletter or magazine, *Quest* described itself as a literary and arts annual that 'dramatically reflected our age, its tensions, problems, ideas and achievements'. It aimed high. Edited by Jonathan Stone, published by Paul Hamlyn and retailing at one pound and five shillings – four shillings more than the cost of *We Have Reason to Believe* – *Quest* was a hardback, 120-page, fully illustrated publication, 'unique in concept and distinctive in design'. The book's many contributors included Isaiah Berlin, Arnold Wesker, Danny Abse, Gerda Charles, Chaim Bermant, Ben Shahn, and of course Louis Jacobs. Even the commercial supporters were impressive: Marks and Spencer, Readers' Digest, ATV, Lansing Bagnall and United Draperies were just a few of the prominent names among the 32 pages of advertisements.[29]

Louis Jacobs with his parents Harry and Lena Jacobs, 1928

Wedding photo of Louis Jacobs and Shula Lisagorsky, 28 March 1944

Louis Jacobs, circa 1960

The Jacobs family at the bar mitzvah of David Jacobs, 1965 (*Left to right*) Ivor, Naomi, Louis, David, Shula Jacobs

Louis Jacobs aged two

Louis Jacobs with Ella Jacobs, his first great-granddaughter

Louis Jacobs *(right and below)* at the New London Synagogue

Louis Jacobs receiving an honorary doctorate at the University of Lancaster, 1991

Louis and Shula Jacobs, circa 1990

The opening of Golders Green Yeshiva, 1947

New London Synagogue

10

An International Reputation

Within a year of its formation the New London had achieved all its early aims. It had a building, a growing congregation, well attended weekly services and a vibrant cultural programme. Louis, Shula and family had moved to a flat a short distance from Abbey Road, and with the synagogue functioning smoothly he continued to devote time to his writing and lectures.

In February 1965 a letter bearing a picture of San Francisco's Golden Gate Bridge arrived at the synagogue. Addressed to Rabbi Dr Jacobs, it had come from the San Francisco Council of Churches, announcing a Convocation of Religion for World Peace, to celebrate the 20th anniversary of the founding of the United Nations. The organizers had invited a senior representative from every religious denomination they could identify, including the Pope and the Dalai Lama. They had asked the distinguished religious philosopher Martin Buber to represent Judaism. However, the letter explained, Dr Buber was unable to come, as he was seriously ill. He had suggested that the organizers ask Jacobs if he would attend in his place.

Shula was beside herself. 'Martin Buber named Louis Jacobs as his choice!' she wrote in her memoir. Jacobs, of course, was flattered too, although he was more restrained, noting simply that: 'Martin Buber was invited to represent Judaism but was obliged to decline owing to advanced age and infirmity.'

Louis and Shula were booked to fly to San Francisco on Sunday 20 June. Insisting that the significance of the occasion called for them to travel in style, Jonathan Stone, who edited *Quest*, had bought them first-class seats and offered to drive them to the airport in his Rolls-Royce.

They nearly did not make it. Just as he was setting off for the Saturday evening service at synagogue, Louis came down with toothache. The pain got progressively worse during the evening; by midnight it was unbearable. At 7.30 on Sunday morning Shula phoned the dentist, on the off chance that he might be available. He saw Louis straight away, and by 9.30 had extracted his wisdom tooth. Remarking that he had never met anyone in their mid-forties who had coped so easily with a wisdom-tooth extraction, he drove Louis to the only Sunday morning pharmacy in Central London, loaded him up with painkillers and wished him luck for the flight. The painkillers may not have been necessary; they had never flown first class before and the experience, further enriched by the sight of the cigar-smoking Groucho Marx sitting across the aisle from them, was more than enough to distract Louis's attention from the ache in his mouth.

The Convocation was due to take place on the following Sunday, 27 June, and the organizers had arranged a full programme of preparatory events to honour the participants during the preceding week. As Louis and Shula landed in San Francisco the Chief of Police and the President of the Commonwealth National Bank boarded the plane to greet them. They were whisked to the Hilton Hotel, escorted by two scooter-riding policemen.

Over the course of the next few days Louis and Shula were entertained and feted by their hosts. The were taken on tours of the city and locality, wined, dined, and introduced to local celebrities and communal figures. On the Friday before the Convocation they attended a commemorative session of the United Nations at the San Francisco Opera House, at which President Lyndon B. Johnson, the UN Secretary General U Thant, and Adlai Stevenson, the American ambassador to the United Nations, all spoke.

The Convocation was held on 27 June in the Cow Palace Arena, before a gathering of 40,000 people. A choir of 2,000 conducted by

Lloyd Pfautsch sang as the procession of delegates entered the hall. Shula Jacobs watched from the front row as Archbishop Joseph T. McGucken opened the proceedings.

> Then the first representative was announced. Rabbi Louis Jacobs, rabbi of the New London Synagogue and Director of the Society for the Study of Jewish Theology. We were very proud that our religion was first, but then ours was the first.[1]

Jacobs spoke about the Jewish ideal of peace. Quoting the prophets Micah and Haggai, he discussed the Jewish aspiration for a peaceful world, an ideal to which the message of the prophets would return the ancient Israelite nation, whenever they fell short.

> The Hebrew word for peace, 'shalom', means much more than the absence of war. It represents a shining, positive virtue, best described by the English word 'harmony', in which differing attitudes are rescued from fragmentation in order to form part of a variegated whole. The unity of which Judaism dreams is the unity of a great symphony or splendid painting, not that of drab, colourless and toneless uniformity. For all the Jewish emphasis on the unity of God, or, rather, because of it, the Jewish mystics speak of diverse powers in the Godhead, of the divine wrath and judgment and the divine love and mercy blended together by means of the divine harmonising principle, which they call 'Beauty', because it is the source of all the beauty we witness in the world around us and in the hearts and minds of men. For life is rich and complex and it is only the narrow-minded who wish to stifle the expression of its infinite variety.[2]

LIBERAL SUPERNATURALISM

Jacobs's theological reputation was founded, in the public mind, on his opposition to what he called the fundamentalist position, the literal belief in the Torah's account of revelation. Less well known was his disagreement with those who held the diametrically opposed view, who argued that Judaism was merely the product of a historical development. That, in the words of Louis Ginzberg, 'the sanctity of the Sabbath reposes not upon the fact that it was proclaimed on Sinai, but on the fact that the Sabbath idea found for thousands of years its expression in Jewish souls.'[3]

In 1966 Jacobs published an article entitled 'Liberal Supernaturalism'. The phrase was drawn from Christian Protestant theology, but it was one that he would return to time and again, and make his own. In the article he distinguished between three dominant philosophies of Judaism. The first, Fundamentalist Supernaturalism, was, he averred, the attitude which had prevailed until the Middle Ages. It was supernaturalism because it conceived of God as a Being beyond all natural processes; who could exist without a universe but without whom the universe could not exist. This philosophy was fundamentalist because it believed in the complete truth and infallibility of the sacred sources, notably the Torah. This position, he agreed, had much to recommend it, in terms of its certainty and grandeur. But he argued that it failed, both because the Torah's view of the universe and human history is incompatible with the views of modern science and archaeology, and because it does not take into account the cultural environment in which Judaism developed and the Bible was written.

The second position, Liberal Naturalism, stands at the opposite extreme. It rejects the idea of a personal God, an existent being who revealed himself to the world at a particular moment in history. Nevertheless, it accepts the value of Jewish tradition and religious behaviour because they, and the ideals associated with God, are worth striving for in themselves. In this view, typical of Reconstructionism, God becomes the force that makes for righteousness, a natural characteristic of the universe which guarantees the value of goodness, truth and beauty. Jacobs rejected this position because there is nothing in the advance of human knowledge which demands such a reinterpretation of belief. There is no scientific basis for this position and, given that it wholly fails to account for the psychology of the human mind and the desire to worship, he maintained that it is inferior to supernaturalism.

The third view, to which Jacobs subscribed and which he would spend a considerable proportion of his scholarly career defending, was Liberal Supernaturalism. This, he argued, satisfies both faith and reason. It is supernaturalism because it accepts the idea of a personal God. Not as a mighty power sitting on a throne surrounded by angels, but as a being whom we can apprehend, even though we cannot comprehend. A being who is beyond all human language and knowledge but who can be sensed by the religious mind. But it is also liberal, accepting the findings of science and the conclusions of reason, while rejecting the dogmas of fundamentalism. Liberal supernaturalism was the philosophy that validated the argument he had made in his 1963 lecture 'The Sanction of the Mitzwoth', and which was pithily summed up in the title of his first theological work, *We Have Reason to Believe*. It was the position, he concluded, which 'frees the mind from the fetters of unreason while enabling the heart to sing the song of faith'.[4]

Ending with the words 'to sing the song of faith' was more than just a stylistic flourish. The article was a testament to Jacobs's analytical prowess, but skilled as he was in theological argumentation, he had not written it merely as a scholarly exercise. Jacobs was no dry theologian: his commitment to Liberal Supernaturalism, although expressed in rational language, sprang from the deep well of his faith.

He allowed another glimpse of this faith in an article he wrote for an issue of *Twentieth Century* magazine, in which they invited thinkers from different religions to answer the question 'God Where Art Thou?'

This, then, is the Jewish concept of God. That there is a Supreme Being, all-good and all-powerful. That He is the ground of all there is and that the way to Him is by the pursuit of justice, mercy and holiness. That the people of Israel have their role to play in making these ideals common to mankind. The faith of Israel has been on earth a long time. It has won notable successes and has also suffered serious reversals. Jews believe that their faith is true and that one day it will win over the hearts and minds of all men. Jews believe that when that day comes, to use the language of tradition, the Kingdom of Heaven, with us now even if we do not see it, will be firmly established upon earth.[5]

SEEKING ALLIANCES

In February 1966 Louis appeared on the ITV programme *The Levin Interview*. Hosted by Bernard Levin, a journalist noted for his acerbic interviewing style, the programme specialized in explicating and challenging the ideas of people who, although prominent, were not necessarily in the headlines daily. Levin was Jewish but not observant, and Jacobs sensed that when he described the dietary laws as 'lumber' that had no relevance to the modern world, Levin was challenging him on an issue which bothered him personally.

Levin may also have been talking about himself when he asked whether there was any future for Jewry outside the Jewish religion. He wondered what purpose, in Jacobs's view, God had for the Jew who had no connection with other Jews or Judaism, had no affinity with Israel, and who saw himself as fully integrated into the country and society in which he lived. Jacobs's reply was that he did not see things in such black and white terms.

> I doubt whether we are all complete believers all the time, or for that matter whether anyone is a complete atheist all the time. So that one recognizes the tensions and I would prefer not to think in these exclusive either-or terms. I think one has to recognize the realities of the situation and encourage as many Jews as possible to work for Jewish values, although naturally, as you say, as a rabbi I would prefer that the religious side of it should be emphasized.[6]

The following month Jacobs gave a lecture in Glasgow. The fact that he was travelling out of London to speak was not in itself significant – he frequently lectured to Jewish communities across the country, to university students and occasionally to Christian audiences. But the Glasgow trip was different; there was an air of expectancy overhanging his visit. Rev. Dr Kenneth Cosgrove, the Minister of the Garnethill Synagogue, was an old friend and the *Jewish Echo*, the local community paper, had followed Jacobs's battles with the United Synagogue avidly. There was strife between the town's rabbis, just as there had been when he had visited the town three years before. Ben Azai in the *Jewish Chronicle* claimed that 'for years now it has been the main function of the lay leaders of the community to keep the spiritual leaders from each other's throat',[7] and it was no secret that relations between the Garnethill congregation and the local Glasgow Beth Din were at breaking point. Although nothing had been said officially, rumours had been circulating that Garnethill was about to break away from the auspices of the Glasgow Beth Din and seek an alliance with the New London. Jacobs's visit was widely seen as a step towards that eventual goal.

A few weeks after Jacobs's visit, New London's treasurer David Franklin, who had travelled to Glasgow with Louis, announced that 'a congregation outside London which had disagreed with some decisions of the Beth Din and which liked what we stand for had expressed its interest in forming an association with New London.' From the New London's point of view this would be the beginning of 'a loose federation of like-minded, independent and autonomous congregations'.[8]

The same day, the Council of Garnethill Synagogue agreed that it would call a meeting of members to decide whether to withdraw from the jurisdiction of the Chief Rabbinate and seek an association with New London. A two-thirds majority of those present at the meeting would be required to make the change.

Things did not work out as Louis and David Franklin hoped. Although most of those present at the meeting held on 6 June voted in favour of an association with the New London, the proposers failed to get the two-thirds majority they needed and the motion failed.

Jacobs did receive a letter a couple of months later from the *Jewish Echo*'s editor, Ezra Golombok, telling him that the situation was worsening in Glasgow, that most of the principal opponents of the 6 June resolution had changed their minds, and that opinion was hardening towards a dissociation of Garnethill Synagogue from the Chief Rabbinate. But the following February the annual meeting of the synagogue was told that although feeling ran high at the time of the June meeting, internal harmony had now been restored.[9] An alliance with Garnethill was an opportunity which, although regularly mooted, never quite came to fruition.

Garnethill was not the only community attracted to Jacobs's point of view. A small group in Hendon, North West London, decided to establish an independent congregation. Allied to the New London, it would be called the New Hendon Synagogue. It planned to hold its first service in the Hendon Labour Party headquarters on 30 August. Reverend Leslie Hardman, minister of the large neighbouring Hendon United Synagogue, was in no way put out by the new congregation opening on his doorstep. He wished every success to 'everybody who worships God in the traditional way'.[10]

The New Hendon Synagogue did not survive. As Jacobs and his supporters would discover several times over the coming years, starting and supporting new communities was rarely easy. Nor was it necessarily productive. His outlook had not changed since his days at Jews' College; his hope was for a Jewishly educated, open-minded English community that was able to approach tradition using the tools of modern scholarship. He believed he could achieve this more easily by allying with existing independent congregations like Garnethill, than by creating new congregations.

A reliable option would have been for New London to affiliate to the World Council of Synagogues, the umbrella organization for Conservative Judaism in the United States. They were keen to establish a foothold in Britain and were already looking to Jacobs as their best hope for achieving this. He was considering joining the Rabbinical Assembly, the membership body for Conservative rabbis. But he had strong reservations about an organizational affiliation for the New London with the Conservative movement, fearing that joining an American umbrella body would comprise the Englishness of his congregation's tradition. In any event he did not see that they needed a label like Conservative at all; the New London defined itself as independent Orthodox and he saw no reason why that should change.

A WALK IN THE PARK

In September 1966 the United Synagogue appointed Dr Immanuel Jakobovits as Chief Rabbi. A refugee from Germany who had arrived unaccompanied in England at the age of 15, Jakobovits was just a few months younger than Jacobs. As young men they had exhibited similar promise, standing out as the stars of their generation. In 1945, when Munk's synagogue were looking for an assistant rabbi, they whittled their choices down to either Jacobs or Jakobovits, before finally choosing Jacobs.

Immanuel Jakobovits had studied at Jews' College and progressed rapidly in his career, advancing to ever more senior rabbinic posts in London, before being appointed Chief Rabbi of Ireland at the age of 27. In 1957 he was offered the pulpit at the prestigious Fifth Avenue Synagogue in New York. Despite his barbed criticism of Jacobs's 'bombastic letter of resignation' from Jews' College, he and Louis were on passably good terms. As we have seen he had offered, to intervene, albeit not entirely neutrally, to help find a solution to the New West End crisis.

Before he accepted the offer of Chief Rabbi, Jakobovits came on a reconnaissance visit to London. He asked Isaac Wolfson's secretary, Captain Myers, to fix up a meeting for him with Jacobs. Jacobs suggested that Jakobovits come to his home, but he declined, believing it might look odd for him to appear to pay a courtesy call on the man who'd had such severe disagreement with the departing Chief Rabbi. Instead, Rabbi Jakobovits asked Jacobs if he would call on him at his hotel. But Jacobs would not agree to this. He feared his visit might be construed publicly as him going cap in hand to the prospective new Chief Rabbi, as if he were seeking a return to the United Synagogue.

Finally it was agreed that the two men would meet in Holland Park. Strolling around the flower beds, Rabbi Jakobovits offered, as

Jacobs put it, 'what amounted to an apology for his intervention in the Jews' College affair', implying that had he known that Jacobs relied on the position for his livelihood he would not have intervened in the way that he had.[11]

Jacobs was not greatly impressed by Jakobovits's religious outlook. In a note to William Frankel he wrote: 'His general views on religion strike me as very reactionary, even though he passes as a "modern". For instance, he said that he was convinced that the future of Judaism was with the people in Stamford Hill and that ultimately his religious guides must be the *gedolei hador* [leaders of ultra-Orthodoxy] . . . I found his attitude frankly appalling.'[12]

Shortly before his induction as Chief Rabbi, Dr Jakobovits told the *Sunday Times* that Jacobs could be reconciled with the Orthodox establishment if only he would accept the authority of the Chief Rabbi.[13] Louis published a stinging rejoinder in the *Jewish Chronicle*. His letter included brief extracts from a draft that William Frankel had, somewhat imperiously, drawn up. Frankel's intention seems to have been that Louis would sign a letter written by the editor of the *Jewish Chronicle*, addressed to the editor of the *Jewish Chronicle*, and published in the letters pages of the *Jewish Chronicle*. Louis studied Frankel's draft before composing a less confrontational, more scholarly and far more incisive response.

In his rejoinder Jacobs wrote that not only was the idea of a superior rabbi inimical to Judaism, it involved the subordinate rabbi's abdication of the duties conferred on him by his ordination. Furthermore, in Britain the office of Chief Rabbi was modelled on that of the Archbishop of Canterbury. He asked what reconciliation could mean in this context. 'If it means that our group will engage in friendly dialogue with other groups in Anglo-Jewry and work together with them for the many aims we all have in common, this is already happening and, where it is not, the remedy lies with Rabbi Jakobovits and his colleagues.'[14]

A couple of weeks later Jacobs's review of Jakobovits's new book *Journal of a Rabbi* appeared in the *Jewish Echo*. He said that it was to the author's credit that he declared unambiguously where he stood, 'though whether this is where we would like to see him standing is another matter'. He criticized the thesis implied in the book that Judaism has always been expressed in the language of its times yet remains an unchanging, monolithic structure. He reserved his strictest censure for the author's beliefs, that suffering on a national scale, like that of the Jews under Hitler, is caused by the sins of the nation, or that illness is to be seen as a punishment from heaven.[15]

A PUBLIC FIGURE

In October 1966 Jacobs flew to Montreal to deliver the annual Allan Bronfman lectures for the Shaar Hashomayim congregation in the suburb of Westmount. He spoke on two topics during his 48-hour visit. In his first lecture, delivered to an academic audience, he discussed the philosophical problem of how to talk about God, given that whatever words one uses limits the idea of God within the constraints of human language.[16] The next day he spoke to the congregation at large on the Meaning of Faith. It was the second time within a few days that he had spoken to North American audiences; a week earlier he had been invited by a very different type of organization to take part in a seminar at the Institute of Directors in London.

The Young Presidents' Organization of America described itself as one of the most influential executive bodies in the USA. Membership was restricted to men; exclusively those who had become presidents of major companies before the age of 40. The organization was planning a trip to London for 35 presidents and their wives. The party would stay at the Savoy Hotel and be ferried around the city, as the advance publicity proudly proclaimed, in a fleet of 12 new Daimler cars. Jacobs received an invitation to participate in their seminar on 'Great Britain and Morality in the 1960s' together with other prominent London figures, including C. P. Snow and the former athlete Roger Bannister.

Jacobs's growing stature as an intellectual on the public stage can be gauged from the way in which *The Times* referred to him in the list of seminar participants simply as Dr Jacobs, without further explanation of who he was; his was a name with which

Times readers were expected to be familiar. His picture, in which he looked decidedly shady, had recently appeared on the cover of the *Daily Telegraph*'s Weekend magazine, introducing a 16-page feature on the Jews of Britain. Within the feature Chaim Bermant described him as 'a charming, scholarly man who, but for the grace of God and an over-inquiring disposition, might have been Chief Rabbi'. Bermant explained that when the row over Jacobs's views blew up, it had looked as if the Jewish community might be torn asunder. However, 'Anglo-Jewry is very English and the controversy died down long before everyone was quite sure what it was about.'[17]

William Frankel had always believed that Jacobs had the potential for a national profile, and had laid what he hoped would be its foundation a couple of years earlier. In February 1964 he booked the Small Dining Room in Pall Mall's Reform Club for a dinner in Louis's honour. He invited a group he referred to as 'puzzled Jewish writers', among them the 'angry young men' he had recruited to write for the *Jewish Chronicle* when he first became editor. The invitees included every radical Jewish literary figure in his network, among them Harold Pinter, Danny Abse, Peter Shaffer, George Steiner, Arnold Wesker, Mordechai Richler, Wolf Mankowitz and Emmanuel Litvinoff. Frankel reasoned that Louis's exposure to a cohort such as this could only work in his favour as his public reputation grew.

Louis continued to travel, lecture and write incessantly. He delivered a lecture to St Augustine's College in Canterbury, on a Friday afternoon in November, racing against the clock to get home before the Sabbath began shortly after 3.30. He gave a public interview to the Jewish National Fund on his life, views and Anglo-Jewry, travelled to Lancaster and Cambridge universities to address their students, gave a talk to the Council of Christians and Jews in Birmingham, spoke to students in London on 'What Judaism has to offer', addressed the members of the fledgling New Hendon Synagogue, preached each week in his synagogue and conducted a Talmud class every Monday evening. The class, which attracted a large number of attendees, ranging from deeply knowledgeable to complete beginners, ran, with only brief pauses, for over 40 years.

His desk life was even busier. Apart from answering the questions and correspondence that he regularly received, he agreed to edit a column entitled 'Current Theological Literature' in the quarterly American journal *Judaism*, wrote a profile for the *Jewish Chronicle* of the author Ahad Haam, joined the editorial board of the journal *European Judaism*, and in the biggest commitment of all, undertook to anonymously write a weekly column for the *Jewish Chronicle* entitled 'Ask the Rabbi'. Readers were invited to send in their questions, from which he would select two or three for a brief reply. The column ran weekly for 25 years, the last one appearing in October 1992. In 1998 Vallentine Mitchell published a collection of his 'Ask the Rabbi' columns in a book of the same name.

ABBEY ROAD

The New London's acquisition of its building had been fortuitous. Its location in Abbey Road had appeared to be of little consequence – they would have jumped at a ready-made synagogue building anywhere within reasonable distance of the New West End. But if, in 1967, you took a street map of London in order to decide where to site the capital's most fashionable congregation, culturally active and with a high-profile, media-savvy rabbi, the chances are that your eye would alight on St John's Wood's Abbey Road.

St John's Wood had always been famous for Lord's Cricket Ground, the home of the MCC, still in those days a bastion of old-fashioned genteel Englishness; a sort of non-Jewish version of the New West End where cricket substituted for prayer. But it wasn't so much cricket that made Abbey Road exactly the right location for the chic New London, as the large white Georgian town house 200 yards away. Outside it crowds of teenagers gathered daily, hoping to get a glance of their favourite pop idols; hopefully the Beatles but failing that, Gerry and the Pacemakers, Cilla Black, Billy J. Kramer and the Dakotas or any one of a dozen others. The New London, of course, had little connection with the music being recorded at EMI's studios in Abbey Road, but both venues symbolized the changing mood in British society. They were thrust together on 17 October 1967, when Jacobs conducted a memorial service for the Beatles' late manager, Brian Epstein.

Epstein had died of a drug overdose on 27 August 1967. Born into a traditional Jewish family in Liverpool, Epstein had become increasingly troubled in his personal life and although it was not certain that he had killed himself, his problems had become increasingly apparent to those close to him, among them the Beatles. His father Harry, an active member of the Liverpool Jewish community and treasurer of several charities, had died just four weeks earlier. Brian had sat *shiva* with his family in Liverpool; now he was returning to the city to be buried.

Epstein's family were not happy with the address at the funeral, the presiding rabbi saying later that he had seriously underestimated the significance of Brian's achievement. When it was decided to hold a memorial for him, the family felt that a London venue would be more appropriate, and that Jacobs would be the right person to conduct the service. Unlike many rabbis, Louis understood popular culture. He knew full well who Epstein was, and what he had managed to achieve.

The service was held at 6 p.m. on 17 October. Louis was quite used to preaching to an audience of the wealthy and famous, but he had never had a congregation like this. All four Beatles came, together with their wives, Cilla Black, Lulu, Gerry Marsden, Billy J. Kramer and dozens of lesser-known figures from the pop world. The *Daily Express* took a particular interest in the Beatles' attire: 'formal black suits, though in somewhat way-out styles'. As for the model Patti Boyd, George Harrison's wife, she arrived in a 'cherry-red hat bound with a black ribbon, a black divided skirt, knee-length boots and a black over-blouse held in place with a Victorian brooch'.

George Rothschild conducted the service, assisted by the New London choir directed by Martin Lawrence. In his address Louis described Epstein as an

extremely capable young man with a gift for discerning extraordinary talent and helping it on its way . . . He helped young people to express themselves in song, and to sing of love and peace rather than hatred and war . . . It would be asking too much of us older people to view with equanimity other manifestations of youth's search for self-expression. But we could not fail to recognize the many positive elements in the accomplishments of Brian Epstein.[18]

At the time the Beatles were deeply involved with transcendental meditation. They had been on a retreat with their guru, the Maharishi Mahesh Yogi, when they heard of Brian Epstein's death. Eastern meditation was very fashionable among young people at the time, and Louis would have known many who were attracted to its allure. His encounter with the Beatles led him to consider the similarities and differences between transcendental meditation and Jewish mystical techniques. In his article 'The Maharishi and the Rabbi' he pointed out that in the Habad branch of Hasidism there is something very like transcendental meditation, but with important distinctions. Although both systems strive through contemplation to diminish the ego and attain rapture, Hasidism is monotheistic; the contemplative exercise is, for Hasidim, an act of worship. Unlike transcendental meditation, Hasidism does not use meditative techniques; Hasidic contemplation is reflection on God as he becomes manifest. But the most important distinction between the two systems, Jacobs insisted, is in their reaction to the sufferings of the world.

> Only a bigot would suggest that we have nothing to learn from Eastern serenity or that glorious compassion is not to be found there. For all that, it is Judaism and those influenced by her which have heard the cry of the poor and the distressed. Both Buddha and Moses cannot remain at ease in the king's palace when suffering humanity groans outside its doors, but when Moses leaves it is to go out to his brethren.[19]

Epstein's death had occurred just a few weeks after the Six-Day War, when Israel had defeated a coordinated attack by Arab states across every one of their borders. The disproportionality of the attack was so evident that, in common with Jewish communities across the world, New London members had responded with alacrity to the urgent calls for aid, raising over £100,000 through the synagogue, in addition to funds and practical assistance donated by members through other channels. Many people saw Israel's rapid outright victory against such overwhelming odds as miraculous, and although Jacobs did not disagree with the sentiment, he worried about the theological implications of categorizing the victory in such terms. In particular he took issue with those who pointed at particular incidents, such as the shell which dislodged a water tank so that the dislodged water put out a fire started by the previous shell, as evidence of supernatural intervention. Why, he wondered, was there divine intervention in this case, but not in others? Does it not present God as capricious? What of the skill and courage of the Israeli generals and air force, of the heroism of the ordinary soldiers, of all the human ability and tenacity that made victory possible?

> A more satisfactory way of seeing the hand of God in the June war, is to see God at work not in this or that bit of deliverance but in the process as a whole. The skilful planning of the Israelis, their resistance to aggression, their readiness to sacrifice for a cause they believed to be just, the realization that they were not fighting a war of conquest but were defending their homes and families, the age-old dream which had helped to bring Israel into existence and inspired its inhabitants to keep it in being – all these were God's instruments, as were similar ideas in the miracle of Dunkirk years ago. Our Rabbis say, for instance, that whenever a judge gives a right decision he acts as a co-partner with God in the work of creation. They surely did not mean that the judge should neglect rigorous attention to the legal aspects of the case before him. A judge might well pray to God to help him decide correctly but he would be a poor judge if he relied on his prayers as an excuse for failing to examine with the utmost application the niceties of the law, hoping that God would guide him to pull the decision out of the air . . .

Yet seeing God at work in the process is quite different from sanctifying warfare. One of the most encouraging features of the whole episode is that for all the admiration for the heroic fighters, very few Jewish voices have been raised to glorify military might. The war had to be fought because the alternative was, sooner or later, annihilation. The Israelis looked upon it as a necessity but a tragic necessity, a necessary evil but an evil nonetheless. Thank God, Israel has not abandoned the ancient Jewish affirmation that, as the Rabbis put it, even though there may be times when the Jew has to wear a sword, he must never look upon it as an adornment. When war came and could not be avoided without loss of innocent life and all that had been built up, the soldiers who fought were doing God's work. But as Jews they were duty bound to recognise, and they did recognise, that God's true plan for man was to be found elsewhere, in building a peaceful world and a just society.[20]

Jacobs's insistence on recognizing God's involvement in the totality of events was repeated by Rabbi A. J. Heschel in a midweek lecture at New London in September 1967. Heschel, Professor of Jewish Ethics and Mysticism at the Jewish Theological Seminary, was an eminent theologian with a worldwide reputation. So many people turned up to hear him speak that the lecture was moved at the last minute from the newly built New London hall into the synagogue itself.

Heschel, whose name features prominently in many of Jacobs's writing, spoke movingly about Judaism's preoccupation with the minutiae of religious behaviour and its inability to engage intellectually with matters of theology and belief. Despite important differences in their approaches, both men believed that far greater emphasis should be placed on the intellectual component of Judaism.

The previous few months had been a difficult time for the Jacobs family. Louis's father, Harry Jacobs, and Shula's mother, Jane Lisagorsky, had both passed away in the same week. But on 14 November the family celebrated a far happier occasion, when

Louis and Shula's eldest son Ivor married Tirza Carlebach, younger daughter of Rabbi Alexander and Marga Carlebach. The families had first met when Rabbis Jacobs and Carlebach had worked alongside each other at Munk's synagogue. Rabbi Carlebach officiated at the wedding, supported by Louis and George Rothschild.

The custom in many English Orthodox synagogues in those days was for men and women to sit together at a wedding ceremony. It was a custom that the United Synagogue was in the process of abandoning, but from which the New London never departed. Except on this occasion. Sensitive to the feelings of some strictly observant guests, it was agreed that for this wedding men would sit on one side of the synagogue, women on the other. It wasn't the only innovation that day. The synagogue had just acquired a new *chupa*, a bridal canopy. Although the prevailing practice is to deck the canopy out with flowers, the synagogue officers were keen that the new *chupa* be displayed in its pristine condition. Tradition reasserted itself through the bride's gown and veil, the groom's top hat and, with a wave to the past, a reception at Munk's synagogue.

WORLD COUNCIL OF SYNAGOGUES

In September 1968 Jacobs applied for membership of the Rabbinical Assembly, the international professional body for Conservative rabbis. Although his friend Wolfe Kelman, the Assembly's Executive Vice-President, had been encouraging him to join for some time, Jacobs had been reluctant. He was conscious that it would be a career-defining moment, labelling him henceforth as a Conservative rather than an Orthodox rabbi. But the American Conservative movement of the time was closer to him than any other stream, and like all rabbis he needed collegiate support and a forum in which he could engage openly with colleagues. In the absence of a similar opportunity in England, joining the Rabbinical Assembly eventually seemed to be a necessary move.

The Rabbinical Assembly suggested that Jacobs's forthcoming lecture tour of America would be an appropriate opportunity to formalize his membership. He was coming, at the invitation of the

American Jewish Committee, to deliver a series of lectures over a three-week period in March 1969. The Rabbinical Assembly suggested that at the end of the tour, for which he would be paid an honorarium of $2,000, he join them at their convention in the Catskills. There, elected by the acclamation of all 500 attendees, he would become the organization's 1,000th member. Jacobs later wondered whether the count of 1,000 was precise, or whether it was an approximation designed to add kudos to his membership.

In his election address he spoke on 'The Pulpit as an Instrument of Theological Material'. He began by outlining many different theological, spiritual and mystical themes around which a rabbi might structure a sermon, and hinted at ways in which each theme might best be expounded. Still, he warned his fellow rabbis not to get carried away; should they feed their congregants too rich a diet of such material, it might give them spiritual indigestion.

Jacobs's book, *Jewish Law*, had been recently published by Behrman House. It was the first of five textbooks, in a series entitled 'The Chain of Tradition', that he would write for the publisher. Accompanied by a Teacher's Guide, the books were intended to stimulate discussion in the classroom. He outlined key topics in Jewish law, illustrated them with classical rabbinic sources and added an explanation and commentary. In his introduction Jacobs explained that although the great ideals of Judaism, such as justice, mercy and holiness, are sublime, they can only be put into practice through the minutiae of detailed action, the law itself, as worked out by the rabbis over the centuries.

Behrman House sponsored his lecture at the Rabbinical Assembly by laying on a traditionally British fish-and-chip supper. The chips were wrapped, as was customary, in newspaper. Less customary was the choice of newspaper; each portion came enwrapped in pages from the *Jewish Chronicle*.

The American Jewish Committee's lecture tour had been organized to mark Jacobs's major publication of the year, *Faith*. The book explored the evolution of religious belief, from the biblical notion of trust in God, through the medieval belief in his existence, to contemporary theological ideas. Reviewing the book in the *Jewish Chronicle*, Dr Solomon Goldman praised the author's erudition and his refusal to shirk any of the modern challenges that modern thought presents to religious life. However, he took him to task for digressing, while discussing different approaches to the Sabbath, into a renewed attack on fundamentalism:

> One wonders whether Dr. Jacobs's dislike of fundamentalism is not in danger of becoming obsessive with him, for in this context it is all so unnecessary. If he had been content to state his own (theological) approach according to which the Sabbath is accepted as a day on which God is acknowledged as Creator, even the fundamentalist would have been happy. The pity of it all is that his critics are likely to seize on this one small passage and that the great worth of the book might become obscured in the cloud of controversy.[21]

Dr Goldman was the minister of the neighbouring St John's Wood United Synagogue which had occupied the building in Abbey Road before the New London acquired it. Louis and Shula were good friends with Goldman and his wife Sadie. They would even take holidays together. 'But we always ate at separate tables,' confided Shula, 'so as not to cause them embarrassment and to stop other people from gossiping.'[22]

After joining the Rabbinical Assembly, Jacobs overcame his misgivings about the New London Synagogue affiliating to the Conservative movement's World Council of Synagogues. Apart from their shared theological outlook there were tentative historical connections between the World Council and the New London Synagogue, or at least with the building it occupied. Solomon Shechter, the architect of Conservative Judaism in the USA, had originally emigrated from Moldavia to England, where in 1887 he and his wife Mathilde had been married at the synagogue in Abbey Road. He moved to the United States and in 1902 Schechter became the second President of the Jewish Theological Seminary, the leading organization in the training of American Conservative rabbis. The Seminary's first rabbinic graduate was Joseph Hertz, who preceded Rabbi Brodie as British Chief Rabbi. Like Brodie, Hertz's official seat was at Abbey Road. The synagogue where Louis preached contained a fragment of the history of Conservative Judaism.

In 1967 the World Council wrote to Jacobs saying that they were planning to hold their biennial convention in London in July the following year. He agreed that the New London would act as hosts. In his welcome address to delegates, Jacobs said that as a congregation the New London were happy to engage with every constructive movement in Judaism and that they had a similar approach and special affinity to Conservative synagogues. However, the New London, he stressed, were not a Conservative congregation.[23]

It was his clearest expression to date of his ambivalent relationship with Conservative Judaism, notwithstanding both his own membership of the Rabbinical Assembly and the New London's affiliation to the World Council. The ambivalence would be thrown into sharper focus in the years to come with the establishment of the Conservative-orientated British Masorti movement,[24] of which he was the titular spiritual leader but with which he was never fully comfortable. Jacobs had established New London as an independent Orthodox congregation. Although he profoundly disagreed with the direction in which Orthodoxy was moving, he saw no reason why he should relinquish his identity as an Orthodox rabbi because of what he saw as the inauthentic theology of his opponents.

In his public addresses Jacobs would often sum up his feelings towards the Conservative movement by quoting the German-Jewish thinker Ernst Simon. 'I can pray with the Orthodox,' he would say, 'but I can't talk to them. I can talk to the Reform, but I can't pray with them. With the Conservatives, I can pray with them and I can talk to them.' Jacobs would raise a knowing chuckle from his audience when he said this, as if all were agreed that the American Conservative movement was the only form of Judaism that made sense. But in quoting Ernst Simon's apophthegm, Jacobs skirted around a deeper antipathy which he only articulated in his later years. He could talk to the Conservatives, and he could pray with them. But sometimes that was as far as it went. Jacobs considered the philosophy of Conservative Judaism to be little different from the Orthodoxy of the old United Synagogue. But as a religious denomination, the concerns of the American Conservative movement were not those of his Anglo-Jewish tradition. Jacobs could not fully identify with the American movement, because England was not America. As Elliot Cosgrove puts it, when discussing Jacobs's opposition to a Conservative proposal to modify an aspect of Jewish law:

> As an Englishman observing American Judaism at a distance, Jacobs could not identify with the cultural trends that pressed for modifications of Jewish law . . . Jacobs's derisive attitude regarding the proposed innovation exhibits a total lack of awareness that just as the press for innovation is driven by a particular social context (America), so too his objections to the proposed changes are similarly framed by his particular context and sensibility.[25]

As he grew older Jacobs distanced himself further from the Conservative movement. He perceived a proselytizing element in American Conservatism which he saw as incompatible with the Anglo-Jewish tradition and his perceived role as its custodian. Quite possibly, he would have preferred to be less of a custodian. One of his friends, a former chairman of the New London, believes that the only reason that its service so closely replicated that of the New West End was because that is what his congregation wanted.[26] But that was only in respect of their services. Intellectually Jacobs's conservative Judaism was virtually indistinguishable from the old Anglo-Jewish Orthodoxy.

In August 1969, Louis and Shula's daughter Naomi married an Israeli scholar, Sasson Bar-Yosef. They had met the previous year, at the Hebrew University in Jerusalem. Louis conducted the ceremony at the New London Synagogue, holding the reception in the hall of St John's Wood United Synagogue. Jacobs's relationship with the United Synagogue had improved slightly under the aegis of Chief Rabbi Jakobovits. A few months earlier he had delivered a lecture at the Hampstead Synagogue, at the invitation of Reverend Raymond Apple, who had succeeded Isaac Levy as the congregation's minister.

Later that year the Office of the Chief Rabbi wrote to a correspondent confirming that, providing there were no impediments in Jewish law, marriages at the New London were valid. There was of course no reason why they would not have been valid. But there had been, and would continue to be, occasions when couples about to marry would be advised by United Synagogue representatives that it would be better to not have the wedding at New London. This, it was intimated, would avoid any future problems – the nature of which was generally not disclosed.

11

Stability

Jacobs approached his 50th birthday acknowledged throughout the English-speaking world as a leading thinker in the field of religion. It had been clear for some time that his split from the United Synagogue, rather than consigning him to oblivion, had in fact been the making of his career. It had been an unpleasant episode for all concerned, and it was true that, from the perspective of the mainstream British Orthodox establishment, he and his followers had been shunted into a corner in which they could safely be ignored. But from a global point of view Jacobs was a towering figure, an original thinker whose departure from the mainstream was an indication, not of weakness but of strength. Few Anglo-Jewish rabbis were able, or even wanted, to make their teachings heard beyond their immediate circle, but as his invitation to the United Nations Convocation had foreshadowed, Jacobs's was now an ecumenical voice. He could be heard far beyond the walls of the synagogue.

In October 1969 Jacobs spoke on 'The Use of the Scriptures in the Synagogue' at the delightfully named parish church of St Botolph-Without-Aldgate in the City of London. The following month he addressed a study group of the St Marylebone Council of Churches on the Prophet Hosea. He was corresponding regularly with academics and students across the world. He contributed to books and journals on subjects as varied as ethics, theology, Hasidism, Kabbalah, Halakha and Talmud. He continued to write book reviews and popular articles, including his unattributed 'Ask the Rabbi' column and sermons in the *Jewish Chronicle*.

Although controversy had given Jacobs a wide berth for quite some time, it was not his lot to have it pass him by for ever. When the film producer John Schlesinger needed to use a synagogue to stage a bar mitzvah scene in his production *Sunday, Bloody Sunday*, he approached the New London. The synagogue agreed and many of the congregants took part in the scene as extras. The film, when released, included homosexual scenes which aroused the ire of a prominent lady in the community. She wrote privately to Jacobs expressing her unhappiness:

> Both of us were revolted and shocked at seeing . . . scenes of passionate love making between men . . . It added to our sense of outrage that, in a film on such a subject, a real synagogue had been put at the disposal of the producer and a genuine service arranged for him. It seemed to us that by so doing a seal of approval had been given to the film by Jewish religious authorities, whereas, in our opinion, Judaism had been prostituted and degraded.[1]

Jacobs could only reply that they had made the synagogue available for one scene, that the service arranged had not been genuine, and they had had no say in the making of the film.

In March 1971 Louis and Shula took up an invitation for him to spend a week lecturing in Scandinavia. Unlike their trips to the United States this visit was far more informal. They visited Copenhagen, Oslo and Stockholm, all of which had small Jewish communities, all led by rabbis who were familiar with Louis's work and who occupied similar positions to him on the ideological spectrum.

Shula wrote one of her ebullient, detailed accounts of their trip. She described how the Chief Rabbi of Denmark, Bent Melchior, who had passed his driving test just two days earlier so that he could ferry them around, took them one evening to a guest house attached to the King's summer palace. The King was not in residence and Melchior had been able to use his influence as Chief Rabbi to hire the dining room for the evening.

The beautiful large dining room. Logs crackling away in the grand fireplace. Enormous vases of Christmas tulips. Pots of cyclamen. All the tables were set, although no one else was there. We sat at a large table nearest to the fire. There were four candles alight on our table. The hors d'oeuvres arrived. So many different delicacies. A variety of fish. There was so much that we thought it was one main course. But we were mistaken. We had all the time we wanted to eat. There were so many waiters around us who kept plying us with everything. And then we were told the main dish will be the most wonderful fish we have ever had. And it was. Then after a time cheeses, pancakes with jam and coffee . . .[2]

On his USA tours Jacobs had grown used to delivering keynote sermons on Shabbat mornings in large formal synagogues. He gave a keynote talk in Denmark too, but the environment was very different. Rather than speaking in the main synagogue in Copenhagen, Shula and Louis were taken to a rural farmhouse, used as a community centre. They spent an informal weekend, Jacobs preaching during services and leading discussions, with country walks and social activities in between.

Shula described the invitation to Scandinavia as 'very well received . . . delightful, relaxing, happy and warm'.[3] It came as a welcome interlude in Louis's life, which although still busy, had settled into something of a routine. He was writing as prolifically as ever, but his scholarly output shifted noticeably in the early 1970s away from theology and towards the substance of the Jewish religion. He wrote several articles analysing the literary structure of the Talmud and composed two dozen entries for the new *Encyclopaedia Judaica*. His major article was the entry on Judaism, with other topics ranging from asceticism to tobacco and including several biographies on medieval and early modern rabbis.

SHIFTING VISIONS

Jacobs taught Talmud classes on Monday evenings at the New London, and during the week at the Leo Baeck College, then based at the West London Synagogue in Upper Berkeley Street. Founded in 1956, the college was modelled on two pre-war German seminaries, the Jewish Theological Seminary in Breslau and the *Hochschule*, or Higher Institute for Jewish Study, in Berlin. Neither German seminary owed a formal allegiance to any religious denomination, but their scientific, analytical approach to the authorship of the Torah and the development of Judaism was shared by the Conservative and Reform movements, and of course by Jacobs himself. And although in theory Leo Baeck College was non-denominational, in practice it became the pre-eminent European training seminary for Reform and Liberal rabbis.

The college asked Jacobs to act as Chairman of the Academic Committee and to assist in recruiting additional faculty. One of those he recruited was Isaac Newman, formerly of the Dalston Synagogue, now at Barnet. Newman had been a supporter of Jacobs's during his disputes with Chief Rabbi Brodie, and had lectured for the Society for the Study of Jewish Theology. In January 1964 his support for Louis had led him into a major rupture with his Dalston Synagogue.

It occurred after Rabbi Newman had invited Louis to speak at a study session. The synagogue's honorary officers, refusing to allow Rabbi Jacobs to lecture on their premises, revoked the invitation. As an alternative, one of Newman's study group suggested they discuss Jacobs's book *We Have Reason to Believe*. But even this proved to be controversial; the honorary officers had been instructed by the United Synagogue not to allow any discussion of Jacobs's theological views, and they forbade this discussion too.

Deciding that they would ignore the prohibition, Rabbi Newman and the members of the study group gathered to discuss the book anyway. The synagogue's Board of Management broke up the meeting, kicking in the door and breaking the windows.[4] It was just the first in a protracted series of disputes involving Rabbi Newman, the Dalston Board of Management and the United Synagogue. At one stage the synagogue's members were even advised that, due to his support for Jacobs, they should not attend a tea party to celebrate Newman's daughter's batmitzvah.

Now, several years later, after he had accepted Jacobs's invitation to teach at Leo Baeck College, Newman received a phone call from Chief Rabbi Jakobovits, telling him that it was not appropriate for an Orthodox rabbi to train students for Reform and Liberal ministries. Torn between his career and his long friendship with Jacobs, Newman stopped teaching at the college. Instead, he invited the students to a twice-weekly class at his home, where his wife made them breakfast.

Many years later, in the course of a correspondence about metaphysical aspects of the Hereafter, Jacobs told Rabbi Newman that he was 'the only Anglo-Jewish scholar I can think of who is interested in such discussion. So much the worse for Anglo-Jewry. So much am I fortunate to have him as a friend.'[5]

Teaching Talmud to rabbinic students at Leo Baeck filled the void for Jacobs created by his departure from Jews' College. But it is noticeable that he did not approach his position with the same fervour that he had shown at Jews' College. He had gone to Jews' College with the stated intention of creating a new generation of rabbis for Anglo-Jewry, traditionally observant and academically minded, who would foster a new spirit in the community.[6] Although his students at both colleges held him in high regard, one gets the sense that at Leo Baeck his objectives did not extend beyond the quotidian matters of teaching Talmud and the welfare of his students. Despite being head of the Leo Baeck Academic Committee, he does not seem to have seen his role there in the same way as he hoped it would become at Jews' College. And the reason was not because his students would go on to be Reform and Liberal rabbis rather than Orthodox; even some years later when he could have actively involved himself in training rabbis for the Masorti movement he did not demonstrate the sense of purpose and mission he'd had at Jews' College.

Of course he was older, and the battles he'd fought had taken their toll, but it does seem that he had undergone a fundamental shift in his aspirations. Rather than wishing to train rabbis to inspire a renaissance in British Jewry, he was now content to exert his influence in more scholarly ways, through his writing, lecturing and teaching.

Nevertheless, his lessons in Talmud made a profound impression on his former students at Leo Baeck.

> Louis Jacobs was an incredibly wonderful teacher. I can't believe how frustrating it must have been for him, because he came from a world where people had grown up with Talmud . . . and there he was teaching at a college where most of us had never opened a volume of Talmud in our lives. And he didn't lose patience with us . . . he was really an innovator in this field . . . He would take a subject and look at it *sugya* by *sugya*, he would encourage us to consider the historical boundaries of a text, which certainly wasn't done, I am sure in yeshiva . . . he was at the forefront of doing that . . . Once he had this *sugya* up on the blackboard marked with all the points of connection, he'd written all the connecting bits in boxes, he was writing it all out . . . And I pointed out to him there was a logical problem in what he had written. He was delighted! Thrilled . . . He kept mentioning it to me for years afterwards.[7]

On 4 February 1971, Shula and Louis became grandparents for the first time. Tirza Jacobs, the wife of their oldest son Ivor, gave birth to a baby boy. They named him Daniel. Louis was 50 years old. Two of their children were married, their third, David, was at work proving himself to be a talented photographer. Louis and Shula had slipped into middle age.

The same year they finally moved house into a property that felt as if it would become long-term accommodation. They needed the stability – they had had a dislocated existence since Jacobs left the New West End for Jews' College, moving four times in ten years. This was their third move since the founding of the New London.

The property they moved into in Marlborough Hill was a converted flat in a large house, occupying the ground floor and basement. Leased for him by the synagogue as part of his remuneration package, the flat gave Jacobs more space for his rapidly swelling library, but it had shortcomings, leaving some of the congregants feeling that their rabbi had been short-changed. The house had been built above the underground railway from Swiss Cottage to St John's Wood, on what was then the Stanmore branch of the Bakerloo Line. It is not uncommon for London properties to be constructed over Tube tunnels. Unlike the flat in Marlborough Hill, however, few have a flue from the tunnel emerging in their garden.

Although Louis and Shula didn't seem to mind too much, the flue in the garden rankled with some members of the congregation, who felt that this property was the latest manifestation of the inequitable way in which Louis's employment had always been managed. His salary had never been high, and although he was perhaps too unworldly to appreciate the unusualness of the situation, one or two wealthy members of the congregation had been supporting him privately for many years. When he had been at the New West End a congregant had bought him a car; without it he would not have easily been able to carry out pastoral visits or travel easily to his lectures. There had been no money for Ivor's bar mitzvah, the Jacobs family hoping that they would be able to cover the costs of the celebration from the gifts Ivor received. 'All I got,' he laments, 'were a few books on cricket and art!'

> But whatever the financial situation my parents never complained, or should I say that we never heard. Until relatively recently the norm in the United Synagogue, and thus the New London, was to provide a house, the lowest salary they could get away with, unpaid labour from the rabbi's wife and a working week far longer than that of any of their congregants.[8]

Jacobs belonged to a generation, perhaps the last, in which English rabbis were conveniently imagined by their congregants to be spiritual beings with few material needs, and were paid accordingly.

Jacobs's major publication of the period, *Hasidic Prayer*, appeared in 1972 with an American edition the following year. Based on the writings of early Hasidic leaders, the book explained, to those not familiar with Hasidism, why prayer occupies a central place in Hasidic thought and why contemplation in prayer became the movement's ultimate spiritual expression. He sent copies, as was the custom, to prominent scholars in the field of rabbinics. Norman Lamm, the future Chancellor of Yeshiva University, told him he was so impressed with the book's lucidity and scholarship that he planned to use it in his university teaching. Gershom Scholem, the formidable scholar of Jewish mysticism, told Jacobs he had chosen an important and weighty theme, and offered to send him a copy of one of his articles which he had spotted was missing from the bibliography.

Shifting his focus to the behavioural and social aspects of Judaism, Jacobs began work on a volume for the Israeli publishing house Keter. Entitled *What Does Judaism Say About . . .*, the book explored Jewish attitudes to pressing contemporary problems. Between them, Jacobs and Keter's editor-in-chief, Geoffrey Wigoder, identified over one hundred topics confronting 1970s society. They included Abortion, Democracy, The Hereafter, Business Ethics, Drugs, Change of Sex, Civil Disobedience and Nuclear Warfare. Jacobs's responses to each topic drew on traditional Jewish sources which he reframed in contemporary terms. On the question of Autopsy he noted that although some scholars pointed to the fact that the biblical Jacob was embalmed, a process that required making incisions in his corpse, the prevailing view in Jewish law is based on an eighteenth-century ruling that autopsies are only permitted if there is a direct connection to the saving of life. There the matter rests at present. However 'one or two bold spirits' have argued that medical technology has improved so much since the eighteenth century that every autopsy today can be considered as potentially saving life. 'It can be seen that there are good grounds for favouring a more permissive attitude towards autopsies, but so far the conservative view has prevailed.'[9]

Jacobs returned to theological enquiry with his landmark work *A Jewish Theology*. Published in 1973, it won the *Jewish Chronicle* Book Award the following year. As Elliot Cosgrove notes, 'the indefinite article serv(es) as a mild rebuke to any past or future theologian who dared to speak for the entirety of Jewish theological expression'. Even though he had always defended his theological corner vigorously, even at the expense of his own career, Louis knew that, however much he believed he was correct, he, like anybody else, could only write 'A Jewish Theology'.[10]

New London's success as an independent congregation was leavened by the fact that, as far as the Orthodox establishment was concerned, it remained beyond the pale. Orthodox rabbis could not participate in its services or events. Some feared that such isolation was, ultimately, to the detriment of the whole of Orthodoxy. At the conference of Anglo-Jewish Preachers in May 1973 Rabbi Dr Morris Turetsky, minister of the independent orthodox Western Synagogue, issued a plea for reconciliation. He described the New London, which was now approaching the 1,000-members mark, as one of the major synagogal bodies in London. 'It would be a disaster of great magnitude,' he declared, 'if this large segment of Orthodox Jews – the majority of whom earnestly desire that they and their children remain Orthodox – should, as a result of cold-shouldering, drift into the shores of the rapidly swelling Reform movement.'

Jacobs had approached Rabbi Turetsky some years earlier when he was a dayan on the Leeds Beth Din. Jacobs was exploring the possibility of establishing a Beth Din that would take a more reasonable attitude towards conversion than the United Synagogue, which he believed subjected prospective converts to unreasonable difficulties, far in excess of anything required by Jewish law. Turetsky had replied, saying that he had given Jacobs's suggestion considerable thought but had decided, for several reasons, that he did not wish to be associated with the proposal. One of the reasons he gave was that he could not place himself in the same religious camp as 'the reverend gentlemen you mention who support you'.[11]

Turetsky's reply to Jacobs reveals a gap even between his moderate Orthodoxy and Jacobs's point of view. Nevertheless, a review that Jacobs wrote illustrated just how slight that gap was. The book under review was a study of Genesis by the Israeli scholar Nehama

Leibowitz. Jacobs had given it a glowing approbation in the *Jewish Chronicle*, but had taken the author to task for paying no attention to modern biblical scholarship. 'It is one thing for example, to reject the Documentary Hypothesis. It is quite another to ignore completely all the achievements of modern Biblical criticism . . .' Writing in the *Jewish Review*, Rabbi Turetsky made a similar point. He noted that Professor Leibowitz was willing to quote modern scholars who accepted modern biblical criticism, yet she did not refer to their research or findings. 'The obvious inference is that while one is permitted to obtain the truth from whatever source it emanates, any implication which might impinge upon the validity of the biblical text is completely and absolutely inadmissible.'[12] Turetsky shared Jacobs's views regarding the importance of modern biblical criticism, even though this did not lead him to the same conclusions. Nevertheless, the fact that he could envisage reconciliation between the two camps indicates just how far their differences had been blown out of proportion.

TENTH ANNIVERSARY

The New London Synagogue was approaching its tenth anniversary, now boasting a membership in excess of 1,000 souls. The synagogue was now focusing on itself, rather than on the controversy that had led to its creation. *Quest* had ceased publication after its second edition, but the concerts continued and Jacobs's regular Talmud study groups attracted participants from across the religious spectrum. The synagogue continued to strike out in new directions, its independent status enabling it to host events that almost certainly would not have been sanctioned at the New West End. In November 1973 Louis welcomed the Dalai Lama, the spiritual leader of Tibetan Buddhism, to a symposium at the synagogue. Even though the event was held at 9.45 on a weekday morning, hundreds of people turned up to hear the Dalai Lama speak.

On 2 June 1974, as part of the tenth anniversary celebrations, Anna and Joe Horovitz put on another concert at the synagogue,

William Frankel using his connections to book Yehudi Menuhin and his sister Hephzibah. Menuhin played a solo sonata for violin written for him by the Israeli composer Paul Ben-Haim. Announcing the concert, Atticus of the *Sunday Times* declared that the New London had 'by common consent established itself as the most lively and intellectually active of all the Jewish Congregations', the inspiration for which, he said, was undoubtedly Jacobs's dominant personality. Typically, Jacobs was more self-effacing. In an article that he wrote for the synagogue magazine in the anniversary month of September 1974, he wrote that 'the perfume of praise, even self-praise, is not without fragrance, provided, as Adlai Stevenson once said, one does not inhale.'[13]

Looking back over ten years he reminded his readers that the two questions that had been discussed endlessly were what the synagogue stood for and where it went from here. He rather dodged the first question, his vagueness standing in sharp contrast to the rigour with which he always approached intellectual matters. He acknowledged there were rough edges still to be smoothed out and uncertainties to be resolved, but asserted that on the basic issue of liberal traditionalism versus naïve fundamentalism 'we were certainly right'. Broadly, the approach of the New London Synagogue, 'call it Conservative if you will, . . . was closest to the best traditions of the Jewish past while holding out hope for the Jewish future'. It was a vague statement of the synagogue's ethos and relationship to the Conservative movement that reflected Jacobs's ambiguous feelings about whether to be associated with an ideological religious stream. It led back to the other question that Jacobs posed in his article: where does the New London Synagogue go from here?

In a feature devoted to the New London's tenth anniversary the *Jewish Chronicle* noted that the synagogue's ambitions to expand had been thwarted. The most promising opportunity had been the discussions a few years earlier with the Garnethill congregation in Glasgow. A similar initiative was proposed by members of the Singers Hill congregation in Birmingham, but again it failed to proceed. The *Jewish Chronicle*'s anonymous Special Correspondent wrote: 'The synagogue occasionally discusses its failure to become a movement and is given to frequent bouts of soul-searching. But although there is still a desire to develop into a movement and there are sympathizers throughout the community, considerable incentive is required to establish a new synagogue.'[14]

As things turned out, sufficient incentive was there.

A CHILD IS BORN

The New Highgate and North London Synagogue held its inaugural service at Hanukkah 1974, just over ten years after the New London's formation. Jacobs had a double incentive for supporting the congregation. Not only was it the first attempt at founding a new congregation which appeared destined to succeed, the initiative in Hendon some years earlier having failed to take off, but the energy that led to its founding had come from two New London members, Michael Rose and Louis's own son Ivor Jacobs.

Referring to themselves, variously, as a daughter or sister congregation, or a branch line, the New Highgate and North London Synagogue declared themselves to be a synagogue

> where traditional Judaism is taught and practised in a way which is intellectually honest and satisfying to its members . . . Our theology is based on the teachings of Rabbi Dr. Louis Jacobs. Essentially this means that we regard Judaism as dynamic rather than static and the Mitzvot are valid to us, not because we believe they were dictated at a certain point of time, but because they are founded in Israel's response to God in history. The effect of this is to make the discovery of the whole range of Jewish thought and practice an exciting quest, rather than a burdensome routine.[15]

Louis found it particularly gratifying that they placed an emphasis on theological issues. He surely took note of their use of the word 'quest', which by now he had effectively made his own as a shorthand for his spiritual and intellectual endeavours.

Jacobs's original idea had been to form loose affiliations with established synagogues, all sharing a similar approach to Judaism, each one under the guidance of its own minister. The New Highgate and North London Synagogue, or New North London as it would eventually be renamed, presented a different sort of challenge. The congregation was young, and enthusiastic, considering themselves as pioneers in much the same way as the New London founders had done. But they were still a small group, mostly aged between 25 and 35; they did not have the resources to employ their own rabbi. Gradually, as their numbers grew, they managed to appoint a part-time student rabbi, but at the beginning the burden of spiritual leadership fell on Jacobs. He acted as a guide in religious matters for the congregation and preached there occasionally, staying locally with his son Ivor and daughter-in-law Tirza.

Louis and Shula had not been able to attend the new congregation's inaugural service. They were in the USA, visiting their new granddaughter, Ziva, who had been born to Naomi and Sasson on 11 November. She was their third grandchild, and the second to be born in the space of few weeks; Ivor's wife Tirza had given birth to their daughter Paula on 30 September.

The baby's arrival happily coincided with a short lecture tour that had been arranged for Jacobs a few months earlier. It was his sixth such visit.

The main event on the tour was a three-day public event organized by the Shaarey Zedek congregation in Detroit. Shula didn't join Louis, choosing instead to stay with Naomi and the baby. But he went with her to see a musical comedy on Broadway, as guests of Jacob Behrman, Jacobs's principal American publisher. Before going home Jacobs spoke at a rabbinic convention in Chicago, where rabbis from all three major Jewish denominations came to hear him.

'The Three Ways of Judaism', the theme for the lecture series that Jacobs presented in Detroit, illustrated at a lay level Jacobs's holistic concept of Judaism, his insistence that one could not separate its spiritual, practical and intellectual dimensions. This unifying approach goes some way to explaining why *We Have Reason to*

Believe had proved to be so controversial in Orthodox circles: the book had introduced theology into a religious environment that was more familiar with the practical, legal and ethical aspects of Judaism. One reason why the book's conclusions were not palatable to those who disagreed with Jacobs was that Orthodoxy at the time was out of touch with theological argumentation. This is not to say that his opponents would have agreed with his conclusions, but they might at least have been more willing to consider the thrust of his reasoning.

In *A Jewish Theology*, Jacobs had illustrated the connection between the different dimensions of Judaism by showing how rabbinic responses to certain legal questions led directly to ethical conclusions. He used a similar approach in his next book, and gave it a title, *Theology in the Responsa*, to show exactly what he was doing.

In the introduction he explained that: 'Although most of the emphasis in the Responsa is undoubtedly on practice, there are to be found in nearly all the great Responsa collections discussions of a theological nature; naturally so since new conditions pose problems for belief as well as for practice . . . One result of the investigation is to give the lie to the view that Jewish theology is un-Jewish.'[16]

Theology in the Responsa was the second of Jacobs's books to be published by the Littman Library of Jewish Civilisation, the scholarly publishing house that his congregant Louis Littman had established in memory of his father. Jacobs had been involved with the project since its inception; Littman had consulted him when he was considering establishing the library, and for many years he was one of its editors. At the memorial service for Louis Littman held in 1988, Jacobs delivered a deeply felt, highly personal address, describing him as a man of 'dedication wedded to a highly gifted mind . . . a human dynamo [who] yet managed to preserve his calmness of spirit . . . a deeply religious man [who] claimed little of the credit for himself, attributing his success to God's blessing.' One can read Jacobs's concluding words, understanding them not just as the summation of a eulogy about Louis Littman but as a window into the deep faith of Louis Jacobs. He quoted William Blake, '*To see a world in a grain of Sand, And a heaven in a wild flower, Hold infinity in the palm of your hand, And eternity in an hour . . .* More than once he had held Eternity in the palm of his hand. Now he has grasped it, never to let it go.'[17]

Jacobs's ability to write *Theology in the Responsa* in a relatively short time was due to his retentive memory. Had he needed to reread every one of the hundreds of collections of Responsa written since the Talmudic era this book alone would have been a lifetime's work. But Louis's great talent was that his memory was both retentive and photographic; not only did he remember everything he read, he could invariably recall where in the book it was, and the position it occupied on the page. Generations of his students were astonished by his ability to tell them not only where a particular passage in the Talmud occurred, but which line it was on.

His next book, well advanced by the time *Theology in the Responsa* was published, similarly relied on his prodigious memory. Entitled *Teyku*, it was a survey of every instance in the Babylonian Talmud, over 300 in all, where a problem was left unresolved because the alternative solutions carried equal weight. The Talmud declares these problems *teyku*. The word is a contraction of the Aramaic for 'let it stand', but in the rabbinic imagination it is an acronym intimating that the problem will be solved when Elijah the prophet returns in the messianic future. Although the *teyku* problems had been known to Talmudists for 1,500 years, Jacobs was the first scholar to subject them all to a methodical and systematic analysis. In his conclusion he stressed that the word did not mean that a solution could not be found, but that it was an insoluble problem, even, notwithstanding Elijah, in the messianic future. He drew an analogy with the use of the same word *teyku* in modern Hebrew to mean a draw in a football match, with each side scoring the same number of goals. 'That is it precisely. Wherever *teyku* occurs in the Talmud the meaning is that while other "games" will be played this particular "game" had ended in a "draw" and the problem must go down in history as incapable of a solution.'[18]

IN THE MOVIES

Throughout his life Louis had received job offers from overseas; occasionally he had come close to taking them up. He had nearly accepted a position at the Jewish Theological Seminary, before deciding against it in favour of Jews' College, and seriously considered a move to South Africa at the height of his dispute with the Chief Rabbi. He had turned down numerous requests from that country since. In 1974 he received a letter out of the blue inviting him to become Director of the Jewish Studies Program at Indiana University. It was a tempting idea, being able to work in a purely academic environment, finally having time to work, study and write without the distractions of ministering to a community. But Jacobs was English, in outlook, in manner and in his allegiance to his 'Anglo-Jewish tradition', by which he meant a rapidly vanishing, not too onerous style of Judaism that had enjoyed a heyday in Central London synagogues during the pre-war years, notably in Hampstead, the New West End and the Central. For Jacobs, England was the only place on earth, other than Israel, where a Jew might reasonably want to be:

> Your average English Jew may still believe that he is in *galut* [exile] but he believes that if the Jew has to be in *galut* there is no nicer place to be and nowhere, apart from in Israel, where he can feel more at home than in the British Isles, a little country without much power today but still a green and pleasant land of tolerance, culture and sophistication in which a Jew can breathe easily in freedom and where he can practise his Judaism without let or hindrance.[19]

Rather than move overseas, Louis continued with his lecture tours, Shula travelling with him. They returned to America in March 1978, for a three-week tour – just long enough, as Shula pointed out, to qualify for the discounted Apex fare. The tour began in California with a weekend at the Brandeis-Bardin Institute, a retreat devoted to training American Jewish leaders. The lecture trail then took them through San Francisco, Albuquerque, Cincinnati and Washington, with hosts in every venue introducing them to their communities, showing them the sights and putting on lavish dinners. They ended in New York, where Naomi and Sasson were expecting their second child; their daughter Noa would be born in June.

There were drawbacks to the lecture tours. Louis was now in his late 50s, and although Shula's report of their 1978 tour was as enthusiastic as ever, we can sense that they were reaching a limit. Continually travelling from city to city, being the centre of attention wherever they went, and never staying long enough for Jacobs to build a rapport with his students, was becoming unsustainable. Fortunately the nature of their overseas travels was about to change.

In June 1980 Jacobs spent a month as visiting professor at the Jewish Theological Seminary. Other than his regular teaching at Leo Baeck, it was the first academic position he had held since Jews' College. He lectured on three mornings a week, and although his diary filled up with student appointments and meetings, it is clear from Shula's diary that their month in New York was as much a sightseeing experience for them as it was a professorship.

Their second overseas trip that year could not have contrasted more bleakly with the vitality of New York Jewish life. This was the period when Jewish repression in the Soviet Union was at its peak, when it was all but impossible for Jews to emigrate to Israel. At the request of the Campaign for Soviet Jewry, Louis and Shula spent a December weekend in Moscow, with the intention that Louis would conduct seminars for some of the refuseniks. When they arrived they discovered that the Soviet authorities had tightened their clampdown and that the seminars could not go ahead. Instead, they spent their time in Moscow meeting refuseniks, with Louis doing as much clandestine teaching as was practicable. Shula became particularly scared at one point; they were standing outside the synagogue on Shabbat afternoon, at the regular informal gathering of refuseniks, when she found herself being intensely cross-examined by a man who, under the pretence of conversation, was trying to find out details of her life in London. Just as she was beginning to feel particularly unsettled by the man's aggressive questioning, some of the refuseniks noticed what was going on and joined her, causing her interrogator to back away into the crowd. Her rescuers told her that the man was certainly KGB: he spoke English far too well to be anything else.

The trip was unsettling and, like so many others who travelled to the Soviet Union at that time, Louis and Shula could offer little more than moral support and whatever items of practical or religious value they were able to bring into the country. These didn't amount to much; Jacobs was searched thoroughly at the airport and although they didn't confiscate any of his luggage they did take his *Times* and *Guardian* newspapers. His most gratifying moment on the trip was meeting Ilya Essas, a scholarly, self-taught, Jewishly learned refusenik who, when he did eventually manage to reach Israel, became a rabbi. Essas had been able to obtain and read a copy of *A Jewish Theology* and had disagreed with Jacobs's point of view profoundly. Louis was delighted to debate it with him.

Some months after they returned to London, Louis received a call from the writer Jeannette Kupfermann. Her son had been bar mitzvah at the New London a few years earlier. Kupfermann had been engaged to carry out some research for the American actress Barbra Streisand, for a film based on Isaac Bashevis Singer's short story 'Yentl the Yeshiva Boy'. The story is of a young girl who dressed as a man in order to go to yeshiva. Streisand's film had suffered a number of false starts, but she now had the go-ahead and filming would start in London in a few weeks' time. Although Streisand had been researching the part for years, and had engaged the London-based Jewish playwright Jack Rosenthal to co-write the screenplay with her, she wanted a rabbi to be on hand to give advice as the film went into production. Jeannette Kupfermann asked Jacobs if he was interested in acting as rabbinic consultant to the film.

Of course he was. Always curious to learn new things, movie production was something he knew nothing about. Initially his job was to go through the script with Rosenthal, making sure that there were no errors or howlers. Then, when filming started, he sat on the studio set in Wembley every day, checking for inaccuracies in the production. Other than spotting a couple of photos on the wall of elderly rabbis who would still have been youngsters in the year the film was set, he found nothing untoward. But Streisand appreciated his presence; they developed a friendship and Shula made sure that he invited her home for tea. She paid attention when Jacobs remarked on the *shtenders* on the set: large enough to hold a volume of Talmud, a *shtender* is a wooden lectern used by preachers and teachers. Louis must have said that he had always wanted one, because when filming finished a *shtender* was delivered to their home. It was only then that he realized that film-set props are rarely of the same quality or durability as the real thing.

In his autobiography Louis describes Barbra Streisand's reaction when he told her that the *Yentl* story was unrealistic. He told her that women, at the time when the film was set, could get a good Torah education at home without having to resort to the subterfuge of dressing like a man and going to a yeshiva. It is an odd comment from Jacobs which misses the point somewhat. Yentl, the heroine of the film, didn't want to study on her own at home because she was not allowed to go to yeshiva; rather she wanted to be given the same education as a man, and in the same environment. Streisand was dismissive of his comment: the film, she said, was a work of fiction, not a documentary.

WHEN IS A WEDDING NOT A WEDDING?

Nearly 20 years had elapsed since the founding of the New London Synagogue, and Jacobs could have been forgiven for thinking that his days of controversy were over. He had even won a concession of sorts from the Chief Rabbi's office: he was now allowed to officiate at funerals at United Synagogue cemeteries, if the deceased had been a member of the New London. There was a caveat, however: Jacobs could only officiate when accompanied by a United Synagogue rabbi or, as he put it, a 'minder'.

But controversy did break out again, and although Jacobs described it as 'something of a damp squib',[20] in some ways it was more insidious than his earlier battles, touching as it did on the lives of ordinary people rather than on the fundamentals of Jewish theology.

It started shortly after an off-the-record approach had been made to Jacobs by the executive director of the Chief Rabbi's office. He asked if Jacobs would perform the conversion of a young man who had not been born to a Jewish mother, but had been adopted and brought up in a religious home. He now wanted to marry in synagogue. The London Beth Din had told him that, despite his obvious background and lifestyle, he needed to go through a rigorous period of preparation for conversion; they could not tell him how long this would take. The young man was frustrated by this. The Chief Rabbi's executive director, knowing that Jacobs performed conversions strictly within the bounds of the law but without the additional rigour imposed by the London Beth Din, asked if he could help. Louis agreed.

Shortly afterwards, Jacobs heard that Dayan Swift, his old adversary on the London Beth Din, had delivered a sermon in which he castigated Jacobs for performing 'unauthorized' conversions. He began to hear rumours that Beth Din were telling people that if they married at the New London questions would be raised should their children subsequently wish to marry in the United Synagogue. Every rabbi knew that no Beth Din had the right to unilaterally 'authorize' conversions, and that, provided two people were not otherwise disqualified from marrying (for example through incest or adultery), then the status of their children could not be called into question, even if they had not had a marriage ceremony. If the rumours were true then they amounted, not to statements of law, but to what Jacobs would classify as a 'smear campaign'.[21]

It might have been a smear campaign, but Louis's congregants were disturbed. He went to see Chief Rabbi Jakobovits, who he assumed could not have been unaware of his executive director's earlier approach. He got the impression from Jakobovits that his hands were tied and that there was nothing he could do. He decided therefore to write an article in the New London synagogue magazine outlining the position in Jewish law regarding conversions, marriages and adoptions. He insisted that:

> the procedures of the New London Synagogue in matters of personal status are in full accordance with traditional Jewish law. We cannot claim that we have an especially humane attitude because that would imply that the law is not in itself humane . . . This defence of our procedures would not be required at all were it not that Orthodox officialdom is now determined to act . . . with an attitude beside which the Neturei Karta are a model of tolerance and sobriety.[22]

The *Jewish Chronicle* seized on Jacobs's comparison of the London Beth Din with the Neturei Karta, a vociferous anti-Zionist sect within the Strictly Orthodox world. The whole affair, which up to now had publicly been confined to Dayan Swift's sermon and Jacobs's article, was now sensationalized in the *Jewish Chronicle* under the headline 'Worse than Neturei Karta'.[23]

The *Jewish Chronicle* article did little more than paraphrase Jacobs's piece in the *New London Forum*. It didn't explain why he had written it and, predictably, it generated a backlash from those who saw Jacobs's words as an unprovoked and gratuitous insult, unfortunately made worse by the fact that Dayan Swift passed away two days after the piece appeared. Jacobs had not mentioned Dayan Swift in his article, but the subtext was no doubt evident, to those who looked for subtexts.

On 20 September, two days after Dayan Swift died, the Beth Din issued a statement to the *Jewish Chronicle*. Tactfully, the paper did not refer to it in their following issue, in which they announced Dayan Swift's death. Instead, they led with it the following week on the front page and in their leader column.

The Beth Din's statement, signed by the Clerk to the Court, Marcus Carr, declared that:

> marriages performed by Dr. Jacobs, even in cases where both parties are eligible for marriage according to Jewish Law, have no

more halachic validity than marriages contracted in a Register Office, under Civil Law. Conversions under the auspices of Dr Jacobs have no validity whatsoever in Jewish Law.[24]

When asked by the *Jewish Chronicle* to clarify why they believed that Jacobs's marriages had no legal validity, the Beth Din's spokesman, Dayan Berger, replied that in some cases the status of the two necessary witnesses might not have met the requirements of Jewish law. After further questioning he confirmed that 'in cases where the parties were eligible to marry in Jewish law, an invalid ceremony itself does not affect the status of the children'.

The *Jewish Chronicle* took up the cudgels in their leader column. Under the heading 'Jacobs Affair II' (Louis always referred to it as Stage 3), they declared the problem insoluble:

Dr Jacobs is insistent that all marriages which take place under his auspices – and all conversions, too – are totally in accord with the halakha, Jewish religious law. The Bet Din is adamant that neither marriages nor conversions supervised by Dr Jacobs (the reference to 'Dr Jacobs' in the Bet Din statement is unquestionably intentional) are Jewishly valid; However, the Bet Din does make the important declaration that the children of marriages between people 'eligible to marry in Jewish law' are fully Jewish, that is, they are free to marry Orthodox Jews.

The question for the layman is, then, if the children are totally acceptable to the Orthodox community, how are their parents' marriages invalid? The Bet Din will not explain . . . The furthest its spokesman has gone in supporting the charge of invalidity is to refer to the halachic status of the witnesses. These, we know from Rabbi Jacobs, to be himself and his *chazan*. There are many grounds in Judaism for ruling a witness 'incompetent.' The only presumable 'incompetence' which might be speculated in the case of Dr Jacobs – given the history of his relations with the London Bet Din – is his view that the Torah came from God not by direct dictation – each word spoken by God to Moses – but by divine inspiration . . .

How many marriages have taken place under Orthodox auspices where the witnesses could have been ruled incompetent . . . because they were not religiously observant . . . [25]

The Beth Din's statement had been a response to Jacobs's article in the *New London Forum*. Arguably, the whole matter could have been dealt with more diplomatically had he not written the article, or even if he had refrained from comparing the Beth Din to the oft-vilified Neturei Karta. Jacobs's friends, and his detractors, have often referred to him as politically naïve, but this incident can be understood as him acting with a certain amount of guile. He knew by now that public sympathy invariably rested with him, and that the Beth Din could be relied upon not to turn the other cheek when provoked. Dayan Swift's sermon had sparked the affair, but Jacobs turned it to his advantage.

That the Beth Din bore the brunt of the blame for the dispute can be seen in a measured letter written by Frederick Landau. Landau was a friend of Louis and the father of Anna Horovitz, who organized the New London concerts. As an Elder of the United Synagogue he was a man with a foot in both camps. He told the *Jewish Chronicle* that 'the community has been disturbed and mystified by the recent communication of the London Beth Din'. He quoted the President of the United Synagogue, who had written elsewhere that United Synagogue marriage facilities were open to anyone, provided they qualified to be married by the Chief Rabbi's office.

This should reassure those who fear that children of marriages performed in the New London Synagogue will be ineligible to marry in a United Synagogue. Moreover, I am not aware of any case where the parties to a New London Synagogue marriage, who have given particulars to the Marriage Office of the Chief Rabbi, have had any doubts cast upon the validity of their marriage in Jewish law.[26]

If the affair reached a conclusion at all, it was as implied in both the Beth Din's statement and Mr Landau's letter. Despite the impassioned language there had never been any doubt by either side that the children of a mother whom the London Beth Din accepted as Jewish would be eligible to marry in the United Synagogue. This was the case wherever the mother married, or whether she was not married at all.

In terms of Jewish law, the controversy was meaningless, but that did not prevent it from causing distress among those who were led to believe that their marriages might be invalid or their children's status suspect. Nor was it a controversy that would go away. Jacobs may have considered the affair a damp squib, but it would take more than a decade before it was even tentatively laid to rest.

Jacobs was upset for those of his congregants who were concerned about the status of their marriages and conversions, but on a personal level he was merely irritated. There was no doubt in his mind that all his ceremonies were strictly within the bounds of religious law – indeed he would say that his was the more authentic position, since he believed he acted with greater compassion. He may have regretted his injudicious public comparison of the London Beth Din with Neturei Karta, but privately he would have argued that in this too he was correct; Neturei Kara were notorious for their anti-Zionism, and they certainly would have opposed Jacobs's theology, had they given it a moment's thought. But they had no more interest in his theology than in the New London, its marriages and conversions. They lived in a different world.

12

A Mood, not a Movement

Jacobs published three books in 1984. *The Talmudic Argument*, from Cambridge University Press, a detailed analysis to show how Talmudic reasoning operates, was intended as a textbook for both beginners and advanced students. In the USA, Behrman House published *The Book of Jewish Belief*, an introduction to Judaism aimed primarily at young people that explained the key principles and practices of the religion. And towards the end of the year the Littman Library published Jacobs's book *A Tree of Life*.

Subtitled *Diversity, Flexibility and Creativity in Jewish Law*, *A Tree of Life* set out to show that legal rulings by rabbinic decisors are influenced by their attitudes and environment; that Jewish law, or Halakha, is not fossilized in stone but has developed throughout history in the same way as all other human institutions. It was a detailed book that both analysed and illustrated the principles involved in legal decision-making, showed how subjectivity and the spirit of the law acted upon its strict interpretation, and provided examples of how rabbinic authorities had been creative and flexible throughout history.

The book reflected Jacobs's insistence that Judaism was, and always had been, a dynamic system that was not rooted unthinkingly in unsupportable doctrines or in practices that had lost all relevance and meaning. He concluded with a chapter entitled 'Towards a non-Fundamentalist Halakah' in which he discussed the future of the Jewish legal system in the light of modern science, for those who, like him, believed there was a human element in the Torah, that it had not been literally dictated word for word by God to Moses.

Jonathan Sacks, the Principal of Jews' College and future Chief Rabbi, wrote a lengthy critique of the book for the *Jewish Chronicle*. It was, the newspaper declared, 'the first time in these columns since "the Jacobs Affair" broke twenty years ago, a rabbinical response to the non-fundamentalist views of Rabbi Louis Jacobs'. Sacks began by reminding his readers that 'the worst controversy hits the nicest people . . . It is about to again.' He said that Jacobs's greatest problem was to have held his views in England. Had he lived in America, he would have been seen as a tame non-controversial scholar on the right wing of the Conservative movement. But the combination of British loyalty to tradition and the absence of a Conservative movement in England had left Jacobs a 'lonely and tangential figure, respected and regretted in equal measure'. Worse still, because of Jacobs's lucidity, his insistence on saying exactly what he meant, there was no mistaking his intent, or escaping the confrontation.

Sacks was correct in regarding Jacobs's isolation as due to his desire to remain in England. And he may well have been lonely, inasmuch as he had no interlocutors of similar standing within the English rabbinate. But he did not regard himself as either tangential or regretted. He had an illustrious reputation, a loyal congregation and many friends. He corresponded frequently with his intellectual peers around the world and was free to write, think and teach as he pleased. He still believed that the Orthodox world would, in time, come around to his way of thinking, although he made no predictions about whether this would happen within his lifetime. All he really wanted was for the Chief Rabbi, any Chief Rabbi, to apologize and admit that they had been wrong.

Most of Sacks's article addressed the final chapter of Jacobs's book, in which he had argued for a non-fundamentalist Halakha. He presented five arguments against Jacobs's position, little different in substance from what others had said before, but expressed more cogently. He asked why, if the thesis of *A Tree of Life* is that Jewish law has always responded to the needs of the time, does Jacobs fail to accept that the same process continues to operate today?[1]

A fortnight later the paper carried Jacobs's response. He responded to each of Sacks's five points, refuting the arguments levelled against him but, having already set out his position in *A Tree of Life*, barely challenging Sacks with counter-arguments. He only went on the attack once, saying that Sacks allowed 'the reader to gain the impression that he does accept the assured results of modern scholarship . . . but it would have been helpful, in a serious debate, if he had declared unequivocally where exactly he stands.'[2] It was the first, but by no means the only time that Jacobs would speak about Sacks in this way.

There is truth in Sacks's assertion that Jacobs was an isolated figure, but Jacobs always saw Sacks as something of a protégé, as one of the few people who concurred with his position despite never giving any public hint of doing so. Jacobs had reached this conclusion after they had corresponded when Sacks was a student and later when he had discussed with him the possibility of the younger rabbi lecturing at Leo Baeck College. It was as if he wondered why Jonathan Sacks had not been prepared to do what he had done, and put his career on the line for the sake of intellectual principle. It is equally possible that Jacobs was completely wrong, and that Sacks no more agreed with him than did any other mainstream Orthodox thinker in England.

The *Jewish Chronicle* left it to its readers to decide between the two points of view. The vast majority of published letters supported Jacobs. We do not know how many letters in support of Sacks were not published. One correspondent, a professor of history, took Jacobs to task for confusing history with science, leading him to the 'peculiar and disturbing conclusion' that Halakha should submit to contemporary intellectual speculation. Another wondered how Sacks could accuse Jacobs of treating biblical criticism '"as if it were evidence for what it takes as axiomatic". This has a curious ring from any Orthodox religious thinker. What position does Rabbi Sacks himself take? Does he not accept as axiomatic Revelation of Torah and justify it basically by Torah and its message to the world?'[3]

PATHS OF FAITH

In November 1984 Louis was interviewed as part of Channel 4's *Paths of Faith* TV series. The interviewer was Karen Armstrong, a former nun, now at the start of a career that would see her become one of Britain's best-known writers on religious and interfaith topics. Despite his prominence in the Jewish community, and the few years in the 1960s when his dispute with the Chief Rabbi had briefly placed him on the media radar, Jacobs had done very little television, and the first few moments of the conversation appeared quite awkward for both interviewer and interviewee.

It wasn't until the discussion turned to mysticism that their conversation became less stilted. Louis had explained that the Jewish mystics talk about two aspects of God: God in manifestation, who is perceived through the wonders of the created world, and God as he is in himself, 'of which nothing at all can be said. In fact one of the Jewish mystics goes so far as to say that you can't even say that. And in fact, if you want to be logical about it, you can't even say that either.' By now they were both smiling, and the interview proceeded far more smoothly, Louis explaining why for example there were so few women mystics, and what the essential difference was between Hasidism and other forms of Judaism.

Louis's other TV appearance around that time had consequences that he never knew of and would scarcely have imagined. Late one evening, his son David was becoming particularly friendly with a young woman friend. The TV was on, and just for a moment David glanced at it. He was horrified to see his father's face filling the screen, gazing directly at him, presenting the Epilogue; the religious exhortation at the end of the day's TV.

ANNIVERSARIES

The New London celebrated its 20th anniversary with a souvenir booklet and a reception for its members. In an indication that the communal mood had somewhat lightened since the dark days of 1964, the reception was attended by senior representatives of neighbouring congregations, including several constituents of the United Synagogue.

The souvenir booklet, *New London Synagogue: The First Twenty Years*, available to members at a cost of £6 per copy, contained over 300 pages of articles, reprints and press cuttings, documenting the events leading to the synagogue's foundation and its subsequent history. In a brief preface Jacobs noted that its tales 'of battles long ago might seem to some a little negative but, then, as a Hasidic saying has it, the negative can have positive values. To be sure, controversies are painful and should be avoided where possible. Yet, when our spot of bother did come about, it is good, after twenty years, to see that it resulted in a vibrant community looking forward to the next twenty years with confidence.'[4]

The New London's 20th anniversary fell just a few months before the New North London celebrated the end of its own tenth year. Although it had started as a local offshoot of the New London, New North London served an area with a far larger Jewish population and was rapidly expanding in size and vibrancy. The synagogue was now established in its own premises, with a membership of over 200 families, educational classes for the children and a variety of social, cultural and religious activities. It was time, some in New North London thought, to review the direction of the synagogue and its relationship with its parent congregation, the New London.

Writing in the *New London Forum*, Michael Rose, one of the two founders of New North London, noted that the relationship between the two synagogues had gone through several phases, most recently agreeing to hold joint Council meetings annually. This, in Rose's view, had proved to be not particularly productive; the joint body was too large, met infrequently, and was unlikely to produce worthwhile discussions and decisions. Instead, he proposed establishing a 'jointly elected, advisory body with the task of keeping our wider aims in perspective . . . [its] brief should extend to the roles and responsibilities of the two synagogues as they relate to the outside world.' He quoted the sermon that Jacobs had preached when the New London was founded: 'We are not sectarian in outlook and we want to look beyond our own immediate sphere of activity to the wider community of which we are a part and the wider world to which we belong.'[5]

Michael Rose was the chairman of the M'sorati Association, of which Jacobs was the president. Formerly known as the European Association for Conservative Judaism, the organization had been formed to further the Conservative approach to traditional Judaism. Among its priorities were the establishment of new independent synagogues. Rose had introduced his article by noting that although there were aspects of Jewish practice where New North London were more stringent than New London, unlike the older congregation they had not referred to themselves as Orthodox in their founding document.

Michael Rose's article was part of a conversation exploring the idea of establishing a formal synagogal structure for Conservative Judaism in England. They used the Israeli name M'sorati, later to be contracted to Masorti. The name was the Hebrew word for 'traditional'. The question as to whether to affiliate the New North London and New London into a new M'sorati alliance evoked strong opinions on both sides of the debate. The most prominent dissenting voice was that of Louis Jacobs.

Jacobs expressed his views in the same edition of *New London Forum*. Under the heading 'The New London Synagogue – Platform or Movement?' he pointed out that from the very moment of the New London's founding, 'some of its supporters looked forward to, and some of its supporters feared, the emergence of a New London Synagogue movement, a new, exciting trend in the religious life of Anglo Jewry . . . During the twenty years of our existence, the voices raised in favour of a movement have not been silenced . . . Why are we still doing nothing about it, we are repeatedly asked.'

In a rare instance of rebuke, mild as it was, he asked that 'those who tell us what we ought to have done and what we ought to be doing' give some thought to reality. At the outset New London had tried to establish liaisons with other synagogues, and failed. Painful as it might be to realize it, the issues of theology and Halakha on which the New London had been founded were just not of concern to most people. The New London should not underestimate its achievements – 'we are justified in saying that the New London is now on the map of World Jewry, perhaps marked in very small print but definitely there.' And that should suffice. 'The catalyst for a new movement is simply not there.'[6]

MASORTI

Jacobs's stated objection to the creation of a M'sorati movement was based on his belief that it was an impossible dream, that it would not succeed. He did not seem, at this stage, to object to the principle, simply to the practicality. And, when, in 1985, the Masorti Assembly of Synagogues was formally inaugurated, he said that he saw the formation of the new assembly as creating a 'new empire.'[7]

There were now three synagogues in the Masorti Assembly – a breakaway group from Edgware Reform Synagogue had established the third in November 1984. Known as the Conservative Synagogue of North West London, it would later be renamed as Edgware Masorti.

Despite his stated ambition for Masorti, Jacobs was always ambivalent about its necessity. He was naturally perceived as the organization's leading light, he defended it when necessary and never spoke publicly against it. But those who heard him speak regularly could not fail to notice the words he uttered nearly every time he spoke about Masorti, amended slightly from the title of the article he had written in the *New London Forum*. 'We are', he would repeatedly say, 'a mood, not a movement.'

This was not a view shared by the Masorti lay leadership, particularly Michael Rose, Jaclyn Chernett and Louis's son, Ivor Jacobs. Rose and Chernett were committed to creating an alternative denomination on the religious spectrum, traditional but not Orthodox, progressively minded but not Reform. They were ambitious for a synagogue movement that would attract new communities and become a dominant voice in British Jewry. Although it would be closely linked to the Conservative movement in the United States, the British Masorti movement would reflect the particular nature of the local community, providing an opportunity for open, traditionally minded debate and religious observance. Ivor Jacobs was not as evangelical about the Conservative movement; his interest was to promote his father's approach and to remedy the injustices of the past.

Jacobs, however, was ambivalent. His daughter Naomi believes that he was reticent about the establishment of Masorti. 'He didn't want a movement . . . he wasn't a movement man . . .'[8] Jacobs's ambivalence towards Masorti was illustrated when he addressed a meeting together with a leading American Conservative rabbi. A member of the audience told them that he and his wife had just joined a Masorti congregation, but as it was too far from their home to walk, they could only drive to Shabbat services. They did however have a United Synagogue close to their home to which they could walk. They asked the two rabbis whether they should drive to the Masorti service or whether it would be better for them to walk to the orthodox, United synagogue.

The Conservative rabbi told them that although it was preferable for them not to drive, provided they only used their car to drive to the synagogue and return home, then this was acceptable to Masorti rabbis. But Jacobs recommended they join the United Synagogue, because although driving on Shabbat was a fact of life for many people, it was better to stick to Halakha wherever possible.[9]

Jacobs had said that at the time of Masorti's founding he did not think it was necessary. He insisted that he did not court the title of Founder of the Masorti movement, and that to refer to him in that way was historically incorrect. 'If I have anything to do with the founding of the movement it is only because my views seem to be in line with and offer guidance to the burgeoning Masorti synagogues.'[10]

He made these comments in a video that he recorded in 2005, a few months before his death. Most of the video is taken up with his account of what Masorti stands for, a defence of its intellectual principles and his explanation as to why it became necessary in British Jewry. His ambivalence towards Masorti stems from an ideal, which he knew was unrealistic, that British Orthodoxy would consider his views unremarkable. As he had tried to demonstrate in *A Tree of Life*,

Orthodoxy's inbuilt creativity and flexibility should, in his opinion, have led it naturally and uncontroversially to the same conclusions as he. Masorti would be unnecessary because it would, by default, be Orthodoxy. The unsigned entry about him in the 2007 edition of the *Encyclopedia Judaica* makes no mention of Masorti.

He used the video to illustrate how the authenticity he believed Masorti represented would deal with issues raised by the modern world. In 2005, when the video was recorded, the question of women becoming rabbis was beginning to be debated in the Orthodox world. He explained that there was no objection in Jewish law to having a woman rabbi, because there is no such thing as a rabbi in the modern sense in Jewish law. There are laws about how rabbis should respect each other, and there is a need for legal decisors, but the title of rabbi as such is simply an academic qualification that the law does not require. If a man can be a rabbi, so can a woman.

He had made this point 30 years earlier to a young woman who was studying at Leo Baeck College. She was writing her thesis and had gone to his home for assistance. 'There I was sitting there, and he was passing all these books to me, and he suddenly turned round to me and he said: "You know it wouldn't be against the halakha for you to become a rabbi . . ." And he carried on passing me books. And I was just gobsmacked. And I didn't really have a further conversation about it with him.' It was all she needed to hear. Jackie Tabick became the first Reform rabbi in Britain. Although she had already seriously considered the idea, it was Jacobs's apparently throwaway remark that provided her with the impetus. Nor was Louis simply musing; when Rabbi Tabick qualified, he signed her ordination.[11]

And yet, as Jackie Tabick acknowledges, and everyone who ever worked with Jacobs knows, he would never have countenanced giving her a rabbinic job in his synagogue. The New London held fast to an 'Anglo-Jewish Tradition' which, as defined by Jacobs, more or less replicated the way things had been done in the New West End. Jewish law might not have prohibited women rabbis but the Anglo-Jewish Tradition did. And on that subject there was nothing more that could be said.

13

Out of the Pulpit

In 1983 Louis and Shula moved home yet again. This time the synagogue acquired a house for them rather than a flat. Far better suited to their needs, it was the first complete house they had lived in for over 20 years, since they had moved from their New West End accommodation in 1961. A detached property in one of the most fashionable streets in upmarket St John's Wood, 27 Clifton Hill even had an entire floor on which Louis could keep his books. He needed it.

A year earlier, Jacobs had received a letter from George Rupp, the dean of the Divinity School at Harvard University. Dr Rupp told him that Harvard had received an endowment for a professorship in the department of Jewish Studies. They were inaugurating the endowment with a series of four, one-year-long distinguished senior appointments. He was writing to ask Jacobs if he would join them as the Albert A. List Visiting Professor of Jewish Studies for the academic year 1985–6. In that capacity he would offer two courses per semester and participate fully in university life.

Louis consulted Shula and wrote back almost immediately. Three weeks later his appointment was confirmed. He would be paid according to the university's senior faculty salary schedule, or at the rate of his current remuneration, whichever was the higher. He would be provided with an apartment in Harvard's Center for the Study of World Religions: 'a one-bedroom apartment if you plan to bring your wife, or an efficiency apartment should you decide to come alone'. Louis of course intended to come with Shula – it hadn't even occurred to him that he might not; the idea of him spending a year anywhere without her was an absurdity.

When confirming his appointment the university requested that Jacobs send his CV. In addition to his record of employment and education, he listed over 20 universities, in Britain, America, Canada and Israel where he had lectured. He ran out of steam when it came to citing all his publications. He listed 11 books that he had written, then gave up and wrote 'etc. etc.' Neither *We Have Reason to Believe* nor *Tree of Life* was among them.

The two courses that Jacobs chose for the first semester were an 'Introduction to Jewish Law' and 'Principles of the Jewish Faith'. For the Spring semester he would teach 'Methods of Talmudic Reasoning' and an 'Introduction to Jewish Mysticism and Hasidism'. He lectured twice a week, on Monday and Wednesdays, with an option of delivering a third session on Friday mornings.

Louis and Shula arrived in Harvard on 18 September 1985, the day after Rosh Hashanah, the Jewish New Year. Yom Kippur would fall the following week. It would be the first time in over 20 years that he would not spend the Fast with his congregation. He had left the synagogue in the more than capable hands of its yeshiva-educated cantor, George Rothschild, who would both conduct the service and preach. It is evident from a letter that Jacobs wrote to his congregation a few days after Yom Kippur that he and Shula had missed being with them.

He told his congregation about the Yom Kippur services they did attend. They'd had the option of attending Reform, Conservative or Orthodox services and had chosen Orthodox, because 'from the information we received it appeared that the Orthodox services were closest to those in our own synagogue, in form, music and tradition'. It gave him a chance to observe American Orthodoxy close up, and to notice the gulf between the Jewish knowledge and Hebrew fluency of the orthodox Harvard students, and their peers in English universities. Not that this encouraged him to play down his own Englishness; when he was asked to read the *haftara* on the following Shabbat he sang it according to the English cantillation, and not the American. 'They did not seem to mind but I did have an uneasy feeling that I was rather like Bertie Wooster saying things like "Old Sport" and "What-ho" at an American tea party.'[1]

Shula pronounced the highlight of their arrival in Harvard to be the convocation of the Divinity School, held at the beginning of the Academic Year.

> In this beautiful building over 500 were seated, while the powerful organ was playing Bach, the procession of professors walking slowly down the aisle. Jacobs near the front wearing the Harvard red and black robe. All very dignified, to me, as though it were not true. It seemed as though it were a TV film – but at the same time I felt very emotional to think that this was actually happening. At the luncheon afterwards the tables were groaning with the weight of the food prepared! All kosher for the likes of us.[2]

In 1985 the Archdiocese of Chicago and the Chicago Board of Rabbis held a joint commemoration for the 20th anniversary of Nostra Aetate, the declaration by the Second Vatican Council that the Jews of today should neither be charged with responsibility for the death of Christ, nor be presented as rejected or accursed by God.[3] One of the organizers was Rabbi Seymour Cohen, a former president of the American Jewish Conference on Soviet Jewry, the Synagogue Council of America and the Rabbinical Assembly. Louis and Shula had first met him and his wife Naomi over 20 years earlier when lecturing in the city. They had remained close friends.

Also involved in the event was Rabbi Dr Byron Sherwin, a Vice-President and Professor of Theology and Mysticism at Spertus College, the city's leading higher educational institute for Jewish studies. He and Louis had corresponded extensively over the years on academic matters, and he had written to Jacobs a year earlier to advise him that the college would like to award him an honorary doctorate in 1986.

As soon as they heard that Jacobs would be spending the year at Harvard, Cohen and Sherwin invited him to represent Judaism at the Nostra Aetate celebration. Jacobs would be expected to deliver one of the keynote addresses, the other speaker would be Cardinal Joseph Bernardin, Archbishop of Chicago. Byron Sherwin told Jacobs that Bernardin was considered the most viable candidate to be the first American pope.

Louis and Shula flew to Chicago on 25 October, after his Friday morning lecture. They stayed with Rabbi and Mrs Cohen over Shabbat, so that Louis could deliver a Friday evening lecture on 'The Relevance of Hasidism'. He lectured on his *Book of Jewish Belief* on Sunday morning at Congregation Am Shalom in Glencoe, and at 3.30 p.m. at Spertus College on 'Kabbalistic and Hasidic Attitudes towards Maimonides'. Byron Sherwin then took him to his home for coffee and cheesecake before they headed off to the Nostra Aetate celebration at Mundelein College.

The choral celebration was held in a hall, in front of 2,000 people. Jacobs described it as 'organised with American aplomb, actors declaiming from a stage, a procession, soft music and spotlights; all a little Hollywood but quite moving . . . The Order of Proceedings stated that the Cardinal, the President of the Chicago Board of Rabbis and I were to embrace . . . It was the first time I've ever embraced a Cardinal in public. The first time I have ever embraced *anyone* in public.'[4] The two men then exchanged lithograph portraits of Pope John Paul II and Rabbi Abraham Joshua Heschel, acclaimed as pioneers in Jewish–Christian dialogue. In her letter to New London Synagogue, Shula remarked that she felt even more moved than she had when Louis was the Jewish representative 22 years earlier, at the United Nations anniversary in San Francisco.[5]

THE LUBAVITCH TRIAL

The Nostra Aetate anniversary had been a celebration of friendship and reconciliation between two major faiths determined to put the hostility of former years behind them. In complete contrast, and with more than a touch of irony, Jacobs's other major American experience during his Harvard year drew him into a dispute that was tearing apart a Jewish movement best known for its advocacy of love between Jews.

The dispute concerned the mystically inclined Habad, or Lubavitch, branch of Hasidism. Louis had held a fascination for Habad ever since he had studied under the jovial Rabbi Dubov at Manchester Yeshiva. He had written on Habad thinkers, translating the *Tract on Ecstasy* by Dov Ber of Lubavitch, the movement's eighteenth-century leader, and composing a monograph, *Seeker of Unity*, concerning the Habad theologian Aaron Horowitz of Starosselje. He had focused on Habad in his books on Hasidism and reviewed several books on the movement by other authors. Jacobs knew as much, if not more, about Habad Judaism as anyone who was not intimately connected with the movement.

The dispute concerned the ownership of the library that had belonged to the former *rebbe*, or leader, of the Lubavitch movement, the late Rabbi Yosef Yitzhok Schneerson, who had died in 1950. He had compiled an important library of both religious and secular books which had been seized by the Nazis in Poland in 1939, just before the *rebbe* had escaped to America. The library had eventually been rescued and was now kept in the Lubavitch headquarters in Crown Heights, Brooklyn.

Rabbi Yosef Yitzhok had two daughters. The younger married the man who succeeded him as the Lubavitch leader, Menahem Mendel Schneerson. The older daughter also married and had a son named Barry Gourary. When Barry Gourary retired he obtained the keys to the library, removed 400 books and began to sell them to rare book dealers in Europe, netting himself, according to the *New York Times*, in the region of $186,000. When challenged by the Lubavitch establishment he claimed that the books belonged to him. His grandfather had died intestate. Therefore the books had been passed down through the family via his grandmother and mother to him. The Lubavitch organization disputed this assertion; the books, they insisted, had always been the communal property of the movement, in the keeping of Rabbi Yosef Yitzhok as head of the movement, but not owned by him. They took Mr Gourary to court.

Jacobs used to say that his fondness for reading thrillers had made him want to be cross-examined one day in an American court. He imagined the counsel shouting: 'Objection, your honour' to his testimony and the judge replying: 'Objection overruled.' Now he had his chance. The plaintiffs' lawyers called Jacobs, as an expert on Hasidism in general and Habad in particular, to testify on behalf of their clients.

The first part of Jacobs's examination required him to give a detailed exposition of the history and doctrines of Hasidism, and of the founding of Habad. The questions were so thorough, and his responses so detailed, that the transcript of his testimony at the trial could easily be used in a classroom as an informal introduction to Hasidism. Indeed, after the trial one of the Habad Hasidim in the gallery thanked Louis, saying that as a result of his testimony he now knew what he believed in.

Jacobs explained that every Hasidic movement was led by a *rebbe* who was supported by his followers through a system of contributions and donations. Rabbi Yosef Yitzhok, the *rebbe* whose library was in dispute, had been a superb organizer, whose skills had enabled the movement to flourish and grow. He had utilized his followers' contributions efficiently, particularly in the realm of education. It was true, Jacobs agreed, that some Hasidic groups made a virtue of wealth, believing that a *rebbe* who was rich had the independence to excel as a spiritual conduit. Habad, however, did not hold to this principle: unlike other *rebbes*, Habad leaders did not live like princes, 'wearing gold shoes, riding in carriages drawn by white horses'. Instead, Jacobs explained, the contributions made by the Hasidim to their *rebbes* were not for them personally but to support the organization's educational activities. The same would apply to the library; it was unlikely that Yosef Yitzhok would have used his followers' contributions to purchase books for his own use.

This was borne out, in Jacobs's view, by the content of the library. It contained many books that he did not think a *rebbe* would have any interest in reading. Many were secular books, some anti-religious, some even anti-Hasidic. There were entire collections of academic journals. It did not look like a library intended for anyone's personal use. It appeared to be an academic library, intended to be consulted by researchers, not by a *rebbe* who, apart from anything else, would not have had the time to engage in specialised research.

Jacobs said he could only make any sense of the content of such a research library if it had been compiled for the prestige of the movement. It would have made no sense to compile it for the prestige of the *rebbe*. That was not the sort of thing a Habad *rebbe* would do. It seemed inconceivable to him that a *rebbe* would do this to increase his personal prestige, any more than he would buy splendid paintings or tapestries for himself. If he did buy such things, it would be to make the headquarters of the community resplendent.

It was at this point in the testimony that Jacobs achieved his ambition of having the opposing counsel raise objections to the questions he was asked. Despite the counsel never actually shouting: 'I object, your honour' the objections came at a fast and furious rate, and were nearly always overruled.

A chief argument for the defence was a letter, shown to the court, which Rabbi Yosef Yitzhok had written to Dr Alexander Marx, librarian of the Jewish Theological Seminary, in 1946. The letter asked for Dr Marx's asking for his help in rescuing the library and bringing it to America. The defence counsel emphasized the *rebbe's* references to 'my library' and 'books that I acquired'. This was evidence, was it not, that the *rebbe* considered the library to be his? Jacobs disagreed. Not only did the letter also state that the books were the property of the Chabad movement of America and Canada, the phrase 'my library' no more denotes ownership than 'my students or 'my *yeshivot*'.

It would be an exaggeration to impute the Lubavitch victory in the court case solely to Jacobs's testimony; other important witnesses included the Nobel Prize-winning author Elie Wiesel and, for the defendant, the professor of mysticism and Hasidism Arthur Green. But it is true to say that Jacobs's clear and reasoned analysis of Habad philosophy, before a judge who was the son-in-law of a Protestant theologian, Reinhold Niebuhr, was pivotal in deciding the outcome of the case. Whatever they may think of his theology (they disagree profoundly), ever since the court confirmed their ownership as the owners of the library, the name Louis Jacobs has occupied an exalted position in the mythology of Habad Hasidism.[6]

A SETBACK

Louis and Shula returned from Harvard at the end of the Spring semester in 1986, almost 25 years after Jacobs's resignation from Jews' College. Masorti was in the process of adding two new congregations to its portfolio, taking its tally to five. Dr Michael Weitzman, an impeccable scholar of ancient Semitic languages who had been lecturing at the New London in Louis's absence, had been banned from leading services at his orthodox synagogue in Edgware, his rabbi declaring that his offence was 'the closest to lecturing at a neo-Christian church'. In Dr Weitzman's defence the *Jewish Chronicle* columnist Chaim Bermant described the rabbi's attitude as 'punk-orthodox'. On the other side of London, in Ilford, two choristers had been barred from their synagogue choir for taking part in Masorti services, and the Beth Din of the Federation of Synagogues had threatened to withdraw kosher supervision from a hotel if it allowed a Masorti group to hold services on its premises. British Jewry was as reassuringly disputatious as ever.[7]

Louis was on his way to synagogue for the Fast of Av when he felt a pain in his chest. He had been complaining of a feeling of 'knives' in his throat for some weeks, and had felt a bit funny a few days earlier when walking with Shula on the South Downs.

He did not mention the chest pain to Shula. According to their daughter Naomi she was always complaining of his smoking, worrying that it could cause lung cancer, and Louis had thought when he woke up that morning there might be something wrong with his lungs. So when he felt a chest pain he did what many men do and said nothing. Instead he went to synagogue. Following the service he did mention the pain to Dr Ian Gordon, a close friend who had been his congregant since the New West End. Dr Gordon took one look at Louis and admitted him at once to hospital for tests. As he was being hooked up to the monitor he experienced further pains, and he was taken to the Wellington Hospital for a triple bypass.

Louis did not take kindly to the idea of being a patient. The doctors prescribed six weeks' rest, but he was having none of it. Three weeks later he undertook a lengthy walk to attend his granddaughter Paula's batmitzvah at the New North London, and shortly afterwards travelled to Jerusalem for another batmitzvah, this time of Naomi's daughter Ziva. The only limitation that he allowed his bypass to have on his life was that he never again carried a Torah scroll in the synagogue procession. Not because it was too heavy; he would not even carry a miniature scroll. He feared that another attack may cause him to stumble and drop it, an accident to be avoided at all times.

RECOGNITION

In an article that Shula Jacobs wrote for the New London newsletter she mentioned a phone call that came at a particularly inconvenient moment.

> At that moment my two house helps were working, one hoovering the stairs and the other polishing and moving items of furniture. The door bell rings, the builders arrived with a long ladder, to walk up the stairs to the almost cleaned staircase. The telephone bell rings. I take it from the hall, which I do not like to do. My voice echoes from the high ceiling and the caller's voice isn't too clear either with all the activity going on. 'This is the prime minister's office'. 'Oh yes,' I reply. 'Can Rabbi Jacobs take the call?' 'No he's at a luncheon meeting.' 'It's urgent' says the caller, repeating 'It's the Prime Minister's office'. 'You mean the Israeli embassy?' said I. But when I was given the telephone number and extension I realised that it was the Prime Minister's office and was not a hoax.
>
> When LJ arrived home and telephoned he was asked why he had not replied to the special letter from Downing Street sent ten days ago, 'What letter?' 'One asking you if you will accept a CBE. If I do not have your reply by this afternoon it will be too late.'

Jacobs, who invariably replied to letters the same day as receiving them, had overlooked one offering him a CBE 'for services to the New London Synagogue'. The honour was announced on 16 June 1990, just a few weeks before Jacobs's 70th birthday.

A few weeks after the news of Jacobs's CBE was made public, the Oxford Centre for Postgraduate Jewish Studies announced that it would be establishing a lectureship in Jacobs's name, to mark his 70th birthday. Ten years earlier members of his congregation had endowed the Rabbi Louis Jacobs Scholarship in Jewish Mysticism at the Hebrew University in Jerusalem. His academic honours were coming thick and fast. But the CBE was the only major national honour he received.

Jacobs dressed for the Investiture at Buckingham Palace in much the same way as he had been expected to dress for the High Holidays at the New West End, the only difference being that now he was not wearing a dog collar. Shula dug out his morning suit and grey gloves; they hired a grey tie and waistcoat from the gentleman's outfitters Moss Bros. Obtaining a top hat posed no problem – the wardens at New London still wore them for Shabbat morning services. Louis always enjoyed wearing formal attire, and continued to wear canonicals in synagogue long after the vast majority of rabbis had abandoned them. He struck a distinguished pose at the Palace too; the photos of the occasion show him looking as sober and ministerial as an old-school English rabbi was expected to be.

Louis and Shula were accompanied to the ceremony at the Palace by their sons, Ivor and David. The only other honoree present that he knew was Bernard Levin, the journalist who had interviewed him on TV nearly 25 years earlier.

Louis and Shula had attended many formal occasions over the years, most notably the spectacular massive convocations at the Cow Palace and Harvard. But the pomp and ceremony at which the British Royal Household excels, the carefully choreographed entrance of the Queen, 'hatless and gloveless', accompanied by five Guards in fifteenth-century uniforms, far exceeded anything they had seen before. Shula could only say that they 'sat and gazed in awe'.[8]

LAND OF THE HERRING

While he was convalescing from his heart attack, Jacobs was approached by the Religious Studies department of Lancaster University, set up in 1967 as the first secular Religious Studies department in Britain, asking if he would take up a short-term appointment as Visiting Professor. Its founder, Professor Ninian Smart, was now taking a leave of absence. Jacobs, and the distinguished anthropologist Professor Mary Douglas, were each appointed as Visiting Professors, Jacobs's contract running for three years from January 1988.

Jacobs travelled to Lancaster four times in his first term, delivering his lectures in short, concentrated bouts. He and Shula would regularly take the earliest possible train in the morning, in order to arrive in time. This meant that in the winter months he was unable to wear his *tefillin* or recite the morning prayers until he arrived, an inconvenience that he took advantage of when illustrating the importance of time in Jewish ritual. He lectured on Hasidism, Mysticism, Jewish Law and Theology to packed classes composed of students from a cross-section of faiths, but invariably not including any Jews. He seems to have found this absence of scrutiny liberating. One of his students described the three years that Jacobs taught at Lancaster as being 'as entertaining as they were profoundly informative'.[9]

Among Jacobs's class was a devout young Saudi student, recently married. He invited Louis and Shula to a meal at his home, telling them that they would be able to eat the meat, just as Muslims can eat meat from a kosher butcher. He was somewhat crestfallen when Jacobs explained that was not the case but riposted by warning Jacobs not to shake his wife's hand, as 'we are like the Hasidim you write about in your books'.[10]

While lecturing at Lancaster Jacobs received an invitation to deliver a series of lectures on the Talmud at Utrecht University in Holland. In one of her many reports to the New London congregation, Shula explained that the lectures were sponsored by the Catholic and Protestant communities, largely for the benefit of students for the Protestant ministry.

There's tolerance for you. The students' knowledge of Hebrew and Aramaic was incredible. So, with such a kind invitation, we set off for a five day visit to the Land of the Herring. This is really why LJ accepted the invitation. But what happened? Not a herring was to be seen anywhere! We rectified it on our return to Amsterdam airport by buying herrings galore, a hangover from LJ's *yeshiva* days.[11]

As his three-year contract at Lancaster drew to a close the university awarded Jacobs an honorary Doctor of Letters degree. It was presented to him by the university's Chancellor, Princess Alexandra. Jacobs was introduced by the University Orator, who had evidently read Louis's autobiography. After referring to Louis's work with Barbara Streisand, sharing a first-class cabin with Groucho Marx and wearing a cowboy hat while being made an honorary citizen of Texas, the orator described him as 'one of us, having the good fortune to be born and bred in Manchester. In that city he spent a youth in the good company of Billy Bunter and the *Beano*, cricket at Old Trafford, Gilbert and Sullivan, the *Children's Encyclopaedia*, jazz and Edward G. Robinson gangster films.'

The ceremonials drew to a close at a dinner later in the evening, where Jacobs was asked to deputize for the England and Lancashire fast bowler Brian Statham, who had been booked to respond to the toasts. Statham had not been able to make the engagement but Louis kept to the cricketing theme, expanding on the Orator's earlier comments about his childhood days watching the Lancashire team at Old Trafford.

14

Personal Belief

He may have been among the most widely read Jewish theologians in the English-speaking world, but few of Jacobs's books and articles offered a clear and succinct summary of his personal beliefs. His views on the dynamic evolution of Judaism, the flexibility of Jewish law and of the human element in revelation were well known. But not since *We Have Reason to Believe* 30 years earlier had he written a personal perspective on the theological questions that many people consider the most perplexing: on his relationship with God, his understanding of what happens after death, and what it means to be a Jew, one of the 'Chosen' People. A series of letters from the Hebrew Union College, the leading seminary in the United States for training Reform rabbis, gave him the opportunity to remedy this.

The first letter was addressed to Louis at home and written on 27 January 1987 by the long-serving college president, Rabbi Dr Alfred Gottschalk. It advised him that the Honours Committee had unanimously voted to confer an honorary degree of Doctor of Humane Letters upon him. The degree would be awarded in May at the college's graduation ceremony, at which Jacobs was invited to deliver an address.

This put him in something of a dilemma. He had received an invitation from Spertus College to attend a degree ceremony in June at which they too would confer an honorary degree on him. He wasn't fully back to normal after his heart attack and didn't feel up to travelling to the USA even once, let alone twice in successive months. He agreed with Spertus that they would award his doctorate *in absentia* and that he would record a video address to be shown at the ceremony. He also replied to Dr Gottschalk explaining his reluctance to travel at that time.

Two weeks later he received a second letter from Hebrew Union College. It came from Rabbi Dr Michael J. Cook, a professor at the college, writing in his capacity as chairman of the Efroymson Lectureship Committee, the organizers of an occasional series of lectures. Dr Cook asked Jacobs if he would deliver a series of three lectures in the following academic year, or subsequently. The lectures delivered would subsequently be published as a book, 'if deemed publishable by the Committee'.

Louis and Shula travelled to Cincinnati in March 1989. Over the course of four days he delivered three lectures and attended the college's Founders' Day ceremony at which he was awarded his honorary doctorate. He also managed to have dinner at the home of his old friend Jakob Petuchowski. They had kept up a regular correspondence for years, but Petuchowski had moved to the USA shortly after graduating, after which they rarely saw each other.

Jacobs used the opportunity of delivering three successive lectures to summarize, as best he could, the key aspects of the theological conclusions he had arrived at during his career. He chose the threefold theme, drawn from the *Zohar*, of God, Torah and Israel, to discuss problems of belief, the doctrine of revelation and the concept of a Chosen People. The Lectureship Committee deemed his lectures publishable and Jacobs's 28th book, *God, Torah, Israel – Traditionalism without Fundamentalism*, was published by Hebrew Union College Press the following year. A slim volume of fewer than one hundred pages, it remains the most accessible of Jacobs's theological works, the book that most succinctly sums up his personal belief.

A key idea that he develops in the book is Liberal Supernaturalism. He had first used the phrase in 1966, in an article of the same name, as a device that allowed him to categorize his philosophy of Judaism. Now, 20 years on, he returned to the subject. He defined Liberal Supernaturalism as 'that attitude which affirms the being and transcendence of a personal God, while remaining open to the fresh insights regarding the manner in which God becomes manifest in the universe he has created'. Stressing that to attempt any definition of God is by its very nature inadequate, he suggested that a 'personal God' is 'a Being by whom we were brought into existence and whom we encounter and who encounters us. To affirm that God is a person, or, better, not less than a person, is to affirm that he is more than a great idea.'[1]

In his chapter on Torah, Jacobs attempted to defend the traditional doctrine of revelation, albeit with 'a strong measure of revisionism'. He described his approach as Halachic Non-Fundamentalism, which he illustrated as one which accepts the binding nature of the commandments, without conceding that the command had to come directly from God in order to be binding. The fact that there is a human element in the Torah does not deprive it of sanctity or authority.

God, Torah, Israel is a departure from Jacobs's usual technique of presenting his arguments against a historical background, showing that his reasoning is a natural consequence of developments within rabbinic thought. That he chose to use the lectures and book to state a position rather than to present an argument reflects a sense that as he approached his 70th birthday he wanted to be known, not just as a distinguished scholar, but as a theorist with a distinctive voice. He may have believed that flexibility was a characteristic of Jewish law, but he feared that he was being seen as too flexible in himself, as an iconoclast who would instinctively support a dissenting cause. He had made this clear at a Council Meeting of the Assembly of Masorti Synagogues a few months earlier.

Masorti was in the process of clarifying its religious position and the relationship between its constituent synagogues. It had been suggested that a Presiding Rabbi be appointed – it would of course be Louis – who would have sole authority to make religious decisions. Jacobs saw this as tantamount to appointing a Masorti Chief Rabbi and was implacably opposed. But this wasn't his only concern. He was uneasy about the way in which the Masorti movement seemed to be developing as an offshoot of the

American Conservative movement. He was not enthusiastic about the American movement, he declared that it was 'not his scene', he did not share its ambition for global growth and influence, and he did not wish to be associated with it. Nor was he interested in what was going on in the Masorti movement in Israel. He did not want to be called upon to express any opinion on these matters or .to be used to further the development of these movements. Jacobs had realized, perhaps too slowly, that his name was in danger of being used in ways he had not agreed to, to support movements he did not believe in.[2]

But that wasn't all. He also resented the fact that when he explained Jewish law but without ruling one way or another he was frequently quoted as having provided halachic authority for things on the grounds that he had not prohibited them. His objection was not that these practices were being carried out – after all he had deliberately not ruled against them. His objection was that because he hadn't said no, he was being quoted as having said yes. To most people such an attitude might seem quite naïve. To Jacobs, a master of Talmudic logic, it made absolute sense.

Jacobs's concerns about Masorti did not impede his efforts on the movement's behalf. He lectured at Masorti synagogues, and at the regular study events and conferences held under the Masorti banner. Almost without exception, every time he spoke at a Masorti event he would stress the theological underpinnings of the movement, particularly its views on revelation. It mattered to Jacobs that Masorti members were disabused of the literal understanding of revelation, that they should not imagine, as he put it, that Moses received the Torah on Mount Sinai in the same way as the captain of the winning team receives the FA Cup. He would repeat with dogged insistence that his critics unjustly accused him of not believing in the doctrine of Torah From Heaven. He did believe in it, but declared that it all depends on how one understands the word 'From'.

As Masorti became more prominent, and under increasing fire from elements in the Strictly Orthodox world, he defended the movement from platforms and in print, arguing the reasonableness of its position both in terms of law and belief. He may not have wished to be the Presiding Rabbi but whenever the *Jewish Chronicle* referred to him as Masorti's spiritual leader, he did not demur. He might have been uncomfortable about the direction he feared Masorti was travelling in, but it was founded under his auspices and he was not prepared to abandon it, either to the American Conservative movement or indeed to its own devices.

Rabbi Jonathan Wittenberg, who was the only other rabbi of a Masorti congregation at the time, believes that Jacobs's ambivalence about Masorti was a consequence of his ostracizing from the United Synagogue. Jacobs never again wanted to be pigeonholed into promoting the ideology of any religious denomination, be it Orthodox or Conservative. His views were similar to those of the Masorti–Conservative movement, not because it was an article of faith for a particular movement but because he was an empiricist who believed that the truth, from wherever it comes, is the truth. Jacobs would neither put himself in a position where he might be seen to be rejecting truth, nor would he subscribe to a relativist ideology, be it Conservative or anything else. His belief that the search for Torah is Torah itself, explains why, for Jacobs, Masorti could only ever be a Quest – a mood and not a movement.[3]

To further complicate this already complicated picture, there was an emotional aspect to Jacobs's feelings about Masorti that meant he could not simply disassociate himself institutionally while agreeing with them theologically. Jonathan Wittenberg, who had grown up at the New London, recalls Rabbi Jacobs telling him, in a moment of candour, that since he had been appointed rabbi at New North London Synagogue, Jacobs no longer felt so alone. It was self-evident that Jacobs had been isolated within the British rabbinic community: he was an independent rabbi operating in an institutional vacuum. But his declaration that Jonathan's arrival made him feel less alone was a tacit acknowledgement that he valued being part of something larger, and that what he was part of needed to have more substance than just being a mood.

At one point he said to me I feel less lonely now that you are around . . . and actually on one or two occasions I picked up both from him and from Shula a sense of profound isolation. On the other hand he was, in all kinds of ways sui generis – he was a genius, he was brilliant, and he did not want to be put in any other box after he got out of the United Synagogue box, which is why he had a very ambivalent relationship to the Masorti movement.[4]

Jacobs's sense of isolation was not overwhelming. He had the support and friendship of his community, and of his rabbinic colleagues at Leo Baeck College and in the United States. But the one area of the community where he sought recognition was the one area that would not give it to him. At least, not publicly. At heart Jacobs remained a product of the yeshiva world. He rejected their narrow focus and they rejected him for his theology, but the yeshiva was still his world. In an alternative existence he would have been a *rosh yeshiva*, the head of a Talmudic college.

His daughter Naomi tells the story of a family friend whose nephew was studying at Gateshead yeshiva. One day the young man told his uncle that his teacher, a learned rabbi in the yeshiva, had set the students a very complex Talmudic question, and given them a deadline by which to answer. The boy's uncle, Naomi's friend, suggested that his nephew write to Rabbi Jacobs for help.

The young man took his uncle's advice, wrote to Jacobs with the question and Jacobs replied with the answer. When the rabbi asked for the answer to his question, the student cited what Jacobs had written to him, but without naming his source. The rabbi was amazed at the reply and said that only an *ilui*, an exceptional Talmudic scholar, could give such a brilliant answer. He demanded to know where he had got it from. The student had no choice but to say that Rabbi Louis Jacobs had suggested the answer. The rabbi then told the class all about Jacobs, how he had been a brilliant student, and what a tragedy it was for the yeshiva world that he had not stayed.

The boy's uncle related this episode to Naomi, and on her next visit to London she told Louis. Louis said: 'I'm so glad you told me. I got this barmy letter from Gateshead, really barmy, and I wasn't sure whether to reply because it was such a strange question; I knew hardly anybody would be able to answer it. I thought maybe somebody at the yeshiva was having me on. But I decided, just in case it's a serious question, I'd better answer it.'

His disappointment at being estranged from his peers in the yeshiva world was reinforced by regular requests from Orthodox rabbis asking him to clarify a complex religious problem or explain an abstruse piece of law. These requests were invariably accompanied by a plea for confidentiality, with which Jacobs invariably complied. An Orthodox rabbi, who had secretly voted for Jacobs in the *Jewish Chronicle*'s 2005 competition, confessed to the newspaper:

> As an Orthodox rabbi, it is a sad state but I have to keep my identity confidential for obvious reasons. Without Rabbi Jacobs's inspiration I, and I am sure many others, would have lost our sanity having to work within the intellectual boundaries imposed on us. However, I have often recommended Rabbi Jacobs's books to congregants who share the same doubts as I had. His contribution to Anglo-Jewry is immense and will be recognised for centuries to come. It is good to show my support by a secret ballot.[5]

Fortunately the clandestine approaches that Jacobs received from the Orthodox world only occupied a small proportion of his postbag. Most of his correspondence was with academic colleagues, students, religious ruminants and the Jewishly perplexed. A list of his principal correspondents could almost serve as a *Who's Who* of academic Jewish scholarship in the second half of the twentieth century, with a fair sprinkling of non-Jewish scholars thrown in. His files contain correspondence with a hundred or more of the leading academics and authors of the time, among them Gershom Scholem, Jacob Agus, A. J. Heschel, Louis Finkelstein, Jonathan Sacks, Menahem Kellner, Jakob Petuchowski, Isaiah Tishby and Geza Vermes. He also answered queries from dozens of students. One whom he held in particularly high esteem was Marc Shapiro, now Professor of Judaic Studies at the University of Scranton.

Recalling the letters he wrote to Jacobs, Shapiro admits that at the time, 'I did not realize what an honour it was to have a scholar of Jacobs' stature engaging in correspondence with me.'[6]

THREE SCORE YEARS AND TEN

Louis and Shula returned to the USA just a few weeks after receiving his honorary doctorate from Hebrew Union College. The trip was for Jacobs to receive yet another honorary degree, this time from the Jewish Theological Seminary. The irony did not escape him: Hebrew Union College was America's leading seminary for training Reform rabbis, while the Jewish Theological Seminary fulfilled the same function for the Conservative rabbinate. Jacobs, who had been shunned by the Orthodox world in which his roots and spiritual inclinations lay, was instead feted by the two leading denominations that opposed Orthodoxy, denominations that valued Jacobs not just for his humanity and erudition but for the very fact of his Orthodox training; he was one of the few yeshiva-educated scholars with whom the non-Orthodox shared a common scholarly outlook and critical methodology.

His 70th birthday was approaching, the three score years and ten that the Psalmist declares to be the natural duration of a human life. Louis's friends and colleagues considered what they should do to mark the occasion. The publisher Frank Cass, who in 1970 had bought Vallentine Mitchell, the imprint responsible for several of Jacobs's books, suggested that 70 years was a fitting occasion for an autobiography. Jacobs agreed. It was the first opportunity he'd been given, since the controversy broke out nearly 30 years earlier, to compose a full account of his own story. And even though he self-deprecatingly wrote that his life would have been uneventful had it not been for the Jacobs Affair, he contradicted himself by devoting only one-third of his autobiography, *Helping With Inquiries*, to the controversy and its consequences.

Jacobs was more used to writing objective works of non-fiction than narratives about himself. But as Stefan Reif, one of Jacobs's former students at Jews' College, noted in his *Jewish Chronicle* review:

> The book is not written, and will not be read, for its literary merit, its details of the Jacobs family past and present, its generous number of illustrations, or its pen-portraits of Anglo-Jewish personalities, none of which elements is so exciting as to merit unusually high commendation. It is of special significance in that it confronts the intelligent and committed Jewish reader, as do so many of Jacobs' books, with an intellectual and religious conundrum and, for those troubled by it, offers the author's proposed solution to the difficulty.

The conundrum, as Reif explains, is the contradiction between the traditional, pre-modern view of revelation and the findings of critical historical scholarship. The proposed solution is to acknowledge the human element in the development of Jewish thought and practice, 'while maintaining the supernatural idea of God at work in history'.[7]

While Jacobs was marking his approaching 70th birthday by recounting his life history, his academic colleagues were preparing their own tribute in the form of a Festschrift, a collection of scholarly writings compiled in his honour, presented to him but published widely. The book – *A Traditional Quest: Essays in Honour of Louis Jacobs* – was edited by Dan Cohn-Sherbok of the University of Kent, and published by Sheffield Academic Press, as a supplement to the *Journal for the Study of the Old Testament*. The contributors included Rabbis Albert Friedlander and Jonathan Magonet with whom Jacobs worked at Leo Baeck College, Byron Sherwin from Spertus College and David Patterson, President of the Oxford Centre for Postgraduate Hebrew Studies.

The only contributor with whom Jacobs did not always see eye to eye was the prolific author Jacob Neusner, who at the time held professorial chairs in South Florida and Frankfurt. Jacobs had reviewed several of Neusner's books, often with reservations about some of his conclusions. A few months after the Festschrift appeared he received a very angry letter from Neusner, who took issue with a review that Jacobs had written of a book edited by one of his students. The review had been relatively complimentary but Jacobs had referred to one of the contributors as having 'a wonderful name' and taken issue with some of the editorial decisions. 'In the future,' wrote Neusner, 'I would hope you would refrain from reviewing a book about which you obviously have nothing to say and which you clearly do not begin to understand . . . Our crowd has always treated you with respect, which, clearly, you chose not to reciprocate. I thought things were going better for you guys than that.' Some years later Jacobs wrote to a friend that: 'I used to correspond with Neusner but found it all so irritating that I have given it up.'[8]

Like most people, Louis probably thought that his 70th birthday would herald a change of pace in his life. He wasn't ready to retire yet, and was under no pressure to do so, but with his life divided between his synagogue duties, writing, lecturing, family, and the occasional spot of travel, he and Shula were happy and confirmed in their routines. He spent time with his grandchildren, all of whom recall how easy he was to speak to, how closely he listened to them and how he always wanted to learn new things. Noa still remembers how he suddenly developed a fascination for calculus.

> I had told him of a great textbook, *Calculus* by Michael Spivak, that opened my eyes and how easily it clarified the most confusing notions. The next day he went to the library and took out that Calculus book (together of course with his usual dozen other books he would take out . . .). Yes, Zaida at the time was 76 and took up studying calculus.

> Although Zaida was a living encyclopaedia, he always referenced others and double checked. He taught me how to verify and learn. When the *Gladiator* movie was released (I was 20 at the time) we went out with Booba, my parents and brother to watch it at Swiss Cottage cinema. On the way back Zaida and I walked together and discussed the Roman Empire and how much of

the movie we knew was true and what not. Zaida was not 100% certain on the different Caesars' timelines so the first thing we did when we got home was to take out the massive books in his study to check. Unsurprisingly, he was right.[9]

But just like his biblical namesake Jacob, who according to the ancient commentators found himself beset by troubles as soon as he tried to live quietly, shortly after his 70th birthday Jacobs found himself at the centre of a gathering storm, one that he had played little part in creating. The focus of the problem was Masorti, the issue was the contentious question of religious authenticity, and the setting was the fractious local politics of the British Jewish community.

A NEW CRISIS

In September 1991 Rabbi Jonathan Sacks succeeded Rabbi Lord Jakobovits as Chief Rabbi. At his induction ceremony he proclaimed a 'decade of Jewish renewal', calling on the community 'to liberate spiritual energy so that Judaism lives as if it were given new today'.[10] A few weeks later the United Synagogue, facing a deficit for the year of over one million pounds, announced that the businessman Stanley Kalms would lead a nine-month review into the future of the organization. Chief Rabbi Sacks expressed his delight. 'This is exactly the kind of thing I hoped would happen in my first year . . . It will involve research that has never before been undertaken – why people go to synagogue, what their expectations are and their areas of satisfaction and dissatisfaction . . . Only if we know these things can we direct the renewal of our spiritual life in Anglo-Jewry. Until now we've been flying blind.'[11]

Stanley Kalms published his report in September 1992. Among the areas of review was a survey of the attitudes of United Synagogue members towards other synagogue groups. Masorti was found to be 'a very attractive alternative to the United Synagogue'. It seemed, from the report, that to a United Synagogue facing a substantial deficit, Masorti presented a real and existential threat, both spiritually and financially.

This threat was, apparently, nothing to do with Jacobs. His name does not appear anywhere in the document. Rather, the report tended to attribute Masorti's success to the United Synagogue's own failures; a drift towards the right wing, unwelcoming attitudes in synagogue and a lack of opportunities for women to be involved in synagogal management. However, in one place the report did acknowledge that Masorti's appeal was more than just an absence of negativity.

> The temptation to join the Masorti movement, with its traditional service, greater community feeling and equal place for women, provided some of the respondents with deep feelings of inner conflict. Those respondents would clearly remain with the United Synagogue if only it could provide that feeling of progress within tradition that Masorti appears to generate.[12]

The 'feeling of progress within tradition' was the result of Jacobs's contention, illustrated most forcefully in his book *A Tree of Life*, that Jewish law is flexible and dynamic, evolving in response to new scientific knowledge, technological innovation and social advances. It was under Jacobs's guidance that Masorti could allow women a greater part in synagogue life than could Orthodoxy. Even though he disliked being quoted as having provided a halachic authority for things he had not prohibited, it was his desire to find ways to say yes, rather than no, in response to legal queries that made Masorti 'a very attractive alternative to the United Synagogue'.

The Masorti lay leadership, seeing the Kalms Report as an opportunity to articulate their distinctiveness, organized a symposium. They called it 'The US and Us', and billed it as a 'friendly response to the Kalms Report'. The symposium, held on a Thursday evening in January, was to be addressed by the three Masorti rabbis, Louis Jacobs, Jonathan Wittenberg and Chaim Weiner, who had recently taken up a position at Edgware Masorti Synagogue.

Speaking first, Jacobs made it clear that friendship came with conditions. He argued that the United Synagogue had once occupied a similar position on the religious spectrum to that which Masorti now occupied, one that was greatly at variance with its current religious establishment. It was this rightward shift in the United Synagogue's position that had contributed to Masorti's appeal to many United Synagogue members. Consequently, Masorti had offended the right wing of the United Synagogue, which had responded, as on other occasions, by misrepresenting his views. They had accused him of denying the concept of 'Torah from Heaven', whereas in fact, Jacobs insisted, the dispute was not about the concept itself but about what is meant by the word 'from'. The only question regarding the revelation of the Torah was how it reached human hands.

Jacobs then turned his fire on the United Synagogue establishment. He upbraided them for implying that weddings and conversions carried out under Masorti auspices were somehow illegitimate. He knew of children who had not been admitted to Jewish schools because their parents had married in Masorti synagogues. He insisted that all Masorti marriages and conversions were perfectly kosher and could not be faulted under even the most stringent legal interpretation. The United Synagogue's attitude was unreasonable, caused sorrow and hardship, and was an unwelcome and divisive aspect of communal life. Masorti, he said, should make every effort to counter United Synagogue propaganda, continuing to present itself as a voice or reason, moderation and understanding, in opposition to extremism and religious fundamentalism.[13]

It was the most rabble-rousing speech that Jacobs had given for many years. Of course, as with most political speeches he was preaching to an audience of the already converted. As far as the wider community was concerned, nothing changed. Later that year Jacobs was refused permission, for the first time, to participate in the wedding of one of his congregants that was taking place in the United Synagogue. Attitudes seemed to be hardening, not softening.

Jacobs told the *Jewish Chronicle* that 'The Chief Rabbi's office is throwing obstacles in my path. I'm sore that they're not giving any clear grounds for their actions . . . I want a declaration that the children of Masorti marriages are Jewish. The current confusion is causing a great deal of distress.'[14]

Jacobs returned to the fray a few months later, at a Masorti conference in Bournemouth. He cited two recent cases where a United Synagogue congregant had been discouraged from marrying under Masorti auspices, in case it caused problems in future for the children of the marriage. In one case the Chief Rabbi's office had told the bride's father that the principal issue separating Jacobs and the Masorti movement from Orthodoxy is the axiom that 'the whole Torah is the divinely revealed will of God'. Jacobs knew that Chief Rabbi Sacks knew, even if his office did not, that there was no validity in that statement.[15]

Before the formation of Masorti, Jacobs and the Chief Rabbi had maintained a fragile modus vivendi. It was one in which Jacobs was at a considerable disadvantage, but by and large any disputes had been resolved quietly. There were even times when Jacobs's independent status had proved valuable to the Chief Rabbi, particularly in the days when he was still willing to carry out conversions that the United Synagogue's Beth Din were unable to handle. But Masorti's success, identified by the Kalms Report as a direct threat to the United Synagogue, changed the dynamic. The picture was to be further complicated by another row breaking out in the community.

A few days before the Kalms Report appeared, the Jewish Educational Development Trust had published a report on the provision of religious education in the community. It called for the establishment of a representative umbrella body for Jewish education to facilitate collaboration and planning. Among its tasks would be to raise funds to support projects of strategic British Jewish education.[16]

The report's mention of a representative umbrella body extending across the entire community set alarm bells ringing in some circles. Chief Rabbi Sacks, who was President of the Trust, moved quickly to reassure the Orthodox community that this did not imply loosening any of the constraints on Orthodox–Reform relations.[17] The following April he announced that the representative body was ready to be created. It would be called Jewish Continuity. The objects of the organization included 'the furtherance of education, learning and research for the public benefit of all aspects of Judaism . . .'[18]

It didn't take long to identify a disparity between Jewish Continuity's governance and mission. The organization's purpose was to fund educational projects across the community, including bodies, like Masorti and the Progressive communities, which did not recognize the authority of the Chief Rabbi or his role as representative of the community. Yet the Chief Rabbi was the president of Jewish Continuity, with a veto over the appointment of its trustees.

Even so, those who did not recognize the Chief Rabbi's authority did not complain too loudly about its structure and governance; this was after all an organization that was offering to raise new funds for them. Only Jacobs raised a dissenting voice, and not because of the way the organization was governed. He criticized the organization's intense focus on outreach to those who were not connected with the Jewish community. Far better, Jacobs believed, to place the emphasis on those who were already committed to a Jewish life; there was little point, he told his friends, in drawing people in unless the centre was strong enough to hold and encourage them.

Jewish Continuity began to come under sustained fire once it began making decisions as to where to direct its funding. Orthodox leaders criticized its policy of funding Masorti and Progressive activities, while Masorti and Progressive leaders felt that they were being corralled into supporting Orthodox ideology, in order to receive funds.

While the Jewish Continuity debate was playing out, Louis Jacobs and Jonathan Sacks were trying their best to alleviate tension. When Highgate Synagogue invited Jacobs to speak on their premises the Chief Executive of the United Synagogue wrote to Rabbi Sacks asking him to issue guidance, to be sent to local rabbis and honorary officers, advising them 'as to the permissibility of extending invitations to non-Orthodox rabbis'. Sacks replied that although the custom was to not invite non-Orthodox rabbis onto United Synagogue premises 'the case of Highgate was different

. . . under such circumstances I believe discretion should always lie with the local Honorary Officers and the Rabbi.'[19]

Jacobs and Sacks also seemed to be making some progress on the vexed question of Masorti marriages. Rabbi Sacks had received a letter from John Levy, son of Reverend Dr Isaac Levy, who had resigned as minister of Hampstead Synagogue over the Jacobs Affair. John and his wife had married 18 months earlier at a Masorti synagogue; Dr Levy had been among the officiants at the ceremony. When their son was born the *mohel* who had been engaged to perform the circumcision initially refused to carry out the procedure, on the grounds that their marriage in a Masorti synagogue was not evidence that the baby's mother was Jewish. He only relented when shown further evidence of the mother's Jewish status. Later the family was told by a head teacher that they may face difficulties in placing their son at a Jewish primary school because of their Masorti wedding. When Mrs Levy wrote to the Beth Din for clarification of their status in Orthodox eyes, she was told that their marriage was 'no worse than cohabitation'.

John Levy wrote to Chief Rabbi Sacks, saying that 'at no time could I have imagined the nightmare scenario that membership of an independent orthodox community could produce an official attempt to delegitimise our marriage.' He said that he did not wish to make the issue public, but would do so if the situation was not rectified.[20]

Jacobs contacted the Chief Rabbi's Office and arranged a meeting. They met on 9 February 1994. Two weeks later Jacobs wrote to Sacks, thanking him for his telephone call 'in which you repeated what we both and everyone else knows to be true, that the Jewish status of their children is in no way affected by the fact that a couple were married in the New London Synagogue or any other Masorti Synagogue.'[21]

A few weeks later Chief Rabbi Sacks wrote to John Levy, confirming the policy of his Office:

If it can be established that there is no barrier to the marriage of a Jewish couple under the auspices of the United Synagogue, then our Office will recognize the children of such a marriage as Jewish regardless of the Synagogue in which the marriage took place.[22]

It was not a perfect solution, as couples were left with a lifelong requirement to prove there had been no barrier in the eyes of United Synagogue to their marriage. But it was the best that Masorti and Jacobs were likely to get.

That should have cleared the air. But Masorti was becoming embroiled in a new row, in Manchester, a city with a large and dominant Strictly Orthodox community. A small group in the north of the city had begun holding services under Masorti auspices, provoking a fierce backlash from the Orthodox community. Four hundred people attended a meeting to hear a panel of rabbis condemn Masorti. The chairman of a synagogue believed to be considering Masorti affiliation was vilified. The four-year-old child of one family was banned from her kindergarten because her father attended a Masorti service. The *Jewish Tribune*, the 'Organ of Jewish Orthodoxy', styled Masorti a:

> 'New *Magefoh* (Plague) . . . even more insidious than Reform, the Jewishly uneducated an easier target for the 'Masorti' religion than the Reform religion . . .'[23]

Much of their opprobrium was directed, unfairly, against Chief Rabbi Sacks, who was seen as too willing to compromise. Ben Yitzhok, the lead columnist of the *Jewish Tribune*, who was 'convinced he means well', opined that 'once one opens the floodgates of compromise – as he has done – there is no power that can resist the baying for more and more and more'.[24] To top it all, the Masorti journal printed a facetious article claiming that as a result of the earlier conversation between Rabbi Sacks and Rabbi Jacobs, Masorti marriages were now considered kosher.

Coming under considerable pressure, and, like any leader of the fractious Anglo-Jewish community, unable to please all of its sectors at once, Jonathan Sacks published an article in the *Jewish Tribune* condemning Masorti. Avoiding any mention of Jacobs, he condemned Masorti as 'intellectual thieves', and their campaigns as 'dishonest, disreputable and unforgivable'.[25]

Chief Rabbi Sacks had avoided mentioning Rabbi Louis Jacobs's name in his article, but the national press had no such qualms. *The Times, Independent, Daily Telegraph* and *Evening Standard,* covering the controversy with almost as much gusto as they had the Jacobs Affair, all referred to Jacobs as either the founder or the head of Masorti. And although Jacobs, still regarding Masorti as a mood and not a movement, insisted that he was neither of those things, he realized he could no longer keep out of a political dispute that showed every sign of worsening.

Jacobs took up the cudgels on behalf of Masorti. He and the other Masorti rabbis held a day of seminars and lectures in Manchester Town Hall. Jacobs, who delivered the keynote speech to an audience of about 250 people, had no intention of trading blows about the dangers of Masorti to Manchester Jewry. Instead, he took the opportunity to return to the question that had defined his career for the past 40 years. 'I am more than a little fed up', he told an audience in Manchester, 'with being told we don't believe in *Torah min Hashamayim.* We do believe in it, but have a different interpretation.' He accused Rabbi Sacks of causing unnecessary anxiety to Masorti families by hinting that Masorti marriages were not acceptable. 'Our marriages are recognized in Israel, and the children of our marriages certainly can be married in an Orthodox synagogue.'[26]

Over the next few months, Jacobs and the Masorti rabbis held similar meetings in Leeds, Birmingham and across London. But of all these locations, Leeds was the only city where an enduring Masorti congregation was founded.

It is not easy to know whether Jacobs was really as resilient as he appears in some of his correspondence, or whether he just put a brave face on things. In a letter to his friend Alex Tobias he made light of the *Tribune* article, while at the same time poking fun at Jonathan Sacks:

Now for my spot of bother with Jonathan Sacks. He is a captive not only to his Bet Din, who refer to him, so I am told, as the '*boychick*', but also to all the young *frummies* who are, in the main, 'ministering' to Anglo-Jewish communities. They got at him until he was forced to write an article in the *Jewish Tribune* . . . stating that Masorti have severed their links with the faith of their ancestors. He telephoned to me, during my visit to Israel, to say that he did not mean me. But, inevitably, I was drawn into the affair and my old troubles began again. Actually, by now, I am not troubled at all by all this and even treat it as a bit of fun . . . when others commiserate with me, I quote Chesterton, the advantage of constantly being in hot water is that one keeps clean.[27]

Vallentine Mitchell lent their support by bringing out a new edition of *We Have Reason to Believe*, the first for 30 years. Jacobs wrote a new preface, in which he summarized the book's reception and the events that followed. He set himself more clearly than ever against contemporary Orthodoxy, ridiculing the then fashionable theory that the Torah contained secret codes that could predict or confirm world events:

> This results in such weird and wonderful ideas as that the Torah, when uncoded, refers to Aids and to Hitler. This kind of nonsense succeeds only in reducing Torah Judaism to a kind of *Old Moore's Almanac* . . . If Orthodoxy means a belief in the God who plants false clues, the God who gave us our reason but condemns us for following where it leads, then those of us who have been trained to think historically not only reject Orthodoxy but believe that our conscience demands that we reject it.[28]

Jacobs was always convinced that any serious Jewish scholar who had been educated in Western universities could not deny the reasonableness of biblical criticism, and therefore a critical–historical view of revelation. He thought this of the Chief Rabbis whom he had known, and he forcefully rejected the idea that they had the authority to rule on what could not be believed, while not being specific themselves about what they did believe.

> On the personal level, I have been on friendly terms with Chief Rabbi Brodie and with his successors in that office, Lord Jakobovits and Rabbi Jonathan Sacks, though, naturally, we differ on important theological matters. And indeed, I sometimes wonder what exactly these Chief Rabbis mean by *Torah min HaShamayim* since none of them has ever tried to spell it out. It is not for a Chief Rabbi in any event to define Jewish dogmas in Papal fashion. The office of Chief Rabbi has no support in the Jewish tradition, and even the Pope is held to be infallible by his followers only when he speaks ex cathedra. In view of this, it is disconcerting to find Rabbi Sacks implying that I adopt the secularist position, a position against which I have fought all my career as a rabbi.[29]

Unusual as it was to have the preface to a book of theology single out any individual for personal comment, Jacobs's comments on Chief Rabbi Sacks should be understood in the context of how he viewed their personal relationship. Jacobs had known Sacks since he was a young man, had long assumed that they shared similar views and had more than once challenged him to make clear his views on revelation. He still could not fathom why the Chief Rabbi of Britain's largest Modern Orthodox synagogue grouping would not give him a categorical answer.[30]

FIGHTING ON

Louis's friends and congregants approached the controversy differently. They had long felt that, notwithstanding his academic reputation and the high regard in which he was held by the non-Orthodox community, he had never received the public recognition they believed he was entitled to. To them he was more than just a scholarly, humble and caring rabbi who had been badly treated; Jacobs, more than anyone else, personified the unique contribution made by the British Jewish community to national life. Margaret Thatcher had ennobled Chief Rabbi Jakobovits, and it was widely assumed that this was the start of a precedent in which succeeding Chief Rabbis would be elevated to the House of Lords to sit alongside bishops of the Church of England. Yet Chief Rabbis only represented a proportion of British Jews and his friends saw no reason why the community should not also be represented by a rabbi of Louis Jacobs's standing, despite him not having the word Chief appended to his clerical title.

Eleanor Lind, an influential Queen's Counsel and chairman of the New London Synagogue, took the lead in seeking support for Louis's peerage. She collected approbations from other peers, members of the Judiciary, academics, philanthropists, public figures and clergy, both Jewish and non-Jewish. Only Isaiah Berlin declined to send an approbation, describing himself as an ignoramus in matters of Jewish scholarship, so that any sentiments which he might utter would be seen 'as mere formal compliments by a friend and admirer'.[31]

The application did not succeed and Jacobs did not seem to mind. He was nearly 75 years old, and his mind was more on retirement than a new career in the House of Lords. But although he told Eleanor Lind that he wanted to retire, she could see that he was not fully committed to giving up his career, to walking away from the controversies. 'Every time something blew up again, he was fired up again.' Others in the synagogue were reluctant to see him go. After some discussion he bowed to pressure from the synagogue council and agreed to stay on, with no end date set for his eventual departure. 'It is a bit in the air at the moment,' he told the *Jewish Chronicle*. 'I was supposed to retire next July but now I don't know when it will be. We are thinking of the future and we are all looking around for a successor but I like the synagogue, I like the members and, thank God, I am happy to continue.'[32]

Jonathan Sacks telephoned Louis Jacobs on the eve of the Day of Atonement, a few months after his controversial *Jewish Tribune* article. He could hardly have imagined that Jacobs would announce to his congregation in his sermon the next day that he had rung to express 'remorse for the intemperate tone of his criticism' and that 'while it was nice of the Chief Rabbi to make the call it did not mean very much in practical terms'. For all his humility, Jacobs had always been a fighter when it came to intellectual principle. It explains why he had refused to back down in his early battles with Chief Rabbi Brodie and Dayan Swift; it may even explain why as a teenager he was determined to pursue a Talmudic education even though his parents would have preferred him to follow a more conventional route. As he got older he became less and less inhibited about making his feelings known. He told the *Jewish Chronicle* that he had not been personally offended by Rabbi Sacks's article. 'I don't need an apology . . . while I do not wish to start up a new controversy, neither do I wish to let this matter [concerning marriages] be swept under the carpet.'[33]

But he did allow the matter to rest. For the past three years he had been working on *The Jewish Religion: A Companion*, a one-volume encyclopaedia of Judaism, containing over a million words, in which he displayed the depth and extent of his learning in typically effortless, easy to read prose. The book's only serious drawback is that it contains no index, which would have been valuable because many important entries appear as sub-entries of others, rather than as an alphabetically ordered topic. One reviewer wrote that:

There are a number of single-volume encyclopedias of Judaism of varying worth, and one might wonder why there is need for another. Yet only a short glance at Rabbi Louis Jacobs' latest book will convince all that it differs from other works of this genre. To begin with, the breadth of knowledge Jacobs exhibits is astounding. A reader unaware of Jacobs' many publications would assume that one author could not have written all the entries. It is an easy task for a scholar to write banal entries on topics of which he knows only very little, but this is not what one finds in Jacobs's book.[34]

As always Jacobs was even-handed and straightforward in his discussion of the entries in the book. But he could not stop himself driving a point home, even if it was fairly peripheral to the topic under consideration. Under the heading 'rabbis' he devoted several thousand words to explaining what a rabbi was, how the idea and purpose of a rabbinate developed, and the different sorts of rabbi one might encounter. Then he turned to Chief Rabbis.

> According to the tradition, no Rabbi has authority over his colleagues, no matter how learned he happens to be. The British Chief Rabbinate was instituted after the patterns of the Anglican Church with the Chief Rabbi being the Jewish equivalent of the Archbishop of Canterbury, with similar or even greater power over his colleagues.[35]

The entry is not incorrect, but unlike the rest of the article in that one senses in equating the British Chief Rabbi with the Archbishop of Canterbury, Jacobs is letting his feelings override his objectivity. The British Chief Rabbinate was established to fit in with the mores of the host culture. The United Synagogue, the only section of the community under the Chief Rabbi's authority, does not conform to the same structure as the Anglican Church and the question of the Chief Rabbi's powers owes more to the personality of the office holder at any particular time than it does to diocesan seniority. Indeed, in his next book Jacobs conceded that:

> One should not be too scathing about such conscious assimilation to the Christian pattern. Jews, prominent by this time in English political and social life, had a need to show non-Jews they were respectably English.[36]

Jacobs also thought England's Jews should appear respectably English. It was one of the reasons why the New London continued to uphold many of the arcane customs of Anglo Jewry, and why he still wore canonical garb in synagogue services, long after most rabbis had discarded them. But his early yeshiva education had taught him that some Strictly Orthodox groups had their own way of doing things, far removed from English convention and polite sensibilities. So although he was a little put out, he was not too surprised by a letter purporting to come from the 'United Assemblies of the Land of Israel and the Diaspora'. Written in Hebrew, the letter was purportedly signed by 13 leading sages of Orthodox Jewry and stated that it had been publicly distributed in Jerusalem. It was a condemnation of Jacobs, studded with biblical quotations and written with a traditional flourish of poetic abuse:

> Since it is already known and is renowned that the 'Dr' called Rabbi Doctor Louis Jacobs does not believe in our Holy Torah . . . behold we protest against him with all our might and strength. Let our eyes run with tears and our eyelids drop water over the desecration of the divine name . . . 'Dr' Louis Jacobs is like all the demolitionists and destroyers who rose up to uproot the boundaries and against whom our holy forefathers and teachers so selflessly battled. No guidance may be obtained from him. His sermons are sermons of utter heresy. And it is forbidden to read any printed work produced by this person since these constitute demolitions of the young which overturn eternal boundaries . . .
>
> We the undersigned announce a public protest in demonstration against all the untrue and unfounded biblical statements made by Rabbi Dr Louis Jacobs of the Masorti congregation. We therefore openly publicize that Masorti is not a Jewish society and is a danger to the public.[37]

When he had got over his initial astonishment Louis examined the document more closely. It struck him as more than a little suspect. He doubted that the signatories, leaders of insular sects, would have heard of him. He asked his Israeli son-in-law, Sasson, to look around Mea Shearim, the Strictly Orthodox area of Jerusalem where the walls typically carry all sorts of protests, denunciations and complaints. There was no sign of the public protest announced in the document Jacobs had received. When one of the supposed signatories told Jacobs he had never seen or heard of the document, he was certain that the whole thing was a hoax. Who had written it remained a mystery. Louis suspected that it may have been written by 'erstwhile friends, perhaps from yeshiva days, who wished to have me on their side again after so many years'.[38] But that may have been wishful thinking.

15

Winding Down

Louis could not have achieved as much as he did without Shula's lifelong support. According to his grandson Dan, Shula:

> nannied him. When it came to day-to-day stuff he was totally reliant on my grandma! . . . When she would go away to see my aunt and leave him at home, she'd literally cover the house with notes about how to do even the simplest things. . . . One week, my aunt was over, and before we left the house he said to her that he'd like to buy the kids an ice-cream. He picked up a load of cash and asked her, 'Will this be enough?' He had the better part of £50 in his hands!

But Dan knew something about his grandfather that few, if any, of his friends and admirers knew: 'He'd pick us up from school every Thursday and bring us home and spoil us. As we grew a bit older he and I would study a little together but then it was always up to my room for a game of snooker. He was pretty handy with a cue!' Louis, who had learnt his snooker skills on the billiards table at Balkind's *heder*, had taught his grandchildren that religion was a discipline by which one runs one life. Jacobs had learnt from Jonah Balkind that even snooker can have a place within that discipline.[1]

All Louis's grandchildren emphasize the strength of their relationship with him, his ability to listen to them and to respond appropriately. Naomi's eldest daughter Ziva recalls how she used to share everything with him:

> He always listened no matter what the subject was. Offered advice when needed, never judged . . . liked to ask for advice on many things – whether academic or social. Many times I didn't need the advice as his questions would lead me to a conclusion myself. Even today, when I try to work through a problem I try to imagine how he would guide me . . . He loved it when I sang in Hebrew. When I was young I used to teach him the Hebrew songs we learned at school. He would want to know all the words and sing along with me. We would do that again and again, on all of my visits. As I grew older, I could hear him humming the tunes to those songs on quite a few occasions.[2]

Jacobs's unworldliness extended to his use of technology. For most of his writing career he wrote his books and articles on a typewriter and his letters by hand. He had always been a prolific letter writer, almost invariably responding the same day. And now his teenage grandchildren in Israel were on his list of regular correspondents. His granddaughter Noa had written to tell him about her visit to Safed, the town where Jewish mystics congregated in the sixteenth century. He replied that although he had always found the subject fascinating, some of the contemporary goings-on in Safed were sheer superstition, 'the sort of thing that gives mysticism a bad name'. He told her about a formal dinner he and Shula were going to at the Guildhall, in honour of Ezer Weizman, the President of Israel:

> The invitation says that it is 'white tie' which means a tails suit like one sees on films (British). The invitation also says that decorations are to be worn which will give me the opportunity of showing off my CBE decoration (worn around the neck, I think). A cummerbund (whatever that is, has to be worn). . . . *Bubba* has a special dress and will wear her glittering pearls. All very posh and romantic. I wouldn't be surprised if after all this dressing up Ezer Weizman turns up wearing an open shirt and rolled up sleeves![3]

The Guildhall dinner took place as the various religious factions in British Jewry were beginning to line up for what would become their most divisive battle since Jacobs's expulsion from the United Synagogue over 30 years earlier. Jacobs kept out of it – he rarely involved himself in communal politics unless they involved religious issues. But he made his feelings known in private.

The quarrel had begun when the much-loved Rabbi Hugo Gryn passed away. A survivor of Auschwitz and the leading Reform rabbi in Britain, Gryn's had been a powerful ethical voice, both among Britain's Jews and nationally through his broadcasts on BBC Radio 4's *Moral Maze*. When Chief Rabbi Jonathan Sacks subsequently announced that he would be attending a memorial meeting for Rabbi Gryn organized by the Board of Deputies, he came under attack from the Strictly Orthodox community for preparing to eulogize 'a man responsible for influencing people away from Torah'. Sacks insisted that his status required him to attend the meeting, but he wrote a private letter to Dayan Padwa, head of the Union of Orthodox Hebrew Congregations, declaring his pain at having to be present. The letter, written in Hebrew and marked 'Not for Publication', was, predictably, translated into English, leaked to the press, and published in full in the *Jewish Chronicle*.

There was an outburst of anger when the non-Orthodox community read what he had written. Although his letter was relatively mild compared with some of the dialogue that regularly circulates within the insular, Strictly Orthodox world, such as the hoax 'protest' that Jacobs had received a few years earlier, the mainstream community was shocked. The language and sentiment went far beyond anything that English Jewry expected of its religious leaders.[4]

The leaders of the non-Orthodox denominations met, over a period of several months, to formulate a strategy that would counter the influence and prominence of the Chief Rabbinate. They considered the old idea of appointing a non-Orthodox chief rabbi, and they agreed among themselves that Jacobs would be the ideal appointee. But Jacobs had poured cold water on that suggestion some years earlier when Rabbi Sidney Brichto of the Liberal Synagogue first been proposed it. He had written to Brichto:

> There is nothing in Judaism which requires the Office [of Chief Rabbi], and that religious Jews can manage very well without a Chief Rabbi, can be seen from the great American Jewish community, in which Jews of every persuasion look upon the British pattern with an amused tolerance, and would not dream of surrendering the stern independence of their rabbis and congregations. Judaism does not demand it. Why should they?[5]

The dispute was finally put to rest towards the end of 1998 when an agreement was reached between the leaders of the Reform, Liberal, Masorti and United Synagogues to establish a consultative committee that would meet regularly to defuse tensions. A sense of relief was palpable when the so-called Stanmore Accords were signed. Talk of communal unity was on everybody's lips. Jacobs however was scathing. 'Why do we need unity?' he asked at a meeting of Masorti rabbis. 'We are not all the same. A religious life requires challenge and tension. All that matters is that the United Synagogue stop misleading people into thinking our marriages are invalid.'

In March 1998 Louis and Shula made what would be their final working visit to the USA. Louis had been invited to deliver a lecture in memory of the distinguished rabbinic scholar Jacob Agus. Nearly 40 years earlier Louis had won the affection of the Agus children by going shopping with their father to buy presents for their wives. Both men claimed to be shopping-phobic, yet when they came home with identical presents, one in black the other in white, Shula was so delighted that she exclaimed they should go shopping together more often.

BEYOND REASONABLE DOUBT

It was now 40 years since *We Have Reason to Believe* was first published. The book's impact, and the consequences of its publication, far exceeded anything Louis could have imagined. But he was not satisfied. His opinions, which as the book title suggests he considered to be reasonable, continued to attract controversy. He was prepared to defend his position, but to do so he needed to feel that he had presented his case in the best possible way. So he reacted enthusiastically when Collette Littman of the Littman Library suggested he write a sequel, a reappraisal, or perhaps even an updating, of his views.

Jacobs intended to call the book *On Reason and Belief*, and indeed when it first appeared in the publisher's catalogue that was its title. But the Littman Library editors did not think it particularly commercial, and their aversion to it increased when a *Jewish Chronicle* reporter, misinterpreting the Manchester accent that Jacobs never lost, trailed it as '*Unbelief and Reason*'. When the book finally appeared it was called *Beyond Reasonable Doubt*.[6]

He began the book with a summary of the historical background to the Jacobs Affair, explaining that *We Have Reason to Believe* had its origins in the study group he conducted in the New West End Synagogue during the 1950s, a synagogue whose Orthodoxy at the time was of a wholly different character to that of today.

> I recall that when I paid a courtesy visit to Ephraim Levine after my election, he quite casually offered to give me his set of the International Critical Commentaries, a series based entirely on biblical criticism in the modern vein, to help in the preparation of my sermons. It was taken for granted by my predecessor that I would find nothing shocking in this, as, by this time, indeed I did not . . . If I had given expression to my views in what now passes for Orthodoxy in Anglo Jewry, even in the New West End synagogue, it would have been thoroughly dishonest. It was neither deceitful nor disloyal to what passed for Orthodoxy in this unique synagogue.[7]

It is an assertion which seems to imply that it would be dishonest were he to try to persuade contemporary Orthodoxy to consider his views. Yet a few pages later, when discussing the hoax 'protest' he'd received, he expressed the hope that the book would help those of his former friends in the Haredi community to grasp what he had been trying to say.

Unsurprisingly, *Beyond Reasonable Doubt* pays far greater attention to the question of revelation and the doctrine of *Torah min Hashamayim* than did *We Have Reason to Believe*. It was Jacobs's views on revelation, on the authorship of the Torah and the validity of the scientific method of biblical criticism that had caused all his problems, his 'spot of bother' as he called it. The theological discussions in *We Have Reason to Believe* of topics like Pain, Faith and the Afterlife were relatively uncontroversial. They did not strike at the fundamentals of Orthodox belief. But neither, in *We Have Reasonable Doubt*, did he harness biblical criticism to support his views to the same extent as he had done in the earlier book. Forty years had passed, and he had integrated his theology under the broad heading of Liberal Supernaturalism. *Beyond Reasonable Doubt*, which opens with him declaring its thesis to be the interpretation of traditional Judaism to show its compatibility with modern scientific research, ends with him writing: 'this book has sought to defend the theological position of liberal supernaturalism . . . I have tried, in this book, to show why I still have reason to believe in a personal God and in Torah from Heaven, provided that this latter doctrine is understood in a non-fundamentalist way.'[8]

Beyond Reasonable Doubt was the last book on theology that Jacobs would write. He had said all that he had needed to say on the subject, and he still had other topics he wanted to write about, despite his other duties beginning to weigh upon him. One of his congregants had been appointed Lord Mayor of Westminster, and Jacobs had agreed to be his chaplain, a largely ceremonial role but one which involved him addressing civic ceremonies at both Westminster Abbey and Westminster Cathedral. He continued to lead his Monday evening Talmud class, spoke regularly at Masorti events and seminars, and accompanied an increasing number of his now elderly, founder members to their final resting place. He was still delivering weekly sermons and reading from the Torah at New London, his voice far weaker than it had once been. Congregants started to express their frustration. It really was time for Louis to face up to the question of retirement.

RETIREMENT

On 3 September 1999 the *Jewish Chronicle* carried an article headed 'Jacobs retires – again'. It was the third time in the past five years that his retirement had been announced.[9]

Louis had always been conflicted about retiring. The synagogue had been founded for him, he had always felt a duty to remain as its rabbi, and he considered that duty to be reciprocal. Rather like a Hasidic rabbi, he regarded the New London as his synagogue; according to several of his long-standing members he sometimes felt that when he was no longer able to work, there would be no reason for the synagogue to continue.[10]

But he was also conscious of new voices in his congregation, people who had joined many years after the founding of the synagogue, who wanted a younger rabbi, one capable of creating a more vibrant community, with more children, rather than one that, 40 years later continued to reflect the New West End of the 1950s. They made their feelings known, arguing that Rabbi Jacobs should give fewer sermons, and enable other rabbis, guest speakers and candidates for his job to speak in his place. Few people outside of the family were aware of the pressure that Louis felt at the time, and the hurt he was experiencing.

The hurt was compounded by a feeling that he had always acted in the best interest of his members even if not necessarily his own. He told Anne Cowen, who chaired the synagogue as he retired, that he would have liked to have made changes to the New London service but felt constrained because so many founder members wanted to hold fast to their New West End traditions. From this perspective, Jacobs's self-defined role as guardian of the old Anglo-Jewish tradition was due to his profound sense of duty to his congregants.

It was his conflict over retirement that had already twice led him to remain in post even after announcing that he was to step down. In 1994 he had bowed to pressure from the synagogue council to remain. Four years later he told the then chairman Eleanor Lind that the forthcoming high holiday services would be his last.

'This time it's for real', the *Jewish Chronicle* was told. Finally, in September 1999 he swung open the door to his rabbinic enclosure for what he thought would be the last time and took a seat in the pews. He became, in his own mind, just another congregant.

Jacobs had always been adamant that when he retired he would not subject his successor to the treatment he had experienced as a young rabbi at the New West End, where his predecessor had made his displeasure audibly known whenever Jacobs said something from the pulpit that he did not agree with. But at the age of 80 Jacobs found this resolution harder to keep than he had imagined. St John's Wood was not richly endowed with synagogues. The only one within reasonable walking distance of his home was a United Synagogue, and although he had many friends there and a good relationship with the incumbent rabbi, Dayan Ivan Binstock, it was also where Chief Rabbi Sacks prayed regularly. Neither he nor they would have felt comfortable had he turned up there.

So when the New London head-hunted Rabbi Chaim Weiner, formerly of Edgware Masorti, to become their new rabbi, Jacobs was in the congregation. And, rather like Reverend Ephraim Levine, his predecessor at the New West End, Jacobs found the experience very difficult to bear. Jacobs was quite hard of hearing by now, and his sotto voce travelled far further than he realized. He could not help disclosing his feelings about the new regime to his neighbour, commenting and grumbling more loudly than he was aware. It was not an easy experience for the new rabbi. Nor was it easy for Jacobs, or indeed his congregation.

Chaim Weiner is gracious about those times. 'It was a difficult time' he admits.

I have always been very forgiving towards Louis Jacobs. He was already an old man and it got the better of him. A lot of different factors came together. He was a great academic and a great scholar, a wonderful pastoral rabbi. He knew people's names, and he knew people's lives and he was interested in people's lives but, in my understanding, he wasn't really a community rabbi, in the sense of understanding how communities function and managing them. Louis should have been at the spot in his career where he was thinking about retirement and thinking about continuity and thinking about his legacy: the things that I built during my career, how do I see them continuing? And I think it was beyond him to think in those type of terms. What he wanted to be was the rabbi of New London Synagogue until his dying day.[11]

Louis admitted as much in a reflective letter that he wrote over a year after his retirement. 'It caused me pain', he wrote, 'that when I eventually announced my intention to retire, hardly any of my friends urged me to stay on for as long as I was able to adequately function.'

Louis's hurt was not just that he was urged to retire before he was ready. He felt that 'there should have been a more dignified send off than an 80th birthday present, the funding of which was put forward in an unworthy form as a veritable charitable appeal.' He resented the suggestion that the synagogue was in decline, 'as if I were somehow to blame. The solution was to engage in a dumbing down of the synagogue with all kinds of gimmickry . . . a conversion of a sound philosophy of questing into . . . clap-happy services. I have been obliged to see the noble edifice we all originally built suffer a virtual demolition.'[12]

Louis Jacobs turned 80 in July 2000. *The Times* ran a full-page profile on him. Headlined 'A Quietly Independent Rabbi', it described him as the 'prime mover of a new Jewish movement, the Masorti'. A few weeks later the Anglo-Jewish Association hosted a reception for him at the Royal College of Physicians in Regent's Park. Along with the dozens of personal invitations sent to friends, family and communal figures, the Association advertised the reception in the *Jewish Chronicle*. Tickets cost £25 each.

To mark Jacobs's birthday his supporters once again nominated him for a peerage. His congregant Lord Basil Feldman told him that it would be difficult, as there were over 2,000 applications for only eight places. Anne Cowen wrote to the Appointments Commission telling them that Jacobs had been 'most reluctant to nominate himself as required by the House of Lords Appointment Commission as it goes totally against his lifelong behaviour of intense modesty and of not seeking public recognition. In fact, he quoted a rabbinic saying to me "that a man should not praise himself and should let others do it for him".[13] It was an interesting aphorism for Jacobs to quote. There was certainly a side of him that did crave recognition, and his emphasis was almost certainly as much on the second half of the sentence as the first. His conflict between pride and humility preferred others to seek his recognition for him.

In this case however he had no choice; the selection process did not allow others to apply on his behalf. He was eventually persuaded to submit an application, citing four members of the House of Lords as referees:

> I am an author of over 40 books and over 1,000 articles and have served as a visiting professor at Harvard University and have been a pulpit rabbi in Anglo-Jewry for over 50 years, during which time I have been in close contact with a wide variety of people from every walk of life. In 1999 I served as chaplain to the Lord Mayor of Westminster and preached at Westminster Abbey and Westminster Cathedral. I was one of the invitees to A Celebration of Achievement for people who have made their mark in this country, hosted by the Lord Mayor of London in 1999, in the presence of Her Majesty the Queen. I am considered to be a veteran rabbi and scholar by the Jewish and general communities. I therefore believe that if my recommendation is accepted I shall be a suitable non-party peer with a worthwhile contribution to make.[14]

For Jacobs, though, the most important event of the year in which he turned 80 had nothing to do with the press, pomp or partying. He marked the occasion with a second edition of his book *Tree of Life*, in which he had tried to demonstrate that flexibility, creativity and diversity were essential elements in the development of Jewish law. In his preface to the new edition he argued that it was the final chapter of the original edition that had caused offence. Entitled

'Towards a Non-Fundamentalist Halakha' the chapter had argued that there should be a more dynamic approach to contemporary halachic decision than in the past. Reviewing the book in the Orthodox journal *Le'ela*, Rabbi Jeremy Rosen took Jacobs to task for being too prescriptive in his approach, in trying to project change onto an Orthodox world that was not ready for it. There was nothing wrong with academic analysis of halachic reasoning, but 'nor is this a matter, as Jacobs suggests of "either or", having to stay Orthodox and keep quiet or open your mouth and suffer alienation. It is a matter of going from description to prescription. Jacobs ended up fronting a polemic. It is the clarion call for change that is the problem. Not the analysis.'[15]

Rosen's argument was fair, but perhaps the most significant aspect of his review was the publication it appeared in. *Le'ela* was the house journal of Jews' College, the institution from which Jacobs had resigned in disappointment all those years earlier, the genesis of his ostracisation. The fact that a Jews' College publication was now able to review a book of his suggested, possibly, that some sort of progress towards reconciliation had occurred.

BOURNEMOUTH

But not much progress. Any suggestion to the contrary was refuted by an incident in Bournemouth that upset everybody in Jacobs's circle of friends and family, other, apparently, than Jacobs himself.

It was July 2003, the week before Louis and Shula's granddaughter Paula was to get married. As is traditional, David, her husband to be, was to be called up to the Torah reading at the Shabbat morning service in his home synagogue. David's parents lived in Bournemouth and the whole Jacobs family travelled there for the weekend.

There was no obligation on the part of the synagogue to call up anyone other than the bridegroom to the Reading of the Torah, but it is customary for other people from both sides of the family to be given honours. It was assumed, by those who did not know, that Jacobs would be called up to the Torah; it was the normal way of showing respect to an elderly visiting rabbi, particularly one who was not only the bride's grandfather but was celebrating his 83rd birthday that day, the anniversary traditionally known as a 'second bar mitzvah'.[16] But the minister of the synagogue, a friend of Jacobs, a reasonable man on the tolerant wing of Orthodoxy, felt he had to play it safe. He rang Louis to tell him that he had contacted the Chief Rabbi's office to check that he could give Jacobs the honour. He told him that he had been instructed not to call him up.

Louis was phlegmatic: he had been shunned for years, nothing had changed. The family disagreed, Paula's father Ivor telling the *Jewish Chronicle* that 'the community is being held by the power of the Beth Din. The sooner reasonable people recognise that their organization is behaving in this unacceptable manner, the better.' The Chief Rabbi's spokesman said that it was not the policy for synagogues under his jurisdiction to call up non-Orthodox rabbis. They were comfortable that they had complied with the Stanmore Accords, in which there was 'no expectation that non-Orthodox ministers will participate in Orthodox services'.

Once again, Louis found himself at the centre of a communal row. It was not as fierce as in earlier years but it bolstered the letters pages of the *Jewish Chronicle* for weeks. Paul Shrank, a former chairman of Masorti and a signatory to the Stanmore Accords, wrote an article calling on Masorti to withdraw from the agreement. Listing several recent episodes that seemed to contravene the terms of the agreement, culminating in 'the disgraceful disrespect shown to our learned teacher Rabbi Dr Louis Jacobs', Shrank declared that: 'The dialogue with the US has been a dialogue of the deaf, and the spirit in which we signed the Stanmore Accords has been dissipated. The US has been, and continues to be, in breach, by not producing a rabbinical representative at the consultative committee.'

Jacobs did not involve himself in the dispute. He would not let it overshadow Paula's wedding. She recalls how, in the run-up to the wedding, she and David studied passages of the Talmud with him:

Some to do with marriage but some just based on our own interest. It still astounded me that he knew so much without needing to refer to the text . . . It was as special to have him address us at our wedding as it was at my Batmitzvah (although I doubt I was as appreciative of it first time around!) . . . After our wedding and especially after my *Booba* became unwell and housebound, we would continue our learning with him, but we would pick up fish and chips on the way there and eat with him in their poky little kitchen, before we studied.

I used to love sitting in his study, whilst he worked, reading or drawing. He always had anecdotes to share, stories to tell and took great interest in whatever I was doing. Not only was he a great philosopher, but a great appreciator of literature and English Literature was always my favourite subject at school. His knowledge of literature was almost as good as his theology and he had plentiful quotes to share with me on that subject too. The smell of his study and his pipe is still there when we open the chest of drawers that we inherited from them.

People often asked and continue to ask me what it was like to have him as my grandfather. Although I understood his importance in Anglo-Jewry and loved and hated those involved in 'his story' in equal measure, and was able to call him up with a halachic question, to help with my homework, to read through my finals essay, to pluck a quote out of thin air that would support my argument (a thing I really miss being able to do now), he was ultimately just 'my *Zaida*'.[17]

FRIENDS OF LOUIS JACOBS

Louis learnt about computer technology late in his career. The first book that he wrote using a word processor rather than a typewriter was *The Jewish Religion: A Companion*, published in 1995. A few years later he discovered the power of the internet when, in the course of a discussion, his son Ivor interjected with some unexpected new information he had just looked up. With Louis now curious about possibilities that the internet offered, Ivor pointed out the potential of having a website that would serve as an archive for all his publications and lectures. It would allow him to disseminate his existing work to a wider audience, and he could add new material freely.

Louis was enthused by the idea. He realized that it would allow him to reach audiences who generally did not attend Masorti events and had limited exposure to his ideas. He believed it would inspire the more observant to consider questions of theology. A website would also help inform readers in the United Kingdom about books he had published in the USA; it had long niggled him that his books published in one country were rarely promoted overseas. He and Ivor agreed that the website should come under the umbrella of a wider initiative, Friends of Louis Jacobs, that would propel into the digital age the educational agenda that Jacobs had begun after leaving Jews' College, in his Society for the Study of Jewish Theology.

Over the next few months Jacobs began recording videos to go onto the site. Ivor digitized Jacobs's extensive archive of publications and documents, sought out and uploaded historical material, reprinted those of Jacobs's books which had ceased publication and created an online bookstore. He instituted a programme of events, as Jacobs had done with his Society for the Study of Jewish Theology with the aim of stimulating discussion within the community.[18] Friends of Louis Jacobs continues to promote Jacobs's ideas and works, and is used widely as an essential scholarly archive.

Vallentine Mitchell published two more books by Jacobs at the end of 2004. They were the last books he would write. *Jewish Preaching* was a collection of homilies structured around the weekly Torah reading. As he rarely preached from notes in the synagogue and therefore had no record of what he had said, he loosely based the contents of the book on the 'sermonic ideas' he had published in journals and the *Jewish Chronicle* during the course of his career. Shula and he were now great-grandparents three times over and he dedicated the book to his 'lovely little great-granddaughters, Ella and Hannah Lucie Jacobs and Jordan Hannah Green'.

In his preface Jacobs explained the difference between a homily and a sermon.

> The sermon is more personal, more spontaneous, has greater flexibility and is far more direct than the homily; naturally so since, in the sermon, a live audience is addressed. Every preacher is aware that he is speaking face to face with his congregation. . . . A yawn or a sense that he is boring . . . is sufficient to throw him off his stride. A touch of humour, even an occasional joke, is essential if he is to hold their interest. An element of passion is also an integral part of the sermon, though this can be overdone all too easily. 'What will happen if he gets out?' as the little girl remarked to her mother when listening to a fiery preacher, gesticulating in a high, enclosed pulpit . . .
>
> A homily is more formal, more structured and more contrived. When it is on a Scriptural verse it should come close to Biblical exegesis, albeit in subjective rather than objective form. . . . The homilist is saying something like this: 'It seems to me, from my own experience and from my study of the Torah, that the following idea or ideas can be extrapolated from the verse so as to bear a contemporary significance.'[19]

Shortly after *Jewish Preaching* appeared, Vallentine Mitchell published *Their Heads in Heaven*, a collection of Jacobs's essays on Hasidism. Subtitled *Unfamiliar Aspects of Hasidism*, the book contained articles previously published elsewhere but which he had now revised, and in some cases updated.

Rabbi Louis Jacobs was an immaculately rational thinker. Yet, somewhat paradoxically, throughout his scholarly career he had shown a keen interest in Hasidism and Kabbalah, the mystical aspects of Judaism. He insisted in the preface to *Their Heads in Heaven* that his approach was 'purely phenomenological. I am neither a Kabbalist nor a Hasid but try to be an objective student of mystical phenomena and the mystical approach in traditional Judaism.' But for those who knew him this wasn't the full story.

Jacobs was a rationalist who saw wonder in the universe and perceived the boundaries of rational thought. Although he was no kabbalist, and never engaged in mystical activity, neither did he reject its validity.

His pupil Rabbi Jonathan Wittenberg points out that on the door of Jacobs's study he kept a picture of Rabbi Yitzchok Dubov, the Hasid who had taught him at Manchester Yeshiva, the man who had inspired his fascination with Hasidism and mysticism. He believed firmly in the supernatural aspects of Judaism, in God, in the idea of the revival of the dead. Towards the end of his life he told Jonathan that he wished he had spoken to more people about these subjects.

SHULA

Louis and Shula celebrated their 60th wedding anniversary in March 2004. It was almost Passover and the whole family went to Israel to celebrate the anniversary and festival. For Louis and Shula it was a rare opportunity to be with all their grandchildren at the same time. Naomi watched with a mixture of pride and astonishment as an encounter took place between her son Michael and her father:

> Michael was then in the Israeli army and from afar in the hotel I could see my dad and him having quite a heated discussion about religion and politics. Then I saw them hug each other. Afterwards, they both told me that Michael had suddenly apologised saying, 'Zaida, I think I was being disrespectful by arguing with you. I am really sorry'. To which dad replied that there was no greater pleasure for a grandfather than to have such a good and lively discussion with a grandson.

Louis Jacobs returned to his pulpit at the New London for a few months at the beginning of 2005. Rabbi Chaim Weiner had departed and Jacobs agreed to fill in while the synagogue searched for a successor. But even though he began his first sermon with

a cheery 'I'm back!', things were not the same. His sense of hurt
had barely dissipated, and to make things far worse, Shula had
fallen ill a few months earlier.

Shula's illness was protracted and debilitating. Towards the
end she required constant care. The Jacobs family, always close,
rallied round to support her, David even moving back home for
reassurance. They engaged a full-time carer, Lisa, to look after
her, and of course to take care of Louis, who had always been so
dependent upon her.

When Jacobs had first retired Shula had vowed she would teach
him how to make a cup of tea, and boil an egg, but he needed far
more than that. It wasn't until some months later that the family
realized that while Shula was declining Louis had also been in
the early stages of oesophageal cancer. He had complained of not
feeling well, but the doctors had not found anything. As far as he
was concerned, he said he didn't care too much about his body
as long as he still had his mind. Anyway, Shula's need was more
pressing than his.

Shula passed away on 12 November 2005. She was 83 years old.
She and Louis had been married for 61 years. He had written her
a poem every birthday. As her final days dawned Shula is reported
to have said: 'Don't worry about Louis. He needs me too much. He
won't be far behind.'

Five weeks before Shula died the *Jewish Chronicle* had launched
a poll to mark the 350th anniversary of the readmission of the Jews
to England. The idea was to determine who had been the greatest
British Jew of the past three and half centuries. They could have
just asked Shula.

Over the course of the next few weeks the *Jewish Chronicle*
profiled various candidates who they believed were credible
contenders, at the same time assuring their readers that they were
free to nominate their own choices. Each week they focused on
a different category of candidate: sportsmen, artists, politicians,
business people, community workers, philanthropists and of course
rabbis. Jacobs was the only candidate in the rabbinic category who
was still alive.

His congregation realized that this was the moment they unwittingly had been waiting for. It was generally accepted that in terms of his intellect and scholarship Jacobs stood head and shoulders above every other religious thinker in the community, and all who knew him recognized his deep faith, good nature and humility. But these were mere opinions; at no point in his lengthy career had he ever received a title or accolade from the Jewish community that was in any way appropriate, in the eyes of his supporters, to his status. At this moment in his life, they reasoned, with Louis elderly and increasingly frail and his beloved Shula in terminal decline, what greater garland could be bestowed upon him than the title of Greatest British Jew? Even if it didn't have the quite the same cachet as a peerage.

And so, in their understated, Anglo-Jewish way, the members of New London Synagogue quietly encouraged each other to vote for Louis.

When the results were in it was apparent that Jacobs would have won the title even without the support of the New London membership. He polled twice as many votes as the runner-up, the nineteenth-century philanthropist Sir Moses Montefiore. *The Times* reported that even the *Jewish Chronicle*'s staff were surprised by the scale of his victory.[20]

It was a vindication for Jacobs that would have been far sweeter had Shula lived to share the moment. As it was, it left him feeling 'embarrassed, overwhelmed and quite daft . . . there is an element of the comical in the whole attempt to discover the greatest British Jew . . .' No small part of his embarrassment was that he had polled many more votes than Rosalind Franklin, the late daughter of his early supporter Ellis Franklin, whose discovery of the double-helix structure of the gene had arguably done more for the good of humanity than any amount of theology.

Jacobs, typically, tried to resolve his discomfort logically. He set himself the problem of analysing what was in the mind of those who arranged the poll, and what the title Greatest British Jew actually designated. Clearly, he argued, British Jew did not necessarily mean someone who was born in Britain – Rabbi

Hugo Gryn had not been. As for Jew, this could only be an ethnic, and not a religious description, as Disraeli had been converted to Christianity as a child. The crux of the problem therefore lay in the definition of Greatest. How would one define greatness when comparing Rabbi Hugo Gryn with Sir Moses Montefiore? They were both great but in different senses. It was, he said, like comparing Picasso with Mozart; contrasting unlike with like. He quoted a Tony Hancock sketch, in which Hancock appears with a painting and a violin. 'I did very well,' said Hancock, 'I bought a Rembrandt and a Stradivarius. But the trouble was, the painting was by Stradivarius and the violin was by Rembrandt.'

Since the whole thing was so daft, he wondered whether he should have gone along with it, or should he have repudiated it, saying: 'It is not me'? But, he decided, that would have been even more daft. 'To repudiate nonsense as if it were sanity would be absurd. So I had to go along with it.'

But he did see a positive side to his victory. It vindicated his Anglo-Jewish approach to religion:

> There is a certain urbanity, a certain tolerance, a certain understanding of the meaning of religion and religious life that is typical of Anglo-Jewry . . . We do no service to Judaism by following other Jewrys, no matter how important they may be to their followers . . . From that point of view, I feel, it was worthwhile having a kind of contest in the area of Britishness, Englishness, Anglo Jewry, in terms of religion.[21]

Jacobs's faith in Anglo-Jewish tolerance contrasts sharply with the rejection he suffered during his career. He would not have been ostracized for his views had he lived in America. But he didn't believe that the dominant rabbinic voices raised against him typified the Anglo-Jewish community. It was not to them that one should look for tolerance. He would parody the well-known rabbinic dictum 'The disciples of the wise increase peace in the world.' 'Don't you believe it,' he would chuckle.

UPROOTED

Louis's life after Shula died was not happy. He carried on reading and writing as he had always done, and, with Ivor's encouragement, continued to record his series of video talks from his study.

Although family and friends came in regularly, he had neither Shula's company nor the sense of purpose that being the rabbi of a synagogue had always given him. He rarely admitted it, but he continued to sense that he was growing unwell. To add to his troubles, there had been a change of management at the New London, and the new team had decided that Louis did not need to live on his own in a large house owned by the synagogue. The synagogue had never contributed to a pension for him, an omission he had never thought to challenge, and if he had considered his later years at all it would have been on the assumption that he would stay in the house in Clifton Hill, supported one way or another by funds from the synagogue and his friends.

But the management at New London saw things differently. They had no intention of cutting Louis adrift, but it made financial sense to move him out of the house. They suggested renting a flat for him instead.

Jacobs was reluctant. Not only was he of an age where moving home feels unimaginably arduous, he had no idea what he would do with his books. The house in Clifton Hill was on three stories; the entire upper storey, and much of the other two floors, were taken up with books. He discussed his problems with his children. They took a pragmatic view; the books would have to be moved eventually. Although it was prudent for Jacobs to take legal advice over the New London's proposals, they approached the Oxford Centre for Hebrew and Jewish Studies, part of Oxford University, to see if they would be interested in hosting his library. At that time the Oxford Centre occupied a large manor house and estate outside the city and they agreed to add Jacobs's collection to their holdings.

Louis Jacobs, together with his most important books and mementoes, moved into a flat in Marlborough Place, just across the road from the New London. His health was deteriorating rapidly and it is possible that the move exacerbated his condition. He lasted just two weeks in his new flat. One week before he died the doctors finally discovered the cancer that had been eating away at him.

Looking back on his father's life, David recalled the small things that meant so much. 'My dad would work all day and night, but his favourite thing was to put on his dressing gown, watch *Coronation Street*, have a small bit of milk chocolate and a whisky. And a cigar. He loved it.'

Louis Jacobs passed away early in the morning, on Shabbat, 1 July 2006. He was a few days short of his 86th birthday. He had no doubt where he was going. Shula would be waiting for him.

Notes

INTRODUCTION

1 *Jewish Chronicle*, 6 January 2006.
2 'Greatest British Jew'. Competition, letters and comments, *Jewish Chronicle*, 30 September 2005–20 January 2006.
3 Shula Jacobs, 'Kibbutz & Cocoa', unpublished family diary.

I AN UNLIKELY RABBI

1 Louis Jacobs, *Helping with Inquiries: An Autobiography* (London, Vallentine Mitchell & Co., 1989).
2 E. H., *A Short History of the Manchester Jews' School, 1838–1869–1919* (Manchester, Massels, 1919). http://catalog.hathitrust.org/api/volumes/oclc/319976396.html.
3 Jacobs, *Helping with Inquiries*, p. 23.
4 Ibid., pp. 27–8.
5 Ibid., p. 42.
6 Louis Jacobs, 'The Doctrine of "Bread of Shame"', unpublished, undated article accessible at https://louisjacobs.org/articles/doctrine-bread-shame.
7 Eliyahu Dessler, *Michtav Me-Eliahu* (Jerusalem, 1963), p. 166, translated and quoted in Elliot Joe Cosgrove, 'Teyku: The Insoluble Contradictions in the Life and Thought of Louis Jacobs', unpublished PhD thesis, vol. 1, p. 26.

2 BECOMING AN ENGLISH RABBI

1 Letter of Recommendation, November 1943. Accessible at https://www.evernote.com/pub/ivor/louisjacobsscrapbook.

2 *Jewish Chronicle*, 9 April 1993; 16 October 1953.

3 Rabbi Dr S. Schonfeld, *Jewish Chronicle*, 16 March 1962.

4 Jacobs, *Helping with Inquiries*, p. 97.

5 Miri Freud-Kandel, *Orthodox Judaism in Britain since 1913: An Ideology Forsaken* (London, Vallentine Mitchell, 2006).

6 'Cold and dreary Manchester', Louis Jacobs on Koppel Kahana, https://louisjacobs.org/video/koppel-kahanah/.

7 Jacobs, 'Kibbutz & Cocoa'.

8 Author conversation with Shula Jacobs, circa 2000.

9 Louis Jacobs diary.

10 *Jewish Chronicle*, 28 July 1944.

11 *Jewish Chronicle*, 5 January 1945.

12 Louis Jacobs diary.

13 Ibid.

14 *Jewish Chronicle*, 24 January 1947.

15 Ivor Jacobs disputes this story. The age difference between him and Tirza is too great. He believes that the baby alongside him was her older sister, Susan.

3 A REASONABLE FAITH

1 Louis Jacobs diary, 9 July 1944.

2 *Jewish Chronicle*, 15 June 1962, 29 June 1962.

3 Jacobs, *Helping with Inquiries*, p. 95.

4 Louis Jacobs, 'Laws of Marriage and Divorce in Israel', *Jewish Review* 3 (69) (21 Jan. 1949): 3–4.

5 Louis Jacobs, 'Judaism and Freedom', *Chayenu* 13.3/4 (Mar./Apr. 1949): 2. The reference to '*Harut*- "engraved"' is from Exodus 32:16.

6 Louis Jacobs, 'Modern Problems in the Responsa', *Chayenu* 14.5/6 (May/June 1950): 2–3.

7 Louis Jacobs, 'Jewish Law in the Modern World: An Orthodox View', *Jewish Monthly* 5.1 (Apr. 1951): 7–17.

8 *Jewish Chronicle*, 13 April 1951 to 11 May 1951, weekly.

9 Correspondence with Revd Benjamin Wykansky, 11 October 1949 and 31 January 1950. Quotation from Jacobs, *Helping with Inquiries*, p. 103.

10 See Cosgrove, 'Teyku', vol. 1, p. 128, quoting Aharon Sorski, *Melekh Be-Yofyo: Toldot Hayav, Po'olo Ve-Darko Ba-Kodesh Shel Maran Ha-Gaon Rabbi Yehezkel Abramski Ba'al 'Hazon Yehezkel'* (Yerushalayim: Menahem Ezra Abramski, 2004), p. 686.

11 Louis Jacobs, 'Evidence of Literary Device in the Babylonian Talmud', *Journal of Jewish Studies* 3.4 (1952): 157–61.

12 Louis Jacobs, 'Organic Growth vs. Petrification', *Jewish Spectator* 17.10 (Nov. 1952): 9–11.

13 Ibid.

14 Jacobs, *Helping with Inquiries*, p.103.

4 HIGH SOCIETY

1 http://www.newwestend.org.uk/docs/RH2007/GradeIListing.pdf.

2 Rabbi Dr Raymond Apple, quoting Redcliffe N. Salaman. https://www.oztorah.com/2007/05/sacks-the-singer-siddur/#. XEnJAFz7SXI.

3 'The New West End Synagogue, 1879–2004', an abridged version of the lecture delivered by Elkan Levy BA MHL, Past President of the United Synagogue and son of the late Revd Raphael Levy, on Sunday 11 July 2004, https://www.newwestend.org.uk/docs/EDLlecture.pdf.

4 Obituary, *Jewish Chronicle*, 2 December 1966, 18 May 1979; Jacobs, *Helping with Inquiries*, p. 107.

5 J. Halpern to Louis Jacobs, 19 May 1953, Louis Jacobs Archive.

6 R. Eliyahu Munk to Louis Jacobs, 1954, quoted in Cosgrove, 'Teyku', vol. 1, p. 134.

7 Louis Jacobs, 'Ask the Rabbi', *Jewish Chronicle*, 1 November 1979.

8 'Sermon by Rabbi Dr Louis Jacobs on the occasion of his induction as Minister to the New West End Synagogue 13th February 1954', Louis Jacobs Archive.

9 See above, p. 46.

10 Office of the Chief Rabbi to Louis Jacobs, 7 November 1955.

11 W. Frankel, *Tea with Einstein and Other Memories* (London, Halban in association with European Jewish Publication Society, 2006).

12 'An Editorial', *Venture* 1.1 (April 1956).

13 Louis Jacobs, *We Have Reason to Believe: Some Aspects of Jewish Theology Examined in the Light of Modern Thought* (London, Vallentine Mitchell, 1957), p. 9.

14 Ibid., p. 59.

15 Ibid.

16 Frankel, *Tea with Einstein*, p. 160.

17 *Jewish Review*, 19 July 1957.

18 Chief Rabbi Israel Brodie to Louis Jacobs, 8 August 1957, 20 August 1957, Louis Jacobs Archive.

19 Louis Jacobs to Chief Rabbi Israel Brodie, 2 September 1957, Louis Jacobs Archive.

20 *Jewish Chronicle*, 8 November 1957.

21 *Jewish Chronicle*, 15 November 1957.

22 Rabbi J. Gould to Louis Jacobs, 21 November 1957, Louis Jacobs Archive.

23 Jonah Balkind to Louis Jacobs, 27 May 1958, Louis Jacobs Archive.

24 Correspondence with Maurice Carr and Dayan Morris Swift, 3 February–10 March 1958, Louis Jacobs Archive.

25 Louis Jacobs to Wolfe Kelman, 1 May 1958; Wolfe Kelman to Louis Jacobs, 8 May 1958, quoted in Cosgrove, 'Teyku', vol. 2, p. 228.

5 IN THE LIMELIGHT

1 Jacobs, *Helping with Inquiries*, p. 122. See below p. 77.

2 Letter from Michael Wallach, Secretary of the London Beth Din, 6 February 1959.

3 Norman Cohen in a 1966 article adduced this event to suggest that 'Dr Jacobs had comforted [*sic*: read *comported*] himself in a way that could only make it difficult for Dr Brodie to accept him.' Cohen's article is highly subjective; he quotes no sources and frequently interposes his own opinions. Unfortunately, other scholars have failed to treat this article with caution, relying upon it as a source in their own research. Norman Cohen, 'The Religious Crisis in Anglo-Jewry', *Tradition: A Journal of Orthodox Jewish Thought* 8, 2 (Summer 1966): pp. 40–57.

4 Wolfe Kelman to Gertie Frankel, 28 July 1959.

5 David Cesarani, *The Jewish Chronicle and Anglo-Jewry 1841–1991* (Cambridge, Cambridge University Press, 2009).

6 *Jewish Chronicle*, 24 July 1959.

7 Jacobs, *Helping with Inquiries*, p. 122.

8 Letter from Jews' College to Louis Jacobs, 22 July 1959, Louis Jacobs Archive.

9 Jacobs, *Helping with Inquiries*, p. 122.

10 Jakob Petuchowski to Louis Jacobs, 27 August 1959.

11 Louis Jacobs to Jakob Petuchowski, 2 September 1959, quoted in Cosgrove, 'Teyku', vol. 2, p. 243.

12 Jacobs, *Helping with Inquiries*, pp. 126–7.

13 Author correspondence with Professor Stefan Reif, quotation taken from a forthcoming autobiography, in preparation at the time of writing.

14 Author correspondence received from a former student.

15 Author correspondence with Professor Stefan Reif.

16 Letter from Gertie Frankel to Wolfe Kelman, 17 July 1959, quoted in Cosgrove, 'Teyku', vol. 2, p. 248.

17 Chaim Bermant, *Lord Jakobovits: The Authorized Biography of the Chief Rabbi* (London, Weidenfeld & Nicolson, 1990), p .67.

18 Israel Brodie, *The Strength of My Heart: Sermons and Addresses, 1948–1965* (London, G. J. George, 1969). Interview quotation from South African *Jewish Times*, 13 July,1962. For a comparison of scholarly views about Chief Rabbi Brodie's attitude towards Louis Jacobs, his personal beliefs and theology, see Freud-Kandel, *Orthodox Judaism*; Cosgrove, 'Teyku'; B. J. Elton, *Britain's Chief Rabbis and the Religious Character of Anglo-Jewry 1880–1970* (Oxford, Manchester University Press, 2017).

19 Jacobs, *Jewish Values* (London, Vallentine Mitchell, 1960), p. 23.

20 *Jewish Chronicle*, 1 July 1960, quoting from Jacobs, *Jewish Values*, p. 140.

21 Rabbi Emanuel Rackman to Louis Jacobs, 22 July 1960.

6 JEWS' COLLEGE

1 *Jewish Chronicle*, 7 May 1960, 22 July 1960.

2 *Jewish Chronicle*, 22 July 1960, 29 July 1960. Private correspondence with Rabbi Dr Jeffrey Cohen.

3 Anne Ruth Grunfeld Cohn, *Dayan Dr. Yishai I. Grunfeld, zt'l*, undated, accessed at http://www.alemannia-judaica.de/images/Images%20141/Dayan%20Grunfeld.pdf.

4 Bermant, *Lord Jakobovits*.

5 Author correspondence with Professor Stefan Reif, quotation taken from a forthcoming autobiography, in preparation at the time of writing.

6 Author correspondence with Rabbi Dr Jeffrey Cohen.

7 United Synagogue Papers, London Metropolitan Archives.

8 Alan Mocatta to Louis Jacobs, 12 December 1960, Louis Jacobs Archive.

9 *Jewish Chronicle*, 14 April 1961, 21 April 1961.

10 *Jewish Chronicle*, 19 May 1961.

11 'Jewish Principles and the Eichmann Trial', *Jewish Chronicle*, 17 March 1961. 'And those that remain shall hear, and fear': Deuteronomy 19:19–20'; 'An abhorring unto all flesh': Isaiah 66:24.

12 Shula Jacobs, 'What Happened When', unpublished memoir.

13 *Newsweek*, 21 August 1961; Jacobs, 'What Happened When'.

14 '*Silhouette*', *Jewish Chronicle*, 15 September 1961.

15 'For this is your wisdom': Deuteronomy 4:6.

16 Jacobs, *Helping with Inquiries*, p. 130.

17 Correspondence between Chief Rabbi Israel Brodie and Sir Alan Mocatta, 2 December 1961, 8 December 1981, Latchman Archive.

18 *Jewish Chronicle*, 22 December 1961.

19 Jacobs, *Helping with Inquiries*, pp. 132–3.

20 *News and Views*, Agudas Israel Organisation of Great Britain, 5 January 1962; *Jewish Review*, 10 January 1962.

21 Chief Rabbi Brodie to Michael Wallach, 7 March 1962, Latchman Archive.

7 FRIENDS IN NEED

1 *Manchester Evening News*, 23 December 1961; *Evening Standard*, 29 December 1961; *Daily Express, Daily Telegraph, The Times*, 30 December 1961.

2 *Jewish Chronicle*, 29 December 1961.

3 Ewen Montagu to Louis Jacobs, 18 July 1961.

4 *Jewish Chronicle*, 5 January 1962, 2 February 1962.

5 In 1943, Lieutenant Commander Ewen Montagu devised a hoax in which an unknown corpse would be placed on a Spanish beach, apparently washed up. The corpse carried identity papers showing it to be a British officer, and plans detailing a forthcoming invasion of Greece. The Germans, finding the corpse and the plans, despatched forces from Sicily to Greece, leaving the field clear for the Allies' landing in Sicily. Montagu wrote an account in his book *The Man Who Never Was* (London, Evans Bros, 1953). A film of the same name was directed by Ronald Neame in 1956, starring Clifton Webb, Gloria Grahame and Robert Flemyng.

6 *Jewish Chronicle*, 2 February 1962.

7   Letter to Chief Rabbi Brodie, 10 April 1962, published in *Jewish Chronicle*, 11 May 1962.

8   *Jewish Review*, 7 February 1962.

9   *Jewish Review*, 21 February 1962.

10 Louis Jacobs diary.

11 *Jewish Review*, 16 May 1962.

12 *Jewish Chronicle*, 11 May 1962.

13 *Jewish Chronicle*, 25 May 1962.

14 *Jewish Chronicle*, 8 June 1962.

15 *Bulletin for the Society of Jewish Theology*, March 1963.

16 *Creative Judaism – Some Aims and Objects of the Society for the Study of Jewish Theology*, 1962.

17 *Jewish Chronicle*, 26 April 1963, 10 May 1963, 17 May 1963.

18 Revd Kenneth Cosgrove to William Frankel, 12 July 1962, Frankel Archive.

19 *Jewish Chronicle*, 31 May 1963.

20 'The Sanction of the *Mitzvot*', lecture delivered at Herbert Samuel Hall, 11 July 1963. For full text see https://louisjacobs.org/articles/the-sanction-for-the-mitzwoth/. *Jewish Chronicle*, 19 July 1964.

21 Reconstructionism is the movement founded in the USA in the mid-twentieth century by Rabbi Mordechai Kaplan. Its central conception is of God as a natural power that makes for salvation, or self-fulfilment.

22 *Jewish Gazette*, 18 January 1963.

23 Sidney Hamburger to Louis Jacobs, 15 January 1963. Louis Jacobs Archive.

24 *Jewish Echo*, 23 November 1962.

25 Jacobs, 'What Happened When'.

26 Author correspondence with Naomi Bar-Yosef.

27 Jacobs, 'What Happened When'.

8 A BIGGER AFFAIR

1   *Jewish Chronicle*, 13 December 1963.

2   Louis Jacobs to Jakob Petuchowski, 31 December 1963.

3   Jacobs, *Helping with Inquiries*, p. 160; *Jewish Chronicle*, 15 May 1964.

4   Chief Rabbi Israel Brodie to Alfred H. Silverman, 24 January 1964, printed in 'Statement by the President of the United Synagogue, Sir Isaac Wolfson, to the Council of the United Synagogue at

a special meeting held on 23rd April 1964-11th Iyar, 5724'. United Synagogue Council, 1964.

5 Letter from the New West End Synagogue Board Management to Isaac Wolfson, 17 February 1964, https://louisjacobs.org/the-jacobs-affair/primary-sources/letter-new-west-end-synagogue-board-management-isaac-wolfson.

6 Sir Isaac Wolfson to Frank Davis, 21 February 1964.

7 *Evening Standard*, 5 March 1964, *The Times, Guardian, Daily Telegraph*, 6 March 1964, *Sunday Times*, 8 March 1964.

8 Notice of Question at United Council meeting 23rd March 1964, Office of Chief Rabbi Archive.

9 Correspondence between Isaac and Leonard Wolfson, 10–13 March 1964, Office of Chief Rabbi Archive.

10 Statement to United Synagogue Council meeting, 23 March 1964, prepared 20 March 1964, Office of Chief Rabbi Archive.

11 Rabbi Dr J. Hertz, sermon preached at Great Synagogue, 23 March 1931.

12 *Jewish Chronicle*, 13 March 1964.

13 Jacobs, *Helping with Inquiries; Jewish Chronicle*, 24 April 1964.

14 *Observer*, 22 March 1964; *Jewish Echo*, 27 March 1964.

15 Louis Jacobs to Edward Neufeld, 14 April 1964, Louis Jacobs Archive.

16 Secretary of the United Synagogue to the Honorary Officers, New West End Synagogue, 15 April 1964, Office of Chief Rabbi Archive.

17 Revd Dr. Isaac Levy, sermon preached at Hampstead Synagogue , 25 April 1964.

18 *Jewish Chronicle*, 17 April 1964.

19 *Sunday Times*, 19 April 1964.

20 Author correspondence with Naomi Bar-Yosef.

21 Author correspondence with Ivor Jacobs.

22 *Jewish Chronicle*, 1 May 1964.

23 *Daily Express*, 28 April 1964.

24 *Jewish Chronicle*, 1 May 1964.

25 *Jewish Chronicle*, 8 May 1964.

26 Chief Rabbi Israel Brodie: Statement to Rabbis and Ministers, 5 May 1964, printed in Brodie, *Strength of My Heart*.

27 Louis Jacobs to Jakob Petuchowski, 2 July 1964.

9 NEW LONDON SYNAGOGUE

1 *Jewish Chronicle*, 8 May 1964.

2 Jacobs, *Helping with Inquiries*, p. 181; *Jewish Chronicle*, 15 May 1964.

3 Louis Jacobs to Professor Asaf A. Fyzee, 13 May 1964.

4 'The spirit which imbues the whole code of bye-laws is that of the Progressive Conservatism which the United Synagogue itself exemplifies, rejecting on the one hand the clamour of those who, in the desire for constant change, would recklessly cast aside Tradition; and on the other, the invitation of those who regard all things as settled, deluding themselves with the pretence that time and environment and circumstances are factors of no account, as though our lives and our mutual relationships are not susceptible to change'. *Bye-Laws Made by the Council of the United Synagogue* (London, United Synagogue, July 1936), p. i.

5 Dr Alexander Altmann to Louis Jacobs, 28 March 1964; Rabbi Immanuel Jakobovits to Raphael Loewe, 22 May 1964, Louis Jacobs Archive.

6 Rabbi Immanuel Jakobovits to Chief Rabbi Brodie, 16 April 1964, Latchman Archive.

7 Chief Rabbi Brodie to Rabbi Immanuel Jakobovits, 30 April 1964, Latchman Archive.

8 Rabbi Immanuel Jakobovits to Chief Rabbi Brodie, 6 May 1964, Latchman Archive.

9 Raphael Loewe to Louis Jacobs, 7 June 1964, Louis Jacobs Archive.

10 Reform and Liberal synagogues have a different status in British law and do not need the Chief Rabbi's confirmation.

11 Raphael Loewe to Louis Jacobs, 7 June 1964, Louis Jacobs Archive.

12 Louis Jacobs to Raphael Loewe, 17 June 1964, Louis Jacobs Archive.

13 Vera Sharpe to Chief Rabbi Dr Israel Brodie, 30 May 1964, Louis Jacobs Archive.

14 *The Builder*, London 1876.

15 *Jewish Chronicle*, 17 July 1964.

16 *Jewish Chronicle*, 10 July 1964.

17 *Babel*, Inter-University Jewish Federation, November 1964.

18 Sermon preached at the New London Synagogue, first day of Rosh Hashanah, 7 September 1964, https://louisjacobs.org/new-london-synagogue/what-we-stand-for/.

19 Jacobs, *Helping with Inquiries*, pp. 253, 270.

20 *Jewish Chronicle*, 13 November 1964.

21 Chief Rabbi Israel Brodie to Maurice Edelman MP, 16 November 1964, United Synagogue Archive.

22 *Jewish Chronicle*, 20 November 1964.

23 *Jewish Chronicle*, 15 January 1965; H. A. Simons to Sir Isaac Wolfson, 1 March 1964.

24 The phrase 'Jacobs Affair' was coined by the commentator Chaim Bermant in his Ben Azai column in 1963, after Louis had resigned from Jews' College but before the events at the New West End.

25 *The New Londoner: The Magazine of the New London Synagogue*, vol. 1, April 1965.

26 Jacobs, *Helping with Inquiries*, p. 191.

27 Anna Horovitz, 'Music and Art at the New London Synagogue', *New London Synagogue Silver Anniversary Journal*, 1989.

28 Author correspondence with Professor Leslie Wagner.

29 *Quest*, ed. Jonathan Stone (London, Paul Hamlyn Publications, 1965).

10 AN INTERNATIONAL REPUTATION

1 Jacobs, 'What Happened When'.

2 Louis Jacobs, speech to the Convocation of Religion for World Peace, 1965, published in *New Londoner* 1, (2), September 1965.

3 Louis Ginzberg, *Students, Scholars and Saints* (Philadelphia: Jewish Publication Society of America, 1928), p. 206, quoted in Cosgrove, 'Teyku', vol. 2, p. 322.

4 Louis Jacobs, 'Liberal Supernaturalism', in *Varieties of Jewish Belief*, ed. Ira Eisenstein (New York, Reconstructionist Press, 1966), pp. 111–22. Available at https://louisjacobs.org/articles/liberal-supernaturalism/.

5 'God, where art thou?', *Twentieth Century* 174, 1027 (Autumn 1965): 7–10. Republished as 'The Jewish approach to God' in Louis Jacobs, *Judaism and Theology: Essays on the Jewish Religion* (London, Portland, OR, Vallentine, Mitchell, 2005), pp. 1–9.

6 *The Levin Interview*, Rediffusion, 28 February 1966.

7 *Jewish Chronicle*, 20 May 1966.

8 Ibid.

9 Dr E. Golombok to Louis Jacobs, 26 October 1966, Louis Jacobs Archive; *Jewish Chronicle*, 10 February 1967.

10 *Jewish Chronicle*, 12 August 1966.

11 Jacobs, *Helping with Inquiries*, pp. 186–7.

12 Louis Jacobs to William Frankel, 2 August 1966, Frankel Archive.

13 *Sunday Times*, 26 March 1967.

14 *Jewish Chronicle*, 7 April 1967.

15 *Jewish Echo*, 21 April 1967.

16 Louis Jacobs, *The Via Negativa in Jewish Religious Thought* (New York, Judaica Press, 1966).

17 *Weekend Telegraph*, 1 April 1966.

18 *Daily Express*, 28 October 1967.

19 *Jewish Chronicle*, 1 March 1968; *Jewish Advocate*, 7 March 1968.

20 *The New Londoner: The Magazine of the New London Synagogue*, 1.7 (January 1968).

21 *Jewish Chronicle*, 10 May 1968.

22 Author conversation with Shula Jacobs, circa 2000.

23 *New London News*, September 1968.

24 See below, p. 207.

25 Cosgrove, 'Teyku', vol. 2, p. 336.

26 Author conversation with Eleanor Lind QC.

11 STABILITY

1 Correspondent to Louis Jacobs, 29 July 1971.

2 Jacobs, 'What Happened When'.

3 Ibid.

4 David Brett to the Editor of the *Jewish Chronicle*, 12 March 1989, Isaac Newman Archive. The version of the letter published by the *Jewish Chronicle* on 17 March omitted to mention the Board of Management's breaking up of the meeting.

5 Louis Jacobs to Isaac Newman, 12 January 1988, Newman Archive.

6 Cf. Louis's resignation letter, p. XX.

7 Author interview with Rabbi Jackie Tabick.

8 Correspondence with Ivor Jacobs.

9 Louis Jacobs, *What Does Judaism Say About . . . ?* (Jerusalem, Keter, 1973).

10 Cosgrove, 'Teyku', vol. 2, p. 283.

11 Rabbi M. Turetsky to Rabbi Jacobs, 27 January 1966.

12 *Jewish Chronicle*, 19 January 1973; *Jewish Review*, 14 February 1973.

13 *Sunday Times*, 2 June 1974; *New London News*, September 1974.

14 *Jewish Chronicle*, 17 May 1974.

15 *New London News*, December 1974.

16 Louis Jacobs, *Theology in the Responsa* (London, Routledge & Kegan Paul, 1975).

17 'In Memoriam Louis Littman', *Jewish Quarterly* 35.1 (1988): 6–7. Reprinted https://louisjacobs.org/articles/memoriam-louis-littman/.

18 Louis Jacobs, *Teyku* (London, Leo Baeck College Publications, 1981), p. 301.

19 Louis Jacobs, 'Jewish National Consciousness in Anglo-Jewry: An Analysis', in *The President of Israel's Sixth International Seminar on World Jewry and the State of Israel*, ed. Moshe Davis (Jerusalem, 1981).

20 Jacobs, *Helping with Inquiries*, p. 215.

21 Ibid.

22 *New London Forum* 1, 2, September 1983.

23 *Jewish Chronicle*, 16 September 1983.

24 *Jewish Chronicle*, 30 September 1983.

25 Ibid.

26 *Jewish Chronicle*, 7 October 1983.

12 A MOOD, NOT A MOVEMENT

1 *Jewish Chronicle*, 2 November 1984.

2 *Jewish Chronicle*, 16 November 1984.

3 Professor Joseph Udelson, 'Contemporary intellectual speculation', *Jewish Chronicle*, 30 November 1984; Dr Louis Freedman, 'A curious ring', *Jewish Chronicle*, 23 November 1984.

4 *New London Synagogue: The First Twenty Years*, ed. Anne Cowen , 1984.

5 *New London Forum* 2, 2, April 1984.

6 Ibid..

7 *Jewish Chronicle*, 20 September 1985.

8 Author conversation with Naomi Bar-Yosef, 28 October 2018.

9 Correspondence re meeting at New London Synagogue, 4 June 2000, Louis Jacobs Archive.

10 https://louisjacobs.org/video/masorti/.

11 Author conversation with Rabbi Jackie Tabick.

13 OUT OF THE PULPIT

1 Louis Jacobs to New London Synagogue, October 1985.
2 Shula Jacobs to New London Synagogue, November 1985.
3 *Declaration on the Relation of the Church to Non-Christian Religions, Nostra Aetate, October 28, 1965,* http://www.vatican.va/archive/hist_councils/ii_vatican_council/documents/vat-ii_decl_19651028_nostra-aetate_en.html.
4 Jacobs, *Helping with Inquiries*, p. 247.
5 Shula Jacobs to New London Synagogue, November 1985.
6 Agudas Chasidei Chabad of United States v. Barry S. Gourary, Defendant United States District Court, E.D. New York. No. CV-85-2909 December 5, 1985; *New York Times*, 7 January 1987.
7 *Jewish Chronicle*, 28 February 1986, 7 March 1986, 25 July 1986, 29 August 1986.
8 Jacobs, 'What Happened When'.
9 Adrian Cunningham, 'Psychoanalytic Approaches to Biblical Narrative (Genesis 1–4)', in *A Traditional Quest: Essays in Honour of Louis Jacobs*, ed. Daniel Cohn-Sherbock (Sheffield, JSOT Press, 1991), pp. 113–32.
10 Jacobs, 'What Happened When'.
11 Ibid.

14 PERSONAL BELIEF

1 Louis Jacobs, *God, Torah, Israel: Traditionalism without Fundamentalism* (Cincinnati, Hebrew Union College Press, 1990), pp. 3–4.
2 Council of Assembly of Masorti Synagogues, 29 November 1988.
3 Author conversation with Rabbi Jonathan Wittenberg.
4 Ibid.
5 *Jewish Chronicle*, 30 December 2005.
6 Author correspondence with Professor Marc Shapiro.
7 *Jewish Chronicle*, 23 June 1989.
8 https://louisjacobs.org/reviews-written-by-louis-jacobs/a-history-of-the-mishnaic-law-of-purities/, https://louisjacobs.org/reviews-written-by-louis-jacobs/jacob-neusner-history-mishnaic-law-

women-parts-1-5/ and elsewhere. Jacob Neusner to Louis Jacobs; Louis Jacobs to Alex Tobias, 18 September 1995, Louis Jacobs Archive.

9   Author correspondence with Noa Bar-Yosef.

10 *Jewish Chronicle*, 6 September 1991.

11 *Jewish Chronicle*, 25 October 1991.

12 *A Time for Change*, Stanley Kalms Foundation, September 1992, p. 215.

13 *Masorti Magazine*, January 1993.

14 *Jewish Chronicle*, 17 December 1993.

15 Rabbi Sacks's Office to New London congregant, 15 October 1993, Louis Jacobs Archive.

16 *Securing Our Future: An inquiry into Jewish Education in the United Kingdom*, Jewish Educational Development Trust, 1992.

17 *Jewish Chronicle*, 11 September 1992.

18 Leslie Wagner, *Change in Continuity, Report of the Review into Jewish Continuity*, March 1996.

19 Jonathan Lew to Chief Rabbi Sacks, 3 May 1993; Sacks to Lew May, 1993, United Synagogue Archive.

20 John Levy to Chief Rabbi Sacks, 18 January 1994.

21 Louis Jacobs to Jonathan Sacks, 23 February 1994.

22 Chief Rabbi Sacks to John Levy, 15 April 1994.

23 *Jewish Tribune*, 3 November 1994.

24 *Jewish Tribune*, 24 February 1994.

25 *Jewish Tribune*, 12 January 1995.

26 *Jewish Chronicle*, 27 January 1995.

27 Louis Jacobs to Alex Tobias, 17 April 1995.

28 Jacobs, *We Have Reason to Believe*, 4th edition (London, Vallentine Mitchell, 1995), p. 5.

29 Ibid., p. 6.

30 *Jewish Chronicle*, 10 February 1995, 8 December 1995.

31 Sir Isaiah Berlin to Eleanor Lind, 17 July 1995.

32 Personal conversation with Eleanor Lind QC; *Jewish Chronicle*, 18 November 1994.

33 *Jewish Chronicle*, 13 October 1995.

34 Marc Shapiro, 'The Jewish Religion: A Companion', *Judaism Today* 4 (Spring 1996): 42–3.

35 Louis Jacobs, *The Jewish Religion: A Companion* (Oxford, Oxford University Press, 1995), p. 403.

36 Louis Jacobs, *Beyond Reasonable Doubt* (London, Littman Library of Jewish Civilization, 1999).

37 Ibid., pp. 27–8.

38 Ibid., p. 29.

15 WINDING DOWN

1 Author correspondence with Dan Jacobs.

2 Author correspondence with Ziva Green.

3 Louis Jacobs to Noa Bar-Yosef, 19 February 1997.

4 *Jewish Tribune*, 10 January 1997; *Jewish Chronicle*, 14 March 1997.

5 Meir Persoff, *Closed Doors, Open Minds: British Jewry's Secret Disputations* (London, Academic Studies Press, 2018), p. 178.

6 Jacobs, *Beyond Reasonable Doubt*, p. 3.

7 Ibid., pp. 9–10.

8 Ibid., p. 237.

9 *Jewish Chronicle*, 18 November, 1994, 3 April 1998, 3 September 1999.

10 Author conversations with founder members.

11 Author conversation with Chaim Weiner.

12 Louis Jacobs to Basil Feldman, February 2002, Jacobs Archive.

13 Author conversation with Anne Cowen.

14 Louis Jacobs to House of Lords Appointments Commission, November 2000.

15 Rabbi Jeremy Rosen, 'The Yeshivish and the Academic', *Le'ela*, December 2000, Jacobs Archive.

16 A bar mitzvah is celebrated at age 13. Psalm 90 says 'The days of our lives are seventy years'. An 83-year-old person is therefore 13 years into their metaphorical second life.

17 Author correspondence with Paula Jacobs.

18 See https://louisjacobs.org.

19 Louis Jacobs, *Jewish Preaching: Homilies and Sermons* (London, Valentine Mitchell, 2004), pp. ix–x.

20 *The Times*, 30 December 2005; *Jewish Chronicle*, 30 December 2005.

21 https://louisjacobs.org/video/greatest-british-jew-on-the-greatest-british-jew/.

Glossary

bar mitzvah/bat mitzvah	coming of age ceremony for boys at 13, girls at 12
bashert	destiny, fate
Beth Hamedrash	study room/school
bimah	Raised platform in synagogue from which the Torah is read and many services taken
boychick	young man
bubba	grandmother
chametz	leavened food, not to be eaten at Passover
chazan	synagogue cantor
chupa	wedding canopy
cupel	skullcap
dayan	judge of a religious court (Bet Din)
epikoros	learned heretic
frum, frummie	religious person
gedolei hador	acclaimed Strictly Orthodox rabbis
galut	exile
Habad	Hasidic sect, also known as Lubavitch
haftara	passage from Prophets, read in synagogue
haham	Spiritual leader of the Sephardi community
halakha	Jewish law
heder/hedarim	elementary religious school/s
hizzuk	strength
ilui	Talmudic genius
kehillah	congregation
kiddush	ceremony at onset of Sabbath/light buffet after synagogue service
kolel	advanced Talmudic study group
meshuggeneh frum	crazily religious
mitzvah/mitzwoth	religious duty/duties

mohel	one who performs circumcisions
Musar	ethics/ethical approach to Talmud study
Pesach	Passover
prozbul	device to circumvent the remission of debts in sabbatical year
rabbonim	rabbis
rav, rov	rabbi
rebbe	leader of Hasidic sect
rosh yeshiva	head of yeshiva
seder	festive Passover meal
semicha	rabbinic ordination
Shabbes, Shabbat	Sabbath
shiur/shiurim	religious lesson
shiva	week of mourning for a departed relative
shtender	lectern
shul, shool	synagogue
Simchat Torah	festival when annual cycle of Torah reading is completed
sugya	Talmudic topic or section
tefillin	small leather boxes worn during prayer containing biblical passages; also called phylacteries
Teyku	Talmudic term meaning that an issue cannot be resolved
Torah Lishmah	Torah learning 'for its own sake'; without expectation of reward
Torah min Hashamayim	'Torah from heaven': doctrine that the Torah is divinely given
tuches	backside
Wissenschaft des Judentums	academic, scientific study of Judaism
yarmulke	skullcap
yeshiva	Talmudic college
yeshiva bochur	student at Talmudic college
Yiddishkeit	'Jewishness'
yirat shamayim	fear of heaven
Yom Kippur	Day of Atonement
zaid, zaida	grandfather
Zohar	classic text of Jewish mysticism

Acknowledgements

This book would not have been possible without the constant encouragement and help of the entire Jacobs family, Louis and Shula's children Ivor Jacobs, Naomi Bar-Yosef and David Jacobs, their spouses Tirza Jacobs and Sasson Bar-Yosef and grandchildren Daniel Jacobs, Paula Jacobs, Ziva Green, Noa Bar-Yosef, Michael Bar-Yosef and Abraham Jacobs.

The book would also have been far more difficult to write, and far less comprehensive in its coverage, were it not for the fact that Shula Jacobs kept scrapbooks, diaries and box files of correspondence and press cuttings throughout almost the whole of her married life. These have all now been digitized and were made freely available to me throughout my research by Ivor Jacobs and Dr César Merchán-Hamann, Director of the Leopold Muller Memorial Library at the Oxford Centre for Hebrew and Jewish Studies, to whom I am deeply grateful.

I consulted, corresponded with, interviewed and spoke to many people while writing this book: friends, family, congregants, colleagues and former students of Rabbi Jacobs, keepers of records and representatives of communal bodies. My thanks, immeasurably (and alphabetically) for assistance great and small, for help, information and support, is due to Cyril Barnett, Rabbi Tony Bayfield, Dayan Ivan Binstock, Jennifer Breger, David Cohen, Rabbi Dr Jeffrey Cohen, Rabbi Dr Elliott Cosgrove, Anne Cowen, Andrew Eder, Simon Eder, David Frei, Dr Miri Freud-Kandel,

Daniel Goldwater, Rabbi Jeremy Gordon, Irving Grose, Shemaya Grunfeld, Annette Herson z'l, Ann Horovitz, Joseph Horovitz, Professor David Latchman, John Levy, Mark Lewisohn, Eleanor Lind QC, Freddie Lind, Andrew Mainz, Ezra Margulies, Gillian Merron, Rabbi Dr Charles Middleburgh, Professor David Newman, John Reeves, Professor Stefan Reif, Revd George Rothschild, Cassy Sachar, Professor Marc Shapiro, Professor Colin Shindler, Victor Stone, Rabbi Jackie Tabick, Professor Leslie Wagner, Dawn Waterman, Adam Waters, Rabbi Chaim Weiner, Rabbi Jonathan Wittenberg, Rabbi Dr Rafi Zarum, the Staff of the London Metropolitan Archives and the Staff of the Hartley Library Special Collections.

A special thank you, as always, to my wife Karen, whose support, encouragement and refusal to become a literary widow keeps me sane and focused.

Finally, grateful thanks to Steve Cox for his sharp-eyed copy editing, and to my wonderful publishers at Bloomsbury Continuum: Amy Greaves and Rosie Parnham for their energy and enthusiasm in publicising and marketing the book, and a special thanks to Robin Baird-Smith, one of Louis Jacobs's earliest publishers, and Jamie Birkett. They had the unenviable task of picking up where I left off, and turning a file of more or less coherent words into the designed, edited, proofread and indexed volume you are, hopefully, still holding in your hands. Thank you.

For Further Reading

A fully comprehensive resource for further information on Louis Jacobs is the website www.louisjacobs.org. It contains many of his articles, sermons and book reviews, as well as biographical portraits, historical information and a remarkable series of videos, mainly recorded towards the end of his life, in which he discusses his ideas, outlook, and life story.

The website also contains a full bibliography of all his writings, reached through the menu on the Home Page.

Many of Louis Jacobs's books are still in print and can be obtained through booksellers. You can also download an extensive library of his books, by subscription, from www.booksof.louisjacobs.org.

Index

A Note on the Author

Harry Freedman is Britain's leading author of popular works of Jewish culture and history. His books include *The Talmud: A Biography*, *Kabbalah: Secrecy, Scandal and the Soul*, *The Murderous History of Bible Translations* and *The Gospels' Veiled Agenda*.